50 UNIFIED YEARS

BUILDING A TRADITION OF EXCELLENCE IN CLOVIS UNIFIED BEFORE, DURING AND AFTER UNIFICATION

**Compiled and edited by
Susan Sawyer Wise
with Kelly Avants**

Watercolors by Pat Hunter

produced by Clovis Unified School District
in conjunction with Craven Street Books, Fresno, CA

50 Unified Years:
Building a Tradition of Excellence in Clovis Unified Before, During and After Unification

Watercolors provided by Pat Hunter.

This volume is an authorized version produced by Clovis Unified School District of the original hard cover edition (ISBN: 978-1-933502-49-6) published by Craven Street Books, an imprint of Linden Publishing.
2006 S. Mary, Fresno, California, 93721
559-233-6633 / 800-345-4447
CravenStreetBooks.com

Craven Street Books is a trademark of Linden Publishing, Inc.

135798642

Printed in the USA on acid-free paper.

A Letter to the CUSD Family of Employees

When you were invited to join the CUSD family, you became part of our living history, taking on the traditions that have developed over the past 50 years since unification, and in the many years leading up to that monumental event. Each employee is receiving a copy of *50 Unified Years* because we believe it is an important story for you, as a member of the Clovis Unified family, to hear. For some, the following pages will serve as a stroll down memory lane while, for others, they will provide insight into the foundations of today's Clovis Unified School District, of which you are a vital part.

> **THIS** book is about you; it is a living, breathing testimony to the thousands of people who, over the years, have instilled education and the passion to learn into the hearts and minds of our children.

It is our hope that through this book you will understand our district better, feel more connected to it, and have a greater sense of pride in Clovis Unified, from where we have come and where we are going in the coming years. This book is about you; it is a living, breathing testimony to the thousands of people who, over the years, have instilled education and the passion to learn into the hearts and minds of our children.

On behalf of the CUSD Governing Board, I want to thank you for the important role you play in shaping the future of our district. May you find inspiration and wisdom in the pages of this book as we embark on the next 50 years of our shared journey in Clovis Unified.

Sincerely,
Ginny Hovsepian
CUSD Governing Board President

ACKNOWLEDGEMENTS

To assemble a book of this nature requires the assistance, cooperation, time and support of many. "50 Unified Years" could not have been possible without the resources and support provided by the current CUSD Governing Board. Thank you to each Governing Board member and to everyone inside and outside the district who contributed to the completion of this book with special thanks to:

Marjorie Allen
Duane Barker
Jim Benelli
Peg Bos
Dr. Terry Bradley
Dr. Floyd Buchanan
Dick Gates
Alyson Gorubec
Carole Grosch
Naoma Hayes
Linda Hayward
Edna Herstein
Earlene Holguin
Ginny Hovsepian
Pat Hunter
Charlotte Hutchison
Linden Publishing
Carol Lawson-Swezey
Carole Linenbach
Kathleen Lund Coates
Susan Moranda Vigil
Everett G. "Bud" Rank, Jr.
Linda Robertson
Bill Secrest, Jr.
Kimberly Sherman
Robyn Young Stafford
Janice Stevens
Monica Stevens
Ron Webb

...and to all current and past CUSD employees, administrators and board members who graciously supported this project by contributing their knowledge, experience and resources all in the name of bringing the district's history to life, and to everyone who generously reviewed the chapters of this book prior to publication. Thank you!

CONTENTS

Note to readers: Clovis Unified's Communications Office has made every effort to assure the accuracy of this text. If you have additional information about CUSD's history, please contact the CUSD Communications Office at 1450 Herndon Avenue; Clovis, CA 93611; 559-327-9094.

FOREWORD

Fifty years ago, we had no idea where the dream of a unified public school system would take us. We knew we wanted to create an educational program that would equip every child in our community to succeed; not just in school, but in life. We knew we wanted to help build a district that would become a lighthouse in education to our entire nation. And, we knew that we wanted to help students become givers, not takers, in society. But as we and thousands of others cast a "yes" vote on our unification ballot in December of 1959, we had no idea where the journey toward that dream would take us.

Today, we know it has led Clovis Unified to a position of national recognition as a place where the community enjoys a great pride of ownership in its schools, and where kids receive a high-quality, well-rounded education in mind, body and spirit. The district's story is about a team of people coming together to build a world-class educational destination; and chances are, if you've picked this book up, this story has touched your life in some way.

The district's roots stretch far deeper than 50 years. Instead, they start in the Central Valley's pioneering history. Many of the schools and the school names you know today trace their beginnings back to tiny schoolhouses built by families who invested their own money, time and talents to help bring public education to the area. These families offered room and board to the first teachers who came to instruct their children and were willing to make sacrifices in order that their children would be able to learn.

The history of Clovis Unified, and therefore this book, is filled with examples of dedication to a goal. Today, our community and our students benefit from high quality, successful schools staffed with outstanding educators. But, today's success comes only because of the battles that were fought and won over the past 50 years.

The first battle was unification itself. The elementary school districts spread across the area were good school districts, but lacked uniformity and common goals. Even so, there was a lot of contention around the idea of individual school districts giving up their independence and autonomy over a hope that education could improve if everyone worked together. Not everyone agreed with the idea, and several neighborhoods chose to go their own way or join with a neighboring school district rather than buy into our dream.

Maybe you lived during these years of debate and dispute, and your memories of Clovis Unified include the battle over unification, the battles over which members of seven different school boards would come together to serve as one governing board, or the knock-down drag-out fight over who would be the leader of this new district. These fights didn't really end until the 1964 recall election, organized by those opposed to the district's leadership and the direction the schools were headed, failed by a 70 percent majority. Only then could we move forward toward the fulfillment of our dream.

Clovis Unified began as a group of diverse communities coming together in order to get better, and our community has won many battles by holding on to that attitude. We set goals that 90 percent of students would be able to reach grade level in reading and math (at the time the numbers in our district were closer to 30 to 40 percent), and worked together to get it done. We set goals to compete, both with ourselves and with others, that led to the district's first valley championship football title in 1970 and many, many more championships to follow. And, we set a goal to be a team and to stick together through tough economic times, like those following the 1978 passage of Prop 13 and its revolutionary change in funding to public schools, and those facing public schools today. A commitment to keeping the team together without laying anyone off created a unified group of employees dedicated to Clovis Unified and its students.

You may remember these building years; when Clovis Unified was a good school district heading toward greatness. In fact, you may have been one of the employees who fought these battles, or one of the students who were the real winners. Or, your interest in this book may be as a local history buff or as a new or current parent, employee or community member building the future story of Clovis Unified.

Whatever your reason, something about this book caught your eye, and we're glad it did. Education is about building the future, and you can't do that until you understand the past. So, hold onto this book. Read it cover to cover, or jump back and forth between the stories of each individual school as you see fit. You'll find a story reflective of our very community itself; filled with courage, care and compassion for the young people who walk through the doors of our schools and, before we are ready to see them go, exit as the next generation of our great American society.

Floyd B. "Doc" Buchanan, Ed.D.　　　　Everett G. "Bud" Rank, Jr.
First Superintendent of Schools　　　　First Governing Board President

INTRODUCTION

The colonies of early California were essentially planned agricultural communities. To create these colonies, investors would purchase land and water rights, and then build canals to deliver water. Once the land was inhabitable, the investors would sell off portions of the land to smaller investors who would then sell parcels to families.

In Fresno County, hundreds of thousands of acres of land were bought from the government by a group of investors from San Francisco. To draw settlers to the area, the land was advertised across the United States. In 1875, emigrants poured into the area to claim their part of the 192 twenty-acre properties selling for $1,000 each for just $150 down and payments of $12.50 a month, interest free. The landscape of the Central Valley changed quickly with the emergence of homes, ranches and farms.

Within the colonies across Fresno County were families whose children needed education. To meet this need, the colonists would assemble to create a school district within the colony. With California's public school system having begun in 1852, rules were in place to form schools. New districts had to be approved by the County Board of Supervisors. Members of the settlement then had four months to begin operating a school. By following this time line, the schools would receive state and county funds.

Ever since what is now today's Office of Education was formed in 1860, schools received funding through taxation support. However, this often wasn't enough to cover expenses, so residents would pitch in to build schools, donate land, and even fund and house teachers. Colony residents served as trustees of their district.

Schools that would later become Clovis Unified schools and were started by colony residents include Temperance (1878), Garfield (1883), Jefferson (1884) and Kutner (1892).

From 1866, when Dry Creek Elementary opened to its first students until 11 schools unified in 1960 to become Clovis Unified School District, a series of metamorphoses occurred that brought the schools to the point of unification. Districts formed unions; others were annexed into other districts; while others simply lapsed for lack of enrollment. Simply, "union school districts" were formed with the joining of two or more school districts in the same county. "Annexed" districts refer to territory taken from one school district and annexed to another. Depending on the nature of the reorganization, the annexed territory could be a portion or the entirety of the former school district. A district would lapse when, after having been organized for more than three years, the registered electors in the district fell below six, or if the number of students in the school(s) fell below six in grades one through eight or below 11 in ninth through twelfth grades.

In 1883, the state recognized a need for public high schools. Before 1899, the year Clovis High School was founded, students in Clovis who attended area elementary school districts and wanted to earn a high school diploma had to apply to go to Fresno High School. Boys could also choose to travel to Stockton, Sacramento or the Bay Area, while girls went to San Jose, if they went at all.

On June 27, 1899, seven school districts — Red Banks, Jefferson, Garfield, Mississippi, Wolters Colony, Temperance and Clovis — organized to form Clovis Union High School District, with each elementary district agreeing to send its ninth-graders to Clovis Union High School. In general, a high school district comprising two or more elementary school districts lying wholly in the same county is considered a "union high school district."

Each district elected one trustee to the board of the new Clovis Union High School District. The children of these outlying farming communities were often partial to the more rural, agricultural Clovis Union High School than the urban Fresno schools.

As was established by unification in 1960, Clovis Unified encompasses close to 198-square miles. Today, 42 percent of CUSD's boundaries reach into the City of Clovis, another 42 percent reach into the City of Fresno, and the remaining 16 percent extend to the unincorporated areas of Fresno County. The boundary lines may give pause, but looking at the history of Fresno County and its development, the area that makes up Clovis Unified is comprised of what were once the outlying, rural areas of the more metropolitan town of Fresno. These communities banded together in their educational endeavors through shared interest and common ground.

On its 50th anniversary, Clovis Unified today is comprised of 31 elementary schools, five intermediate schools, five high schools, four alternative education schools, one adult school, one outdoor and environmental educational school, one Center for Advanced Research and Technology, and one online charter school. Clovis Online School, CUSD's most recent school to open and the first of its kind in the district, welcomed students for the 2009-10 school year. The full-time online school, created under the umbrella of a charter school, offers all the general core education classes needed for graduation, as well as electives such as art history, Spanish, graphic arts and photography. The school first opened to ninth- and tenth-graders, and as of the 2010-11 school year, Clovis Online is open to a full complement of ninth through twelfth grade students. The tuition-free school is available to students in Fresno County, as well as the neighboring counties of Madera, Merced, Mono, Inyo, Tulare, Kings, San Benito and Monterey. CUSD's online school is designed to deliver a high-quality Clovis Unified education to students who may otherwise choose to drop out or leave the district.

Opening in time to begin the 2011-12 school year will be Roger S. Oraze Elementary School located at Dakota and Armstrong avenues serving students and their families living in the southeast section of the school district. Board members chose the name of the new school in honor of longtime CUSD teacher and administrator Roger Oraze, Ed.D., who is credited with the development of the district's current high-quality facility program. Oraze's 38-year career prior to his retirement June 30, 2004, included serving as a math teacher, learning director, deputy principal, principal, assessment administrator and as the district's first assistant superintendent of facility services. The new elementary school is the latest example of the district's continued growth and commitment to provide outstanding facilities for students to attend as enrollment continues to grow.

Today, the more than 38,000 students enrolled in CUSD, and the 2,100-plus certificated and nearly 1,800 classified employees who work in the district, look forward to a future of progress, innovation, achievement, opportunity, high-quality academic programs, support for the arts and athletics, the development of good character, and the excitement of what the next 50 years have in store for the tight-knit community that is Clovis Unified School District.

UNIFICATION DIVIDES BEFORE IT UNITES

By Charlotte Hutchison

In a pig's eye!

In the beginning, Clovis was a fiercely independent, dusty, farm community with a great deal of pride. The people of Clovis had no desire to see their little town swallowed up by the rapidly expanding Fresno. But even as that big neighbor to the southwest expanded its borders toward Clovis, it looked down its blue nose in disdain at the country bumpkins next door.

In his July 31, 1990, editorial appearing in the *Fresno Bee*, sportswriter Bob McCarthy concluded that Clovis High School's pre-unification athletic status ". . . in the North Yosemite League was pretty much of a joke." An intense rivalry existed between Clovis High and Fresno's Bullard High School. The Friday night football games between these two schools were animated events. The Bullard Knights and their fans arrived at game time waving posters printed with mean-spirited putdowns. They labeled Clovis as a "cow-town," and called Clovis kids "cowboys" and "cow pies." On game-night, the Clovis Cougars made the heartrending trip to the stadium with the knowledge they would probably lose the game. But after the game, the growling Cougars piled into pickup trucks with a determination to win the after-game fight. "Matter of fact, matters got so ugly one year that they threatened to cut off sports competition between the two schools — until cooler heads prevailed," wrote McCarthy.

Before unification, the Clovis schools had little to appeal to parents who were looking for a quality education for their children. McCarthy, in his 1990 editorial, wrote a vivid and colorful summary of the unpopular Clovis school situation:

> Move to Clovis? In a pig's eye! Back then, no self-respecting urbane Fresno family would even consider living there — and the Clovis area schools certainly had little to offer to counteract that attitude. The prevailing theme was "Mamas, don't let your daughters grow up to be cowgirls."

The move to unify

Fresno city schools and Calwa schools merged on July 1, 1948, to form the Fresno Unified School District. The new district was organized under Chapter 16 of the State Code, which permitted land annexed by the City of Fresno to automatically be incorporated into the Fresno Unified School District.

By 1958, Fresno had annexed over 40 percent of the assessed valuation of the Clovis district. Wolters Elementary School District, Scandinavian School District, Sunnyside and the Manchester Shopping Center areas were located in the Clovis Union High School district before they were annexed by the City of Fresno. Later, Fresno expanded even further into Clovis territory by annexing the areas where Hoover and McLane high schools are now located.

The Clovis Union High School Board of Trustees, as the primary catalyst moving to unify, was aware that if Fresno continued on the course it was pursuing, Clovis High would soon be left with only the feeder schools located within the city of Clovis, Dry Creek Union and a portion of Jefferson Union. Unifying the six individual Clovis elementary districts with Clovis

Union High School appeared to be the only way to stop Fresno's encroachment and preserve the Clovis High School population base.

The new organization

In December 1959, the unification proposal was placed on the ballot. Clovis residents living in school districts that had organized between 1866 and 1935 and had joined to form the Clovis Union High School, were eligible to vote. On December 22, 1959, the unification issue was passed by 80 percent of the voters.

Clovis unified under Chapter 19 of the State Code, which prevented outside agencies from taking land without the approval of both school boards. In essence, Chapter 19 stopped all further encroachment by neighboring Fresno Unified.

Because each of the original Clovis districts desired to retain local autonomy over school issues, the new seven member governing board included one trustee from each of the original districts. The board's first trustees were William B. White, Area 1; Everett G. "Bud" Rank, Jr., Area 2; F. L. "Kelly" Parks, Area 3; James E. Oliver, Area 4; Einar P. Cook, Area 5; James B. McCrummen, Area 6; and William F. McFarlane, Area 7. During the first 10 minutes of the organizational meeting, the trustees selected Oliver to be the acting chairman (president) and McFarlane was to be the district's first secretary (clerk). Rank was then selected as the board's official president.

In 1960, enrollment in the original 11 component schools (Temperance-Kutner, Jefferson, Tarpey, Cole, Sierra Vista, Fort Washington-Lincoln, Pinedale, Nelson, Dry Creek and Weldon elementary schools, and Clovis High School) totaled 5,037 students. The combined elementary schools' average daily attendance of over 1,500 gave the governing board the status of a city board of education and provided the new district with full instructional control for grades kindergarten through 12. This centralization of authority was essential to providing a single, continuous program of education for the children of Clovis.

Some of the items on the board's first agenda were to decide the terms of office for the board members, the place and time of future meetings, dealing with immediate costs to the district, and a motion to name the district. The following item was entered into the minutes of the meeting:

> DISTRICT OFFICIALLY NAMED. It was moved by Mr. Parks, seconded by Mr. Cook, and unanimously carried that the district be named "Clovis Unified School District."

With the motion carrying unanimously, the new Clovis Unified School District began its first year of operation with 5,037 students and a $3,000,000 budget.

The four-to-three vote

From the beginning, the unification issue continued as a source of controversy for the new governing board. Local control of school issues was very important to the people, and local powers were not willing to give up any of their authority. The chasm that divided the members of the board into pro-unification and anti-unification was evident long before their first meeting in April of 1960.

The pro-unification faction consisted of trustees Rank, Cook, McFarlane and McCrummen. They were aware of some of the more immediate benefits unification offered, like pooling services such as purchasing, bookkeeping and transportation to eliminate the need and expense of duplicating these services in each district.

The anti-unification faction of Oliver, White and Parks, favored keeping the status-quo and allowing each of the seven original districts to continue to operate as separate entities with separate administrations, budgets, curriculum and transportation.

The first major item of contention among the two factions was the appointment of a district superintendent. Each trustee was looking to the future and what he felt was the best direction for the Clovis educational system to take. They interviewed many applicants for the position, including the former superintendent of Jefferson Union School District, Dr. Floyd B. "Doc" Buchanan.

The pro-unification trustees were aware of the changes and improvements Dr. Buchanan made during his three years at Jefferson. They thought Buchanan and his visions for a unified district would serve the best interests of Clovis. On the other hand, Oliver, White and Parks viewed Buchanan as a newcomer and saw him as a threat to the farming community's status-quo. Most early board meetings ran late into the night, and many did not end until the early hours of the next morning. Discussions became heated and tempers flared. During a recent interview, former trustee Everett G. "Bud" Rank, Jr. described how, at the board's first meeting, "… the [acting] president got so angry that he threw the gavel at me."

On April 29, 1960, with a simple majority vote of four in favor and three opposed, a motion passed to appoint Buchanan as superintendent of the Clovis Unified School District. But at that time, Buchanan's appointment was not a done deal. Three days later, a large group of citizens arrived at the board meeting to voice their opposition to Buchanan's appointment. The trustees went into executive session to discuss the matter further and agreed to table further consideration of Buchanan's contract until additional applicants were interviewed.

Over the next 10 days, the board continued the interview process for the superintendent position. When they met on May 12, the four-to-three vote remained unchanged, and the motion to offer a four-year contract to Buchanan passed again with a simple majority vote. Afterward, a second motion to appoint Buchanan acting superintendent until the district became an official entity on July 1, 1960, carried unanimously.

The clerk phoned Buchanan and invited him to come to the meeting. Buchanan arrived at 9:25 P.M. and accepted the offer to be the district's first superintendent. Ten Clovis teachers submitted letters of resignation. By the time the board met on June 9, another 10 teachers had resigned, and the pro-unification and anti-unification factions evolved into pro-administration and anti-administration factions.

The four-to-three vote became a mainstay for deciding district issues until October 21, 1960. On that day, William B. White submitted his letter of resignation as the Area 1 trustee to Walter G. Martin, superintendent of schools for Fresno County. Martin forwarded White's letter to the Clovis board, informing them they could legally accept the letter of resignation and appoint a successor. With a four-to-two vote, Phillip V. Sanchez was appointed to fill the seat vacated by White.

Two weeks after he was appointed, Sanchez presented his letter of resignation to the board. He described the dissension among the board members and cited their factionalism as the basis for his withdrawal:

> I have become aware of the existence of two distinct factions [a pro-Buchanan and an anti-Buchanan faction] within the membership of the board, and a decided rift between the two. . . . On this board there exists a minority group opinion which seeks to maintain its status as such, regardless of the consequences. This. . .is unfortunate. . .these [two factions] could more logically, intelligently and profitably be merged into one faction: *a pro-Clovis Unified School District* faction.

After all six trustees refused to accept Sanchez's resignation, "It was moved by Mr. Oliver and seconded by Mr. Parks and carried unanimously that the governing board give Sanchez a unanimous vote of confidence."

The recall election

Over the next four years, some of the faces on the board changed. In 1963, Ralph J. Lynn was appointed to fill the vacancy left when William F. McFarlane did not run for re-election. Other new members were Alfred P. Biglione, Claude B. Shellenberger and Douglas R. Dresser. Even though some faces had changed, the division between the pro-administration and anti-administration factions remained intact and spilled over into the general public. Many items on the agenda still produced heated debates and caused board meetings to continue well into the early morning hours.

On March 31, 1964, the evening before the next regular school board meeting, a Citizens Committee met to discuss how they might help unite the members of the governing board and find a way to resolve the anti-administration problems that were surfacing at the high school. When the trustees met on April 1, a large number of Clovis citizens were in the audience to ask the board to develop a plan that would give rise to harmony in the district. After considerable discussion by visitors and board members, the following Five Point Program was adopted:

1. The board unanimously resolves that the present administration is doing a good job and will have the complete support of the entire board.
2. The board expects the unanimous support of the administrative staff and all the employees in carrying out the policy set by the board.
3. The board desires that the superintendent meet with the president of the board and discuss the agenda before it is mailed.
4. The board requests that the people of the community act with dignity and restraint in matters involving our school district.
5. The board pledges they will work together in accord, realizing that there is room for differences of honest opinion commensurate with our duties as a policy making body.

Perhaps in retrospect, there was a bit of irony in the fact that the Five Point Program was passed on April Fool's Day. During the summer of 1964, the discord between the two factions reached fever pitch. When the board met on May 6, the factional split had not changed, and members of the Citizens Committee attending the meeting concluded that the problems facing the board had existed for so many years that they must find a way to resolve it. Charles Preuss, chairman of the Citizens Committee, informed the trustees during this meeting ". . . that certain people had been receiving anonymous phone calls late at night or early in the morning." This was later reiterated by Myrlee "Molly" Buchanan. In a statement to the *Fresno Bee*, she recalled the anger and threats made against her husband (Dr. Buchanan) during the first four years of consolidation in the Clovis district. She said, "I used to get phone calls at night after meetings, saying he wouldn't make it home."

Petitions to recall the four pro-administration trustees — Rank, Lynn, Shellenberger and Biglione — were submitted to the County School's Office on September 11, 1964. Two of the most controversial issues contributing to the Recall Election were ousting Buchanan and opposition to the proposed location of the new high school at the corner of Fowler and Barstow avenues. The status-quo trustees were opposed to using sixty-acres of good farmland to build a school.

However, all seven members of the board were aware that the discord within their group was creating animosity throughout the community. With the Recall Election coming up, both sides agreed that after the election, the losing side would quit (Rank). In order to ease the tension on the board, on December 14, James E. Oliver sent his letter of resignation to Fresno County Superintendent of Schools Harold L. Coles.

On December 22, 1964, exactly five years to the day after voting to unify the district, Clovis voters elected to retain Rank, Lynn, Biglione and Shellenberger as trustees. Oliver's resignation was effective January 15, 1965, and on that day the board appointed John E. Coffman to fill the Area 4 vacancy. Parks chose not to run for re-election and retired in June 1965. A short time later, Clovis voters elected Calvin F. Wise, D.D.S., to represent Area 3 on the governing board.

Build it and they will come

After the recall failed, tension and discord during board meetings eased up and the members of the board united to assess the district's curriculum. On April 15, 1964, they passed Resolution No. 92 to purchase the land located on the corner of Fowler and Barstow avenues, and the plan to build the new Clovis High School went forward. Architects were appointed and construction began in 1965.

Four years later, with construction of the new school complete, the former high school, located at 902 Fifth Street, was converted into the district's first intermediate school. Both the new Clovis High School and C. Todd Clark Intermediate School opened in the fall of 1969.

The new high school campus was state-of-the-art, and included 74 classrooms, a multipurpose building, TV laboratory, kitchen, administrative offices and a swimming pool. The intermediate school retained its swimming pool, tennis courts, gymnasium, boys' and girls' locker rooms, band room, and other athletic facilities. With bragging rights to one of the finest high schools in the state and a modern intermediate school, CUSD helped to place Clovis on its path to "A Way of Life." Developers came to Clovis to build houses and shopping centers, and families moved to Clovis to provide educational advantages for their children.

War on illiteracy

The result of the recall election was the turning point for uniting the trustees. The pro-administration and anti-administration factions were gone, and a strong governing board united in efforts to support a rigorous educational program. However, the district had no centralized curricular schedule in place and fewer than 50 percent of Clovis students were on grade level in reading and math. In his "Historical Overview of Clovis Unified School District," Buchanan described the low student achievement:

> By 1968, it was possible to review student achievement results to determine how well the district was preparing its students academically. The figures were staggeringly appalling: only 42 percent of the students were on grade level in mathematics, and 44 percent were on grade level in reading. Realizing that fully six of every 10 students in school were able neither to read their books nor to do their math at the appropriate grade level, district administrators knew something had to be done.

During the administrative staff meeting in December 1969, Buchanan outlined a plan for getting 90 percent of the district's students on grade level in three years. The method for accomplishing this goal was competition.

The 90% Goal

The governing board's reaction was that a 90 percent goal seemed outrageous and unattainable. In a 2008 interview, former trustee Ralph J. Lynn described his reaction to the administration's proposed 90% Goal.

> At the time, the 90% Goal appeared to be unrealistic. It was BOLD — it was VERY BOLD!!! But, it turned out to be a very wise move. . . . Doc had a very picturesque way of putting it. I remember his saying, "Well, a lot of people are happy or content with this fifty-percent. But, how would you like to line up fifty-percent of the parents and tell them, your kid can't read and he's not going to be able to read. Ask the teachers, do you want to tell these parents that their kids aren't going to be able to read?"

Eventually, the governing board saw the necessity and the advantage of getting 90 percent of Clovis students on grade level, and the 90% Goal was adopted. Afterward there was a lot of laughter and disbelief on whether the new goal was attainable. In a 2009 interview Buchanan described the teachers' reaction: "When I told the teachers we had to get ninety-percent of Clovis students on grade level in reading and math, they thought I was absolutely out of my mind. I asked them, 'Well, look, do you want to have a conference with the parents and tell them which ones aren't going to be able to make it?' Everybody in the state laughed at Clovis. Two of my teachers came in from Jefferson. They sat down to talk to me. They said, 'Doc, do you mean all we have to teach is reading and math?' I said, 'Well, if the kids can't read, what else are you going to teach them?'"

By implementing the 90% Goal, the governing board and the administration declared war on illiteracy, and in Clovis that meant that low test scores were no longer accepted as the norm.

The Competition Model

To achieve the district's goal of getting 90 percent of Clovis students on grade level, the administration implemented Buchanan's Competition Model, a program he began developing while earning his doctorate degree at the University of California at Berkeley. He based his competition program on the theory that every organization must have a product if it is going to succeed.

"In education, we don't admit we've got to have a product," Buchanan said. "If we don't have a product, this is going to be useless, why do we stay in business? . . . In Clovis, I tried to develop a product. . .we defined the product. And you know how we defined it? If you're going to be in business, [and if] you're going to be successful, you've got to decide how successful you're going to be. So, we set a ninety-percent goal in reading and math. So that was the start with the reading and math programs. . . . You have to have a product, and you have to define what it's going to look like when it graduates from the twelfth grade."

Competition was instituted as a means of evaluating students' performance. Its success depended on monitoring the work of everyone involved in each child's education at intermediate and long-range levels. Every child must feel important, and everyone involved with a child's education must give evidence that they are concerned with the child's performance. The theme of the competition program implemented in CUSD was designed around a concept of teams of schools, teams of teachers, and teams of students competing against each other and against themselves to improve.

In 1976, construction on CUSD's second high school was complete. When the new Clovis West High School opened, the district was divided into two competing teams. Clovis High and all of its feeder schools made up the "Blue Unit," and the "Red Unit" was comprised of the new Clovis West and its feeder schools.

State-mandated testing provided feedback for the effectiveness of the educational methods in Clovis Unified. The evidence of success in the Clovis system was available at the end of the 1970-71 school year. Test results revealed that the number of students on grade level had increased by 25 percent, and the results continued to improve.

Site-based management

One of the most unique elements of the Clovis Competition Model, site-based management, was implemented in 1972. Site-based management consisted of four elements: mission, content, method and accountability. Mission and accountability were the responsibility of the governing board and the administration. Content and method were delegated to the site manager/principal.

The role of the superintendent was to provide leadership. The principal of each school was given the authority and flexibility to evolve their programs at the site level. Every teacher developed an individual program for his or her own classroom, and the administration provided all tools and supplies that each teacher requested.

In 1972, the laughter stopped and the disbelief was replaced by amazing pride in the district's 90% Goal when Tarpey Elementary School's first grade teachers, Leola Minors, Dorothy Luthord and Ester Smith, reported 90 percent of Tarpey's first grade students were on grade level. In 1977, Fort Washington Elementary School was awarded the district's first Golden Bell Award as the first school to have 90 percent of the entire student body on grade level.

Together we stand

The momentum of increasing student performance and athletic excellence continued to build through the 1970s, with community and staff fully behind the district's efforts to build a school system that served its students well. In 1978, what could have sent this momentum to a crashing halt became another defining moment in Clovis Unified history. California voters, frustrated with soaring property tax rates, passed the Jarvis-Gann Act (Proposition 13) in June of 1978. The bill would revolutionize both the way the state calculated property taxes and the way it funded its public schools.

Immediately, school districts around the state were thrown into disarray. Unsure of what was to happen to their ability to pay for teachers, textbooks, classroom supplies and the other basic necessities of education, schools began to lay off teachers and slash transportation, performing arts and athletics programs. But, not in Clovis Unified. Spurred by mounting panic among other education agencies, Buchanan called an emergency meeting of all Clovis Unified employees in the summer of 1978. Tucked into an un-air conditioned Clovis High School gymnasium, employees listened as Buchanan laid out Clovis Unified's plan to respond to the state's new funding mechanism: Clovis students weren't going to lose important resources or the programs that had begun to define a Clovis Unified education, and Clovis Unified employees weren't going to lose their jobs. Buchanan told the assembled employees, "We're all in this together, and if we have to close school early and all go home, that's what we're going to do."

Confident that their jobs were secure, teachers, custodians, bus drivers and school leaders threw themselves into working even harder to build an unmatched educational experience for their students. When the end of the school year rolled around and classes were still in session, employees knew that Clovis Unified could get through anything so long as they remained united.

In 1973, six years before California voters passed Prop 13, the Clovis community expressed strong support for Clovis Unified's building program through the passage of a special override tax. The facility tax was used to establish a recreation, cultural and athletic (RCA) fund specifically for special facilities and is credited with setting the standard for high quality facilities for CUSD students. This emerging commitment by the local community to provide resources for school facilities was stalled by the passage of Prop 13, which removed local tax override measures then in place and prohibited future measures at the local level. Though CUSD continued to receive approximately 90 percent of the original RCA fund from the state, it was not until 1986, when Prop 46 modified the prohibition on school facility bonds included in Prop 13, that the CUSD community was able to cast their vote in support of a $59 million school bond measure, which they did again in 1993 ($49.2 million), 1996 ($98 million), 2001 ($79 million) and 2004 ($168 million).

The continued support residents in Clovis Unified have shown for facility bond measures demonstrates their faith in how the district has managed tax dollars and the importance placed on state-of-the-art schools and athletic/performing arts venues in providing an outstanding educational experience for students.

The Sparthenian Concept

A cornerstone of Clovis Unified's successful educational system is Dr. Buchanan's revolutionary Sparthenian Concept. His idea of a "Sparthenian" education was derived from two ancient Greek words, Spartan and Athenian, and epitomized the district's goal to raise students who were well-rounded in mind, body and spirit. The Spartans were physically fit and courageous, while the Athenians were intellectual and artistic.

Accountability Model

During its first 30 years, the Clovis administration and governing board concentrated on building the proverbial "better mousetrap," and "the world beat a path" to their schoolhouse doors. By 1990, approximately 22,000 students were enrolled in Clovis schools. And at that time, fewer than 50 percent of the people in Clovis had lived in the district for more than five years.

New people meant new ideas. During the late 1980s, some of the newcomers began rejecting the values that had created CUSD's successful approach to education. They joined forces with those who had been anti-Buchanan from the past and attacked the district's most basic concept: competition.

In 1985, the faces on the governing board began to change again when voters elected Jan M. Biggs to serve as the trustee for Area 1. During his campaign, Biggs openly opposed the district's use of competition.

Two years later, the Competition Model continued to be a highly visible issue. In a déjà vu mode, an anti-Buchanan faction materialized during the hotly debated campaigns to fill three seats on the board. On November 3, 1987, incumbent board members John E. Coffman, Paul C. Anderson and John W. Davis lost their bids for re-election. They were replaced by three more new faces, Ralph E. Lockwood, Jr., Richard V. Powers and Allen O. Clyde, D.P.M. In 1988, the Competition and Testing Advisory Committee was organized to study the district's competition program.

During the summer of 1989, the governing board combined the analysis provided by CTAC's studies with responses and recommendations garnered from of the annual School Assessment Review Team (SART) survey and the Superintendent's Advisory Committee (SAC). One of the results of these studies was to incorporate Buchanan's Sparthenian Concept into the Clovis mission statement:

> The mission of the Clovis Unified School District is to provide excellence in education through exemplary programs, services and activities to a diverse community that fosters lifelong learning, service to society and a commitment to the Sparthenian concept — be the best you can be in mind, body and spirit.

A list of seven priorities was appended to the new mission. The following seven areas were identified as relevant to accomplishing the objective and guiding Clovis schools into the next decade: developing the Sparthenian concept, student achievement, human resources, financial resources, cultural diversity, organizational effectiveness and community involvement. It was the responsibility of the superintendent and administration to develop a plan and to monitor the progress of the governing board's clearly defined mission.

The feedback from CTAC, SART and SAC also led to, in 1990, the Competition Model being replaced with a revised Accountability Model, and the red and blue attack units were formally disbanded, but competition remained ingrained in CUSD. The new model retained some the elements in the old program by reiterating an emphasis on mission statement, clearly stated goals and methods of tracking progress. One major difference was to replace "ranking" with "rating" in a move toward the creation of a model that emphasized continuous improvement and individual competition. At this time, many longtime Clovis residents would probably agree with Deborah Strother's lamentation in her book *Clovis California Schools, A Measure of Excellence* that "Clovis Unified was the only district in the United States to change its program because children were achieving so well."

The five-to-two vote

Turmoil continued on the governing board and in the community, and on the evening of July 11, 1990, more than 500 Clovis citizens attended the Clovis Unified School District board meeting held in the Clovis High School cafeteria. On the agenda was a decision whether or not to extend the contract of Superintendent Dr. Floyd B. "Doc" Buchanan, and the large turnout was indicative of the passionate opinions on both sides of the debate. Many people in the audience carried banners that read "Don't Knock the Doc" to show support for the current leadership. Later in the meeting, the trustees retired into executive session to discuss and vote on whether to renew Buchanan's contract. At approximately 2 A.M., with a five-to-two vote, the decision was made to allow Buchanan's contract to expire on June 30, 1991.

New leadership

The challenge of finding a new leader led to a widespread superintendent search. On July 1, 1991, Dr. David Sawyer became the new superintendent. Sawyer came to Clovis Unified from a South Carolina district without any existing ties to Clovis Unified. But, the stormy waters from Buchanan's departure were still churning.

The depth of the early 1990s disconnect between the changing community and the school district also revealed itself when a $95 million facility bond measure failed in November 1991. The bond measure was desperately needed to keep pace with an ever-increasing student population. The district failed again the following year, when voters rejected a $79 million facility bond.

By 1992, resources to build new schools had stalled, and Clovis Unified had to turn to alternate student housing plans. Cole, Gettysburg, Tarpey, Miramonte and Weldon elementary schools opened in 1992 on year-round, multi-track schedules in order to obtain 100 percent state funding for school districts with 30 percent of K-6 students enrolled in year-round programs. This would help accommodate swelling enrollments and to allow the district to find classroom seats for a student population that hit 26,000.

The tide began to turn the following year. With enrollment continuing to grow, a $49.2 million bond measure was finally approved by the community. In 1994, the state's year-round school funding rules changed and the district's 21 elementary schools returned to a traditional calendar year, poised to begin building new schools to accommodate enrollment.

Governing board stability was slow to return but first began to turn around when, on November 5, 1991, Ginny L. Hovsepian, William C. "Clint" Barnes and Susan M. Walker, D.H.Sc., defeated incumbents Christine A. "Kris" Maul, Ralph E. Lockwood, Jr., and Richard V. Powers to gain seats on the governing board. R. Kent Kunz was elected to replace the seat vacated by the earlier resignation of Allen O. Clyde, D.P.M. In 1992, Richard P. Lake, C.P.A., replaced Barnes, who resigned shortly after being elected. A year later, Jan M. Biggs announced he would not seek re-election. That November, his seat was assumed by Sandra A. Bengel; Jim Van Volkinburg, D.D.S., defeated incumbent Naomi P. Strom; and Robert H. Rowley defeated incumbent Elizabeth J. "Betsy" Sandoval. In 1996, Brian Heryford was elected to replace Kunz and Sandoval was re-appointed following the resignation of Rowley. The board of Hovsepian, Walker, Lake, Van Volkinburg, Bengel, Heryford and Sandoval served together for many years and brought stability to the district on many levels. In 2008, board members Lake and Walker retired from service on the board and were replaced by F. Scott Troescher and Christopher S. Casado, respectively.

During the tumultuous years of the late 1980s and early 1990s, many of the district's long-time school principals and teachers remained and kept the educational focus on providing students with the high quality education expected from Clovis Unified. Sawyer departed after just two and a half years as superintendent. He was followed by long-time Clovis Unified administrator Dr. Kent Bishop as the district's next superintendent. A year later, Bishop's term ended when he was dismissed due to misconduct, and Chief Business Official Dr. Terry Bradley took the reins on an interim basis. In 1995, the governing board selected another newcomer, Dr. Walt Buster, from Northern California's Cotati-Rohnert Park as CUSD's next superintendent. Buster focused on rebuilding lines of communication and the understanding that the desire for every child to succeed in mind, body and spirit was still the shared goal of both the district and its community. When Buster retired in 2002, Dr. Terry Bradley was appointed to the district's top post.

Bradley first came to Clovis Unified in 1976 from Wisconsin, and had played a large role in developing Clovis Unified's financially stable foundation. Having served twice as interim superintendent, he brought to the job a well-defined sense of the district's history. During his seven-year tenure, Clovis Unified saw student achievement and co-curricular performance soar to some of the top levels in California. On Bradley's retirement in 2009, Dr. David Cash joined the district from Southern California's Claremont Unified and assumed the leadership role. With funding to California's public schools slashed as a result of a nationwide recession, Cash's initial year in the district was focused on balancing the budget while avoiding employee layoffs and preserving high quality educational offerings to students in good times and bad.

Epilogue

Looking at Clovis in a rearview mirror might reveal a deeply embedded competitiveness ingrained in the little town itself. Early Clovis residents competed city to city with Fresno. A basic competition was highly visible in the board room during the early days of the pro-unification/administration and anti-unification/administration school board. It was an angry competition that raised its ugly head during the 1964 recall election. At times, during later Clovis school board elections, "political competition" over Buchanan's Competition Model received a great deal of unflattering attention in the local press. And through it all, the district kept winning its war on illiteracy.

The district's history was fraught with divisiveness, turbulence and "competition" as new trustees, administrators and staff members came and went. But even though they did not always agree, most of the district leaders always kept one important goal in sight, to make Clovis Unified students the best they could be in mind, body and spirit.

In 2010, Clovis Unified celebrates its fiftieth anniversary, but 1970 will long be remembered as the district's defining year. By 1975, the board had adopted a strict dress code that not only changed the look of Clovis students, but flew in the face of the anti-cultural movement of the "Flower Power" generation. Long flowing locks and headbands were prohibited. Shoes, socks and shirts superseded sandals, fringed vests and love-beads. It was the year students were first in attendance at the new high school and C. Todd Clark Intermediate School. It was the year the 90% Goal was adopted and the Competition Model was implemented. And it was the year Dennis Lindsey was hired as the new football coach for the Clovis High Cougars.

In 1970, the rivalry between the Clovis Cougars and Bullard Knights was still ongoing. In a recent interview, Buchanan described the animosity that had existed between the two schools during his first ten years as superintendent:

> Before Dennis came to Clovis High, all the Clovis kids wanted to do was fight. They didn't have discipline. They didn't know how to play football, but they wanted to be physical . . . and to beat up the other team so bad that they wouldn't be able win their next game. And, they used to spend Friday nights down in the parking lot behind Bob's Big Boy at Shaw and Blackstone and have fights with the Bullard High kids.

The 1970 North Yosemite League football championship was up for grabs when the Cougars and their new coach met the Bullard Knights at Radcliffe Stadium. The teams were already on the field, when suddenly a blue and gold helicopter appeared overhead and descended down, down, down onto the playing field. The Clovis band began marching and playing as the Clovis cheerleaders jumped out of the chopper, bounced across the turf, cheering and waving their pom-poms.

That night, with a final score of 21-7, the Clovis High Cougars wrested the valley championship away from their arch rivals. And, after the game, the parking lot down behind Bob's Big Boy was quiet, because back in Clovis these "cowboys" were heroes.

FORMING CLOVIS UNIFIED:
THE GONE YESTERDAY SCHOOLS

By Charlotte Hutchison

The one-room schoolhouses that once dotted the valley floor around what is now Clovis Unified School District have all slipped into local history along with the Pollasky Railroad, the Enterprise Canal, and the Fresno Flume and Irrigation Company's canal and planing mill.

Early schools were often built on land donated by or purchased from area farmers. Parents and other residents in the area who valued a local educational system for children volunteered labor and supplies to create these early public schools. Once the building was finished and workers laid down their hammers and saws, the school became the center of education where children spent the day learning. And when school was out and the children went home, the schoolhouse became a gathering place for social and political meetings, dinners, dances, and church services.

Over time, many of the area's early elementary schools, such as Dry Creek, Jefferson, Garfield, Lincoln, Fort Washington and Clovis, evolved into the modern multi-building plants that grace the district today. Other early schools annexed to neighboring districts to form unions, and then there were those that lapsed and eventually closed their doors for lack of attendance. These long-gone schools are profiled here in recognition of the important role they played in shaping what is today Clovis Unified.

Mississippi School District

The first Mississippi School District organization occurred on May 4, 1869. The schoolhouse was built a quarter mile north of Little Dry Creek, between present-day Behymer and Perrin avenues, by volunteers on land donated by J. M. Heiskell. The first schoolhouse was built of rough lumber and the desks were handmade. In 1903, the building was moved to Clovis and used as a residence. The first Mississippi School was annexed by Millerton District on December 5, 1871, two-and-one-half years after it was first organized.

The second Mississippi District organization occurred June 4, 1877, on the petition of James Darwin Collins, who had been responsible for the Academy School (later Dry Creek Elementary School). Mississippi's new schoolhouse and the desks were built with finished lumber. In an article appearing in the *Fresno Weekly Expositor*, the schoolroom was described as comfortable and commodious with new patent seats and desks with the capacity to seat 50 students. M. W. Mathews was the first clerk of the board, and early teachers included Bettie Heiskell, Harold Bowman and Mrs. G. W. Oman.

Like other schoolhouses in the area, Mississippi served as a community meeting place for many social activities, and the Methodist Church held services there on Sundays. In *Those Were the Days*, Mrs. C. Todd Clark described how the early circuit riders used Mississippi and other schoolhouses for Sunday services:

> In the early years of our state and country there were no churches outside of towns and cities, so activities of the communities were in the schoolhouses.

> The Mississippi School District was so named because several of our early families were from the state of Mississippi. The Ships, Nelsons and Samples were some of these families. The Mississippi District was part of the Big Dry Creek circuit. A circuit would be a number of Methodist Churches linked together with one pastor who lived in the community where none of the churches were located, and he was a circuit rider. . . . In those days they had circuits and preached three times on Sunday. . . . After the Clovis church was organized and had their own service the services at Mississippi School were discontinued.

On June 27, 1899, twenty-two years after the second organization, the Mississippi District was one of the seven elementary schools that came together to create Clovis Union High School District for the education of older students. Four years later, on March 14, 1903, it was annexed by the Clovis Elementary District, comprised of Clovis Grammar School. After the second Mississippi School closed, the building was moved to 304 Harvard Avenue in Clovis, and used as a residence.

Letcher School District

The small settlement of Letcher was a stage stop located on Tollhouse Road near Sample Road. The settlement and later the school district were named for F. F. Letcher, a county supervisor and area farmer.

The Letcher post office opened July 8, 1886. The following year on May 7, 1887, the Letcher School District was organized. Mrs. I. H. Chapman was the first teacher and H. H. Budge was the first clerk of the board. Other early teachers at Letcher were Elsie Peck, Grace Spence and Anita Shade. During the school year of 1896-97, fifteen students graduated from Letcher.

After operating 25 years, the Letcher School was suspended and lapsed in 1912 for lack of student enrollment. Three years later, on January 15, 1915, the Letcher post office closed. And on August 6, 1916, the Letcher School District was annexed to Dry Creek District.

Nees Colony District

Organized on February 6, 1906, the Nees Colony District was created from a portion of the Clovis Elementary District. The first schoolhouse was built that same year and located at Armstrong and Nees avenues. As were many of the early schools in the Clovis area, the first Nees schoolhouse was a traditional one-room building. Laura Hole was the first teacher, and the average daily attendance during the district's first year of operation was 26 students.

Six years later, in 1912, architect A. C. Swartz designed a new one-story brick building with three classrooms and a belfry. The new structure was located on the northeast corner of Armstrong and Nees near the original one-room school. During Nees Colony's last year of independent operation, May Mathews was the principal and 107 students were enrolled.

On May 16, 1947, the Nees Colony District was annexed to Dry Creek District to form Dry Creek Union School District. The new district continued to use the three-room brick building on Armstrong and Nees avenues until around 1954, when a new Dry Creek Union schoolhouse was built, using bricks salvaged from Nees Colony schoolhouse which had been torn down.

Wolters District

The Wolters District was organized on February 29, 1892, with a schoolhouse located near the present intersection of Shaw Avenue and First Street. Elsie Clark was the school's first teacher.

On June 27, 1899, after John Rutledge and Lee Beall's petition for a new high school in Clovis was approved, seven elementary school districts came together to form the Clovis Union High School District. One of those districts was Wolters. The high school district existed as a separate entity from these seven elementary districts, but the schools committed to sending their young students on to Clovis Union High School for a local secondary education. At that time, Mrs. Hattie Hopkins was the teacher, and M. Coppin, H. V. Parker, and H. J. Jorgensen were trustees of Wolters.

In 1906, average daily attendance at Wolters was 47 students and Asa Whitaker was the principal. Ten years later, in 1916, a new schoolhouse was built. By 1952, when the 36-year-old building was replaced with a modern stucco school, Wolters' enrollment was 367 students.

Portions of Wolters, as well as the Lincoln, Fort Washington and Bullard districts, became part of the Pinedale School District when it was organized February 8, 1924.

In 1959, as Clovis was proposing to unify, voters in Wolters District elected on June 16 to leave the Clovis Union High School District and annex to Fresno City Unified District. After voters from seven other districts approved unification on December 22, 1959, another delegation from Wolters and Bullard protested the new district's boundaries. Their claim was denied by Fresno County Board of Supervisors, and the new Clovis Unified School District's boundaries remained intact.

Scandinavian District

When the Scandinavian Colony was settled in 1878, it was advertised as the Scandinavian Home Colony. Residents were mostly of Danish ancestry.

The Scandinavian School District was organized July 6, 1883, on a petition headed by Fred Anderson. The first Scandinavian schoolhouse, built in 1891, was located on Central Street.

In 1965, it was relocated to the corner of Shields and Sierra Vista avenues. The first teacher was Grace Morley. Early trustees included J. W. Hinds, D. A. Spence, A. Hennigson, and Rudolph Leohnard.

In December 1959, seventy-three years after organization, the residents of the Scandinavian District voted 1,087 to 408 to join the Fresno City Unified School District. Dr. Paul Nielsen was principal during Scandinavian District's last year of separate operation. The district's annexation to Fresno City Unified School District was effective July 1, 1960, thus removing Scandinavian's 17-square mile district from the new Clovis Unified School District.

Sunnyside Unified District

The Sunnyside Unified District has probably the most unusual history in the Clovis Unified area. This district was formed automatically when voters in the area within Kings Canyon Road and Fowler, Clovis, and California avenues rejected the idea of joining other districts forming

Clovis Unified School District, even though its students had been attending Temperance-Kutner Elementary and Clovis Union High School. The people in Sunnyside were determined not to be included in the new district and withdrew from the Clovis Unification proposal.

On January 19, 1960, the Fresno County Board of Supervisors officially approved a portion of Temperance-Kutner Union as the Sunnyside Unified District. In *History of Public School Organization and Administration in Fresno County*, John Dow described the new, one square-mile district.

> Sunnyside, reported to be the youngest and smallest school district in the nation, voted itself out of existence January 10, 1961. The district with approximately 200 children never had a schoolhouse or a teacher and officially became a part of Fresno City Unified School District July 1, 1961. Sunnyside was the seventh district to annex to Fresno Unified since 1947.

Epilogue
The majority of the pre-unification schools in Clovis began in less complicated times as one-room schoolhouses. Whether they evolved into modern day multi-building campuses, were annexed to unions or simply faded into history, the one-room schoolhouse has disappeared from the valley floor many yesterdays ago. But, today, those simple structures are remembered and celebrated as the roots of this district's most basic philosophy, "A fair break for every kid."

AGRICULTURAL EDUCATION

By Susan Sawyer Wise

The history of Clovis' student agriculture program and the Clovis chapter of Future Farmers of America (FFA) are intricately woven into the history of the community.

Clovis has long been an agriculture town, home to ranchers and farmers. Early rural elementary school districts in nearby farming communities often chose to align themselves with Clovis Union High School, sending their ninth through twelfth grade students there to receive their secondary education with the opportunity of benefitting from the high school's agriculture program offerings.

"Vocational agriculture, or 'vo-ag,' education in the United States has been an integral part of secondary education for many years. With California and Fresno County being leaders throughout history in agricultural production, it is natural that vo-ag has long been a part of the Clovis curriculum," said Dick Gates, former Clovis FFA chapter president and member of the national champion meat judging team, FFA State Star Award winner, Clovis High class of 1959 graduate, and father of two Clovis FFA chapter national champions. Like many in Clovis, for the Gates family, agricultural involvement and FFA participation is multigenerational.

Clovis High's agriculture program

Clovis Union High School's first official agriculture program started in 1933 at its campus on Fifth and Osmun streets in downtown Clovis. The program, housed in two portable classrooms, began so students could learn more about agriculture to improve their own farms and ranches at home. Through the Clovis FFA chapter housed out of Clovis High, students could also compete against other high school students to show the quality of their crops and livestock. Clovis FFA, since its inception, has been one of the leading chapters in the state and nation.

Agriculture classes were open only to boys until 1969. Until that time, girls could show their animals through 4-H and could only participate in FFA as a Sweetheart, the chapter's elected queen for the year.

Overall, agriculture and FFA programs have made considerable transformation over the years. "Prior to World War II many agriculture students returned to the farm to continue generations of work on the farm," said Gates. "As the country became more industrialized in the 1940s and beyond, many agriculture students chose higher education and vocations related to agriculture. This was a transition from cultivating the soil to cultivating the mind to be prepared for a broader-based capability and knowledge to compete in life."

A significant first for Clovis FFA came in 1942 when Clovis High student John E. Coffman, who attended CHS from 1939-43 and was very active in the agriculture program during that time, was the first Clovis FFA member to receive the coveted State FFA Degree from the California FFA organization. The competitive award is given to members with projects that are considered outstanding in areas including performance, leadership and animal projects. After reviewing members' achievements, officials give only a select number of awards each year. Since Coffman's receipt of the award, Clovis FFA members have been honored numerous times with the State FFA Degree as well as a few members earning the prestigious State Star Award, which is given to a State FFA Degree recipient who exemplifies excellent records, scope and depth in a supervised agricultural experience (SAE) project.

Clovis FFA achieved notable status for Clovis High and the community in the 1950s and 1960s. Under the instruction of such men as Hugh Carter, George Middleton and Max Henderson, Clovis FFA competed successfully locally, regionally, statewide, and even nationally in numerous contests such as parliamentary procedure, judging and evaluation, public speaking and academic testing in various agriculture-related subjects. Nearly every week of the school year, a Clovis FFA team was competing somewhere and many were winning. In the late 1950s, there were approximately 240 high school chapters in California and more than 4,000 chapters nationwide. The Clovis High chapter had more than 100 members at that time.

The school year of 1957-58 was particularly successful for Clovis FFA. Numerous first place and grand champion awards were achieved by Clovis FFA students that year. In addition, Clovis FFA was the premier sweepstakes winner at the state championships by winning more competitions than any other high school in California. Also that year, the meats judging team of Bob Smittcamp, Al Gould and Gates participated in the national competition in Kansas City and became Clovis FFA's first national champion judging team. Since that time, the Clovis chapter has had 10 national champion meats judging teams, coached by Ken Dias, and two national champion horse judging teams and one national livestock champion, all coached by Susan Henderson-Perry.

The agriculture program and FFA remained at Clovis High until the 1990s. At that time, students were finding it nearly impossible to fit agriculture classes into their schedules due to an increase in state-mandated academic class requirements. California FFA in general was in jeopardy due to these new academic standards. FFA programs had to change their teaching to accommodate the standards, which proved to be too difficult for some sites. Clovis Unified's long-standing, well-respected agriculture program would not however fall victim to these circumstances. Former trustees John E. Coffman and William F. McFarlane, then-Deputy Superintendent Dr. Terry Bradley, local farmer Pat V. Ricchiuti, Jr., Dr. Monte Person, whose interest came from his son having very successfully graduated from the CHS agriculture program and FFA, and agriculture teachers Ken Dias, Susan Henderson-Perry, and Kevin Woodard, worked relentlessly to save CUSD's agriculture program by involving industry, curriculum and community.

Through their efforts, the agriculture program was kept alive financially by a local school bond and a state grant for $5 million, as well as generous in-kind donations from local supporters. Other avenues of funding that support the program include federal Regional Occupational Program funding, an annual $35,000 Agriculture Incentive Grant matched by the district and various booster events.

McFarlane-Coffman Ag Center: The facility

After four years of planning, CUSD's agriculture program re-opened in the fall of 2000 at the Reagan Educational Center, located near Gettysburg and Locan avenues in southeast Clovis, where it could benefit from improved facilities and increased acreage for production. It was housed in the state-of-the-art McFarlane-Coffman Ag Center, so named for John E. Coffman and William F. McFarlane, former Clovis FFA members and Clovis High Class of 1943 graduates, who were instrumental in reinvigorating Clovis' agriculture program. Both men currently serve on the advisory committee.

The first phase of the agriculture center included an academic wing (with two biology labs, a traditional classroom and a distance learning facility), a 7,000-square-foot agriculture engineering facility, space for beef and sheep, and four acres of pastureland. Through a school bond passed by the community, the second phase of the center was completed in 2003. A biotechnology classroom and a state-of-the-art swine breeding facility were added. Extensive lab space would enable students to research genetics, breeding, DNA fingerprinting, plant tissue culture and more. An orchard to the east of the buildings allows students to experiment in crop development.

The center's main buildings are comprised of traditional classrooms. A metal and wood shop connects to one of the classrooms where students can learn to cut metal using lasers and build and repair agriculture equipment and irrigation systems. Next to the main buildings are a barn and a 20-acre farm. Through a loan program offered by the school, students can buy and house their animals in the barn.

McFarlane-Coffman Ag Center: The programs

Since opening at the Reagan Educational Center, home to Clovis East High, Reyburn Intermediate and Reagan Elementary, CUSD's agriculture program has increased its enrollment from 220 to 680 students. Student projects such as beef, swine, sheep, mechanics, crops and nursery have also increased, and staff has grown from two teachers to six.

Courses are categorized into five career certificate programs and are derived from basic core and advanced clusters. The programs, most of which are aligned to state science standards, are Agricultural Engineering, Animal Science, Environmental Science/Natural Resources, General Agricultural Science and Plant Science/Ornamental Horticulture. These certificate programs align with Fresno City College, Reedley College and California State University, Fresno, and also allow students to meet all University of California lab science requirements as well as college prep electives within the agriculture program.

Courses offered include agriculture engineering, agriculture science, botany, animal science, veterinary science, biotechnology, natural resources, agriculture business, environmental science, and fruit, vegetable and nursery landscape.

For Reyburn Intermediate students, five periods of exploratory agriculture are offered. More than 300 Reyburn students per year take advantage of these classes.

Grant enhancements

The agriculture department staff has written and received numerous grants in an effort to provide as many opportunities to their students as possible. One of these grants resulted in the development of the School of Agriculture Science and Technology (SAST). The SAST places teachers from the English, math, social science and agriscience departments together with a common group of students in an academy-type structure where agriculture is the main focus.

As part of a career technical education (CTE) facilities grant awarded to Clovis Unified by the State Allocation Board in 2008, Clovis East's agricultural mechanics program received $2,762,300 to construct a new 11,668-square-foot shop at the McFarlane-Coffman Ag Center. The funding, matched by the district, was part of a statewide effort to enhance career tech facilities in order to better prepare students for careers after graduation.

Through the CTE grant, the program was able to grow by nearly 200 students and the agriculture mechanics shop — woodworking, basic and advanced welding, and cold metal manufacturing — now had its own teacher. Additionally, the grant was used to purchase equipment and metalworking materials to sustain the expansive program.

McFarlane-Coffman Ag Center: Clovis FFA

Clovis FFA has also changed since arriving at its new Reagan Educational Center home-base including increased technology offerings, increased enrollment and the opportunity to develop more leadership skills and career skills for students. It has also seen many highlights in that time such as producing a national FFA president, a California state president and other state officers. In fact, when Clovis FFA and Clovis East High School alumni Beau Williamson served as national FFA president and Catharine Kuber served as California FFA president in 2007-08, it was the first time in FFA history that both a national and state officer originated from the same school district, much less the same school.

Since making its home at the McFarlane-Coffman Ag Center, Clovis FFA has produced national champion career development teams in meats evaluation, livestock judging and horse judging, and several other state champion teams. The chapter has also earned national beef proficiency awards, the California Top Agriculture Department Award, and several reserve and state champions and supreme champions at the State Fair, Cow Palace, and Fresno Fair. The program's instructors have also been celebrated. Kevin Woodard, Clovis East High agriculture science teacher and FFA coach, was named California Association FFA's 2008 Star Agriscience Teacher of the Year for the State of California. Additionally, agriculture teachers and FFA coaches Ken Dias and Susan Henderson-Perry have both been named Teachers of Excellence by the California Agriculture Teachers Association.

The benefits of FFA are many, according to Dias. "FFA makes a positive difference in the lives of students by developing their potential for premier leadership, personal growth and career success through agriculture education," he said. "Students are exposed to being part of a team, competition, earning awards and money, traveling and having fun through it all. They also learn about the agriculture industry and get exposure to potential careers in the industry."

Added Gates: "In my estimation, there is no youth organization in America greater than FFA that prepares students for the real world. Citizenship, scholarship, accountability, leadership and responsibility are traits well-endowed in FFA students. They represent far more than straw hats, bib overalls and tractors!"

ALTA SIERRA INTERMEDIATE SCHOOL

By Susan Moranda Vigil

Culmination of a dream

The building of Alta Sierra Intermediate School was the culmination of a dream for former Superintendent Dr. Floyd B. "Doc" Buchanan, Clovis Unified's superintendent of 31 years (1960-1991). He had envisioned an education complex comprised of an individual elementary, intermediate and high school on one parcel of land. A child's education would be streamlined from grades kindergarten through 12; facilities and resources could be shared; cross-age tutoring could take place. The benefits were many, and Clovis Unified School District was poised to bring the dream to fruition with the need to build schools to accommodate rapid population growth to the northeast of the heart of Clovis.

Alta Sierra's official opening in 1991 marked the beginning of the Buchanan Educational Center, the first educational center built in Clovis Unified, with Buchanan High School to follow in 1993 and Garfield Elementary in 1994.

Alta Sierra, named for the ranch that had previously occupied the land where the school was built, is positioned on the northwest corner of the education complex bounded by Peach, Minnewawa, Nees and Teague avenues.

The school was designed by Darden Architects and built by Swinerton-Walberg. It includes 47 classrooms, a library media center, administrative offices, a gymnasium and a multipurpose room, all centered on an open-air amphitheater located at the heart of the campus. Dr. Buchanan once explained to Devin Blizzard, recent principal of Alta Sierra, that he believed all of the administrator's eyes should be toward the students and not facing the streets. It is for this reason that the school's three cluster offices and the principal's office face the amphitheater.

In the beginning

It took approximately 16 months to complete construction of the school. In the beginning, it was surrounded on all sides by orchards. Original staff members reported that when the wind blew, the campus was often covered by topsoil.

There was not a kitchen or cafeteria window when the school first opened. Students lined up outside the attendance windows to be served their hot lunches. Large portable restrooms complete with sinks and running water had to be used before the completion of the permanent structures.

But, despite the challenges, said Donna Wetzel, who served as ASI's first activities director, "opening a new school was a wonderful experience, and the staff really became a family. We really had a wonderful time building all of the traditions that would mark the level of excellence that Alta Sierra enjoys."

Wetzel recalled several memorable "firsts" at Alta Sierra. "The first rally that we had was out on the Alta football field because there was no gym yet. I had the Bruin mascot dropped in by helicopter — you sure couldn't do that now!" she said. "I also remember that the first formal for the Buchanan High students was held in the Alta Sierra multipurpose room. We didn't realize that we had a silent fire alarm, and right in the middle of the dance the fire department showed up! Apparently, our smoke machine for the dance had triggered an alarm and we didn't know it."

> **ESTABLISHED:** 1991
> **GRADES:** 7-8
> **MASCOT:** Bruins
> **COLORS:** Red, white and Air Force blue
> **MOTTO:** "Building Unity, Pride and Champions"
> **LOCATION:** 380 W. Teague, Clovis
> **ACREAGE:** Part of the 160-acre Buchanan Educational Center

Randy Rowe was Alta Sierra's first principal. The first students at Alta Sierra were eighth- and ninth-graders who had previously attended Clark and Kastner intermediate schools.

"Getting those Kastner Thunderbirds and Clark Chieftains to love each other and blend into being Bruins was a challenge," said Wetzel.

During its second year of operation, 1992-93, Alta Sierra consisted of eighth, ninth and tenth grades, which then became the first student body of Buchanan High School when it opened in 1993. From that point forward, only seventh and eighth grades were taught at Alta Sierra.

Enrollment as of 2010-11 is more than 1,300 students, but at times has swelled to more than 1,800 hitting an enrollment high in 2006-07, just prior to the opening of CUSD's Granite Ridge Intermediate which alleviated Alta Sierra's overcrowding. To create a small school feel within its large school enrollment, Alta Sierra created three clusters: Polar, Kodiak and Grizzly, each with its own guidance instructional specialist, teachers and administrative staff. Every student is assigned to a cluster for both of their intermediate years where they receive individual counseling and guidance as needed, creating a closer relationship between students and staff.

Principals who have served at Alta Sierra in addition to Rowe and Blizzard have included Gary Giannoni, Gabe Escalera, Carlo Prandini, Don Ulrich and as of 2010, Steve Pagani.

Building unity, pride and champions

"Building unity, pride and champions" was established by the Alta Sierra community in the late 1990s as the school motto. The concept of being united as a learning community remains solidly at the core of everything done today at Alta Sierra, according to Blizzard, exemplified by the fact that since the 1999-2000 school year until the present, the school's principal has taught a lesson to every incoming seventh-grader about the school motto and how it applies to student success.

"We continue to instill student pride in themselves, their school and their country. Ultimately, our students and professional faculty aspire daily in our actions to do all that is requisite to truly be a champion," Blizzard said during his principalship. "As part of being a champion, we hope that each member of the faculty and, additionally, each student embraces service to the community. The entire Buchanan Educational Center has become very well known for community service including the region's largest blood drive, annual clothing donations, food donations and fundraising for charities."

Bear Nation

The Bear was designated as the mascot for Buchanan High School, a nod to Dr. Buchanan, who received his doctorate at UC Berkeley, which boasts the Golden Bear mascot. Alta Sierra immediately adopted the Bruin as its mascot. Buchanan High's Bear, Alta Sierra's Bruin and Garfield Elementary's Cub mascots form the educational center's "Bear Nation."

Unique school firsts

The campus at Alta Sierra features nine full-sized soccer/football fields which are shared with Buchanan High School. These facilities, as well as the softball complex and the football stadium, the three schools serving grades kindergarten through 12, and the Medical Therapy Unit housed on Garfield's campus, make the Buchanan Educational Center the only complex of its kind in the state.

Alta Sierra was the first school in the San Joaquin Valley to incorporate an Anytime Anyplace Anyone Laptop (AAAL) Learning Program which extended laptop usage in classrooms across the domains of English, social studies, science and mathematics. The school's strong laptop program was reinforced early on by placing additional computers in academic block classes and making additional laptops available to loan students unable to purchase their own laptops. Don Ulrich, principal of Alta Sierra in 2001, said that the laptops were used as a technology tool to help students access a higher level of research, make presentations using video and Power Point, and enhance their writing skills to prepare them to use the tool in high school, higher education and throughout

Recognized Excellence

Alta Sierra Intermediate has received:

>> State Distinguished School Award (1996, 2001, 2005)

>> National Blue Ribbon School Award (2008)

>> National School to Watch Award (2008)

>> School To Watch - Taking Center Stage Model School Award (2008)

>> CSU Fresno's Bonner Center Character for Education's Exemplary Middle Schools of Character Award (1997, 1999, 2001)

their lives. The program used technology as a tool to further enhance and enrich the academic environment for all students.

Alta Sierra and Buchanan were the first CUSD schools to have all staff members on e-mail.

The school presently prepares cohorts of students to participate in Career Technical Education pathways in energy management (environmental energy) and also in the technical fine arts, both of which can be continued through their education at Buchanan High, which houses specialized career programs in these areas.

Alta Sierra developed a unique program called Program Reach to promote cultural understanding and education, which has been shared both state and nationwide. The school was also the first to create a Restorative Justice pilot program, which strives to integrate discipline into the institutional practices.

Alta Sierra was the first school to host a FIRST LEGO Robotics Regional Championship in 1995. Now an annual event, the regional event has grown to be one of the largest in California.

ALTERNATIVE EDUCATION

By Linda Robertson with contributions by Earlene Holguin

In 1970, in an effort to provide all students with equal opportunities in education, Clovis Unified developed its first alternative education school. The school, originally called "Clovis Continuation School," was initially part of Clovis Adult School and overseen by Chuck Peterson, who also served as the principal of the adult school. The continuation and adult schools were located at 901 Fifth Street in downtown Clovis, in the original campus of Clovis High School, which had since moved to Fowler and Barstow avenues.

Since that time, the district has established four separate schools designed to meet the needs of students struggling to succeed at a traditional, comprehensive school. These schools include Gateway High School, Enterprise Independent Study School, Clovis Community Day Elementary School and Clovis Community Day Secondary School. Originally opened in 2003, the Community Day Schools eventually replaced and expanded services previously offered through Excel High School and the Opportunity program.

GATEWAY HIGH SCHOOL

In 1975, Gateway High School, serving grades 10 through 12, as well as providing opportunity for students in grades seven through nine, became the first self-contained alternative education school in Clovis Unified School District. On the school's official opening day, its permanent campus was still under construction, so classes were temporarily housed at the 901 Fifth Street location.

When Gateway's new campus at 1550 Herndon Avenue was complete, it consisted of six modular buildings, which housed 10 classrooms and included a main office and library. The school was designed by Darden Architects with the assistance of Dr. Floyd B. "Doc" Buchanan, superintendent of CUSD from 1960 to 1991. Buchanan wanted modular buildings, what he called "permanent relocatables," on enough land so that if the idea of a continuation school in the district did not work out, he could convert the buildings into an elementary school, and have sufficient acreage to accommodate another school.

Gateway opened its doors surrounded by open fields and cow pastures, adjacent to the newly constructed District Office. CUSD Governing Board members and developers chose this site because it was the geographic center of the district, knowing it would better serve all the students in Clovis Unified.

The school's first principal, Satoshi "Fibber" Hirayama, chose the name "Gateway" from the sign that hangs over Clovis Avenue introducing the City of Clovis as "The Gateway to the Sierras." The green sign was also the inspiration for the school's colors of green and white.

Gateway is unique for having a full-size regulation gym for students to use. The newly built Gateway Event Center gymnasium was dedicated to Hirayama on October 16, 2008, in honor of his commitment and dedication to the school. While he was principal at Gateway, the school was often referred to as "Fort Hirayama."

Following Hirayama, principals at Gateway High School include Betty Caughell, Ralph Lockwood, Steve Weil, Carl Drow, Walt Byrd, Cheryl Rogers, Willie Thomas, Gabe Escalera, Steve France and currently Barbara Parks.

Students

Because of the unique nature of the school, enrollment fluctuates on a daily basis. Between 1,100 and 1,300 students enter the system and then return to their home school in one school year, with an average of 230 students enrolled at any one time in the full day program. Twenty-one teachers are on staff at Gateway.

Students are offered courses in art, English, math, technology, physical education, science and social science. Although Gateway does not have a traditional sports program like most high schools, their students participate in intramural activities such as mushball, bowling, basketball, volleyball and arm wrestling.

Community support

Gateway's Healthy Start collaborative is a partnership of alternative education staff, students, families, public/private health and human service agencies, employment agencies and businesses showing a willingness to "do whatever it takes" to help students in need. Alternative education believes that by combining these services and bringing them to the school site, the students can draw on their strengths to become self-sufficient.

Several community-based organizations, such as Old Town Clovis Kiwanis Club, Clovis Odd Fellows and Rebekkahs, Japanese-American Citizens League and Clovis Rotary provide annual scholarships and community-service awards for alternative education students. The Foundation for Clovis Schools provides financial support through classroom grants, grant-writing support services, funds for teachers and scholarships for students.

Recognized Excellence

Gateway High has received:
>> National Drug-Free Schools Program Award (1995)
>> Model Continuation School (2011)

Students at both Gateway and Enterprise high schools benefit from support programs such as kNOw MORE, a dating relationship violence prevention program; Just Say No anti-drug use campaign; Students against Destructive Decisions (SADD); West Care drug rehabilitation; Clovis Youth Employment Services (YES), among others. For its anti-drug efforts, Gateway was named to the National Drug Free Schools Program in 1994-95.

ENTERPRISE ALTERNATIVE SCHOOL

Enterprise Alternative School serves students in grades kindergarten through 12 whose family, parenting, medical, emotional and/or special circumstances preclude them from attending a traditional comprehensive school on a daily basis, so they use the flexibility of independent study as their learning strategy.

The Clovis Independent Study program was brought to the district by then-Director of Child Welfare and Attendance Dr. Jean Stovall during the 1976-77 school year. Stovall administered the program from his office until January 1978, when it moved to the Gateway High School campus. Steve Weil was assigned as the school's lead teacher and administrator of the program

In September 1983, the Clovis Independent Study Program was relocated to then-vacant Pinedale Elementary School campus. Weil was named coordinator and served as the site administrator. The stay in Pinedale was short-lived; in August 1984, the program moved back to the Gateway campus. Ralph Lockwood, director of alternative education, and Dick Boyajian, the new coordinator of independent study, led the program until July 1988 when Dave Bishop took the reins.

In 1991, Clovis Independent Study Program became a school under the name of Enterprise Alternative School with Bishop as learning director. Although on the same campus with Gateway, Enterprise is not a part of Gateway; it is a separate entity, having gone through a complete accreditation to make it a comprehensive school.

From the beginning, independent study staff have dedicated themselves to teaching students to believe in themselves, strive to better themselves and to work hard to become all they can be in their adult lives — as people, as parents, as employees, and in their business and personal relationships. Enterprise is "not a place to bury kids," said Dave Bishop. Current Principal Barbara Parks has continued this approach to educating and supporting Enterprise students.

Because students graduating from Enterprise needed to show attendance at a Western Association of Schools and Colleges (WASC) accredited institution for college admittance, the school independently pursued a WASC accreditation. The school's WASC accreditation in 1994 made it one of the first independent WASC-created study schools in California.

Enterprise Alternative School serves students through three components. Home Hospital instruction provides educational services to school-aged children who are struggling with short- or long-term illnesses that prevent them from attending classes regularly.

Home School supports families choosing to register and provide instruction to their children in a home setting. The school's Independent Study component allows students who have been identified as being unable to attend classes on one of CUSD's campuses to meet weekly with an instructor and complete work on an independent basis. Entrance to Enterprise is recommended through Clovis Unified's Student Services and School Attendance Office.

Enterprise's campus consists of three classrooms. Centers are available at the school where students can work alone, as are cubicles for individual teachers and their students, a mathematics lab, a book room and a computer lab.

There are nine teachers on the Enterprise teaching staff, all of whom make themselves available to students by phone as needed, working with the students emotionally as well as on their school work. The management staff, shared with Gateway High School, includes a principal, learning director, three academic counselors and a part-time Healthy Start coordinator. In addition, students have access to a nurse, a psychologist and a resource specialist program teacher.

Enterprise's student body population ranges from 130 to 300-plus students in grades kindergarten through 12, averaging 185 during the school year. The school's revolving enrollment fluctuates daily.

EXCEL HIGH SCHOOL

Clovis Unified opened the doors to Excel High School in 1998 as a second continuation school, and closed the school in 2005. Excel was created to meet a specific need for students whose behavior choices jeopardized their attendance at any other Clovis Unified School.

Students in grades seven through 12 were accepted into the program, where they received support, teaching and assistance in modifying their behavior choices. High school students could choose between two separate three-hour sessions, one in the morning or one in the afternoon. They earned school credits through a combination of independent study and direct teaching.

Principal Dave Bishop and his staff of teachers and counselors worked daily to connect with students at the school to ensure that each received a quality education and a chance to graduate.

With state standards increasing for all schools, it was determined that Excel students needed more than three hours of direct teaching every day. With this in mind, Excel High School was closed when Clovis Community Day Secondary School was created in 2005.

CLOVIS COMMUNITY DAY SCHOOLS

Clovis Community Day School was first developed in 2003 as a single school serving severely at-risk students in grades four through six in a six-hour per day program. Students are referred to the school by counselors in the district's Student Services and School Attendance Office.

Clovis Community Day, now divided into both a secondary school (grades seven to 12) and elementary school (grades four to six) campuses, aims to help students be ready to successfully return to their home schools as quickly as possible by providing a supportive and structured learning environment. An educational program is provided offering students opportunities to correct academic deficiencies, demonstrate improved attendance, and provide evidence of improved attitudes and behavior. Students in fourth through eighth grades can complete their educational goals and return to their home school within six to 18 weeks. Those in grades nine through 12 may stay at Clovis Community Day Secondary, or transfer to a comprehensive high school at the end of the semester or to Gateway High School after six weeks.

Dave Bishop was principal from 2003 until June 2008; his successor, Tom Judd, continues to serve in that role today.

Clovis Community Day School began as a single self-contained classroom. The first students were fourth-, fifth- and sixth-graders who had been identified as students who were unable to benefit from traditional classroom settings or on-site intervention programs.

Recognizing the need for expansion of the program to include seventh and eighth grades, two additional classrooms were added in 2004. Prior to this, the only seat-time option for alternative education for grades seven and eight students was a three-hour per day opportunity program that ceased to exist in 2004. In 2005, three classrooms were added to form two separate small schools, Clovis Community Day Elementary (CCDE), serving fourth through sixth grades, and Clovis Community Day Secondary (CCDS), serving seventh through twelfth grades.

Clovis Community Day Secondary

Nearly 400 students each year pass through the doors of Clovis Community Day Secondary (CCDS), where they attend a required six-hour school day. Students may take a full high school credit diploma program.

The campus consists of five classrooms in the high school and two intermediate classrooms that hold approximately 15 students each. With a maximum capacity of 105 students, the attendance averages approximately 30 students in grades seven and eight, 30 freshmen and 45 in grades 10 through 12. An eighth classroom was added in 2007 that serves as a multipurpose room, complete with snack bar, lunchroom, conference room and restroom.

Each student is evaluated individually every six weeks by a Student Success Team (SST) comprised of a counselor, the principal, the student, the school's psychologist and sometimes a special education teacher. Depending on grades and level of education, it may be determined that the student can return to his or her home school. CCDS encourages this; that is their goal. If, after six weeks, the student does not appear to be able to return to his home school, another meeting of the SST is scheduled and the student is reevaluated.

Clovis Community Day Elementary

Students assigned to Clovis Community Day Elementary (CCDE) attend a required six-hour school day, with class size limited to 15 students. The length of a student's stay at the school site varies based on each student's individual circumstance.

In an effort to reduce dropout rates, gang involvement and levels of juvenile delinquency, a 12-month plan for mentoring was developed for Community Day called Project SMART (Student Mentoring and Responsibility Team) for students in grades four through eight. Based on research indicating that the presence of a caring adult and a personal relationship are the most important factors in keeping students in school, the program targets vulnerable youth with a mission of providing a school-based one-to-one mentoring relationship with specific youth populations enrolled at CCDS.

Mentors in the program are selected from a list of local community applicants and are closely screened. Once assigned to a student, they work closely with CCDE and follow the student upon return to his/her home school. There are currently 21 students working with mentors in the Project SMART program.

Results from the 12-month program indicate that participating students have fewer disciplinary actions, improved school attendance and higher academic achievement, and are able to more clearly recognize destructive behaviors such as alcohol and drug use.

The program was initially funded by a discretionary grant through the U.S. Department of Education Office of Safe and Drug-Free Schools along with the Foundation for Clovis Schools. The program's current funding continues through private donations. Attributed to the program's success are the involvement of community and local sponsors. Those sponsors include local businesses, business owners and local attorneys.

C. TODD CLARK INTERMEDIATE SCHOOL

By Linda Robertson

Early years

The facility in which C. Todd Clark Intermediate School is housed had its beginnings as an expansion of Clovis Union High School. Until this new addition was built in 1941, Clovis High was housed completely across Fifth Street in today's San Joaquin Law School building. Clovis Union High School continued to occupy buildings on both the north and south sides of Fifth Street through the unification vote of 1960, eventually outgrowing the campus as the community continued to grow.

The 1941 facility was designed by Fred L. Swartz, a prominent Fresno area architect responsible for collaborating on other local buildings including Fresno State College Library, which is listed on the Historic Resource Inventory List for the City of Fresno, as well as the Fresno County Hall of Records and the Fresno Memorial Auditorium.

In 1969, Clovis High moved from the Fifth Street campuses in the heart of Old Town Clovis to its new location at nearby Fowler and Barstow avenues. With the southern buildings of Fifth Street campus unoccupied (the original Clovis Union High building on the north side of Fifth Street was used to house continuation and adult school classes), Clovis Unified School District opted to fill the available site with its first intermediate school.

Origins of a name

When the new intermediate school began operation in 1969, it was named in honor of Clarence Todd Clark, a Clovis resident who was born on February 13, 1877, and died August 30, 1967. His wife, Kate Potter, followed him in death in May 1969.

James Walker Clark and Mary Magdalena (Hershey) Clark came from Missouri when Todd, their eldest child, was a small boy. They lived on a farm in Zamora, California, in north-central California's Yolo County for more than 30 years, as their family expanded to four children.

C. Todd Clark and his wife lived on a grain farm in the Sacramento Valley. Clark worked his way through college and, at age 21, accepted a Methodist pastorate, filling the position and the pews at various parishes throughout California, including Mountain View, Sacramento, Chico, Santa Rosa and Kingsburg, before moving to their ranch near Clovis in 1920.

It was Clark's devoted service to his community that inspired the naming of Clovis' first intermediate school after him. He served as a trustee of the Clovis Union High School District from 1922 to 1928; was on the Fresno County Board of Supervisors from 1933 to 1949; and served in the California State Assembly from 1931 to 1933. He was also active in the Concordia Chapter No. 320 in Clovis, as well as the Clovis Masonic Lodge, the Fresno County Farm Bureau and the Clovis Grange.

C. Todd Clark
Photo Courtesy of Clovis-Big Dry Creek Historical Society

Creating an identity

Though Clark Intermediate School assumed the space vacated by Clovis High, it needed its own identity. Clark's mascot was chosen to be the Chieftain and the school colors of blue and gold mirrored those of Clovis High School.

The opening of Clark Intermediate was a milestone, marking the district's first school created specifically to instruct seventh- and eighth-graders. Previously, Clovis Unified elementary schools were comprised of grades kindergarten through eighth. With the addition of Clark, all elementary schools would now teach students only up to sixth grade, sending their seventh- and eighth-graders to the new intermediate school.

In 1968, as the campus was preparing ready to be occupied by Clark, the old Clovis High facility underwent structural additions made to the original building by architect David Horn at a cost of $460,000. Electrical rehabilitation was performed by architect Gene Zellmer at a cost of $125,000.

Significant additions and renovations were performed in 1997. The front façade of C. Todd Clark Intermediate underwent a complete "facelift" to match the architectural design of the Mercedes Edwards Theatre prominently located at the entrance of the campus. A wrestling room, new library, science wing, snack bar and team offices for learning directors were also built that year. Additional renovations took place in 2008 including a second major facelift, including new windows in classrooms and exterior updates.

During the 2008 construction, a significant part of Clovis' history was discovered. A piece of the 42-mile-long logging flume that had once snaked its way down the Sierra Nevada Mountains from Shaver Lake to the Clovis Rodeo Grounds was unearthed under Clark. The flume was significant for bringing people seeking work in the logging industry to Clovis in the 1890s and early 20th century.

Supporting students

The teachers and administrators at Clark provide a nurturing and attentive foundation for their students as they transition from elementary school to high school. According to the school's mission statement, students "will be 'connected' to the goals and purposes of our school through their involvement in various academic and co-curricular activities ... and will be academically prepared to meet the challenges of high school and will be life-long learners."

> **ESTABLISHED:** 1969
> **GRADES:** 7-8
> **MASCOT:** Chieftains
> **COLORS:** Blue and gold
> **LOCATION:** 902 Fifth Street, Clovis
> **ACREAGE:** 30

All students are enrolled in an Academic Block class spanning two periods of the day. This class enables students to be with one teacher for an extended period of time learning history, reading and writing. Intermediate students also have the opportunity to take single-subject core and elective classes during the remainder of their school day.

This structure of learning, which set the standard for all future intermediate schools in the district, was developed by then-Superintendent Dr. Floyd B. "Doc" Buchanan. He integrated the full day of learning with one teacher, traditional to elementary school, with the day-long rotation of classes typical to the high school. By exposing students to a half day of each format, he made the transition from elementary to intermediate to high school an easier process for students.

Principals

Principals at C. Todd Clark Intermediate School have included Ralph Lockwood, 1969-72, William F. Noli, 1972-75, Mickey C. Cox, 1975-79, Beau Carter, 1979-1986, Hank Brown, 1986-1994, and Carl Tomlinson, 1994-2005. Since 2005, Scott Steele has served as the school's principal.

Mercedes Edwards Theatre

One of the most remarkable features on the Clark campus is the Mercedes Edwards Theatre, located prominently at the front of the campus facing Clovis' busy Fifth Street.

The theater was built in 1942 through funding provided by the federal Work Projects Administration program started in 1935 to employ millions of Americans in public works projects. It has served the community since as a desirable performing arts location due to its spacious elegance. It has hosted performances of plays, musicals, dance, music, choral and more. It was dedicated May 8, 1982, in honor of Mercedes Edwards, who served for 28 years in Clovis Unified as a music teacher and as Clovis High's choir director when the high school was still located on Fifth Street, where Clark now stands. A Fresno State College graduate, Edwards taught chorus, ensembles, various groups and *a cappella* classes. She was loved by the school and the community, and dedicated herself to her students. Edwards' choices for musicals were almost always operettas, although she was always willing to select pieces to accommodate students' experience. Her "Feast of Lights" celebration incorporating the student body was the highlight of every year she taught, with football players lighting candles and participating with her choirs.

Her attitude and belief was that "the show must go on" no matter what. "She could be hard-core, but it was always for the students. She set the bar high when it applied to the kids. She was the ultimate teacher," said Dan Pessano, local theater legend who has served as the Good Company Players' managing director since its inception in 1973 and who worked with Edwards at Clark Intermediate. He spoke in her honor at her funeral when she passed away in 1975 following a battle with a brain tumor.

In 2000, the original theater building was renovated at a cost of just over $4 million and was reopened as a fully upgraded performing arts facility with seating for 750 people. Architectural and theater consultants firm Landry & Bogan provided the full scope of theatrical consulting for this auditorium, including new performance lighting and rigging systems, orchestra enclosure, refurbished seating, sightline layouts and proper exiting requirements. Other renovated highlights included new gold-patterned charcoal-colored carpet, original seats that had been reconditioned and reupholstered, a spacious women's restroom, and a ticket office to replace the archaic system of using two chairs and a folding table for the "ticket booth." Martin E. Dietz of Darden Architects was the principal architect in the project.

> ### Recognized Excellence
> Clark Intermediate has received:
> - State Distinguished School Award (1997, 2001, 2009)
> - California Blue Ribbon Nominee (1995)
> - National Blue Ribbon School Award (1995)
> - California School To Watch - Taking Center Stage Model School Award (2009)
> - CSU Fresno's Bonner Center Character for Education's Exemplary Middle Schools of Character Award (1997, 1999, 2001, 2003, 2005)

Trading Post

The Trading Post, a mini-store located on the Clark Intermediate campus, offers students and faculty the opportunity to buy school supplies, as well as purchase such items as t-shirts, hats, stationery and various food items. The store serves as a symbol of the school spirit that marks this historic campus that stands as a landmark in the heart of the community it serves.

CEDARWOOD ELEMENTARY SCHOOL

By Marjorie M. Allen

The original waterslide

Cedarwood Elementary's origins begin with a logging flume, a 42-mile-long waterslide that snaked its way down the Sierra Nevada Mountains from Stevenson Creek, culminating at what was to become the Clovis Rodeo Grounds. The flume trough was designed in units called boxes, and each box was made of cedar planks, 1.5-inches thick. A 1911 map showed the 1893 Fresno Flume and Irrigation Co. crossing present-day Herndon Avenue, just east of Temperance Avenue. Mill workers enjoyed taking flume rides on small board rafts called flume boats.

The flume, built from planks of cedar wood, was the historical basis used for naming Cedarwood Elementary. The school is situated only a short distance from where the flume once flowed. Other names were proposed by the Cedarwood community such as "Tollhouse," "Herndon Heights," "Foothill" and "Sample Meadow," before the board made its decision.

Twin ground breaking ceremonies

The rapid growth of Clovis and the large enrollment of two neighboring schools created the need for an additional elementary campus in the mid-1990s. The blending of students from Mickey Cox and Red Bank elementary schools into the new Cedarwood Elementary required intensive planning.

Twin ground breaking ceremonies on October 6, 1995 — one at 9 A.M. and the other at 10:30 A.M. — were held for two new Clovis Unified elementary schools: Cedarwood, built to accommodate the students north and east of central Clovis, and Copper Hills, built to house students in the northeast portion of the City of Fresno located in CUSD's boundaries. There were several similarities between the two campuses. Both school sites covered about 15 acres, and had the same square footage and number of classrooms. Both were scheduled to begin serving their student populations in September 1996.

Cedarwood was designed by Integrated Designs by SO-MAM Inc., a group of Fresno architects, and built by Tech Four Contractors at a cost of $9 million. Landowners in the Cedarwood area were the San Joaquin Co., J. D. Morgan and D. W. Cate.

Principal Colin Hintergardt, who had served previously as the principal of Mickey Cox Elementary from 1989 to 1996, opened the new school's doors in September 1996 to 575 students. Hintergardt held the position until his retirement in 2010 when the current principal, Teresa Barber, took the reins.

ESTABLISHED: 1996
GRADES: K-6
MASCOT: Hawks
MOTTO: "Poised for the Future"
COLORS: Forest green, silver and black
LOCATION: 2851 Palo Alto, Clovis
ACREAGE: 15

A child's right to education

Cedarwood faculty and staff hold steadfast to embracing a shared commitment for student success, and the fundamental educational philosophies, begun in Clovis Unified School District in 1960. Reflecting this commitment, Cedarwood's mission statement stresses the need to facilitate the maximum educational growth of each child, and its vision is in the motto, "Poised for the Future." Cedarwood provides exemplary programs, services and activities to a diverse community that fosters lifelong learning and a commitment to society, according to Hintergardt.

Every child in grades three through six maintains a Cedarwood Goal-Setting Card that reflects past achievement and future performance goals. In keeping their cards, students are actively involved in their own academic experience.

Communication is a top priority at Cedarwood, begun with Hintergardt's open door policy. He readily welcomed constructive criticism from the staff and the community. To keep students and families informed of news from the campus, the school established newspapers, the *Hawk Tale* and the *Hawk-Eye*, to be sent home to families on a weekly basis.

School spirit

On the Cedarwood Elementary campus, known as the "Home of the Hawks" in honor of its mascot, students can be seen regularly sporting their school colors of forest green, silver and black.

Every Friday afternoon as students leave to go home, the cheerful song "Don't Worry, Be Happy" is piped through the school's halls and classrooms over the PA system.

First grade teacher Judy Marvin reflected the prevailing school spirit as she said, "I'm proud to be an American because I have the freedom to teach in Clovis Unified at the best school, Cedarwood!"

Recognized Excellence
Cedarwood Elementary has received:
>> State Distinguished School Award (2000, 2006, 2010)
>> California Business for Education Excellence Foundation's Scholar Schools Award (2009)

"Cedarwood is a family-friendly school with strong solidarity between staff, students, and parents," said Hintergardt before his retirement. "We must be competitive. It is our responsibility to orchestrate programs that prove to be progressive and successful for all students. We will be guided by the tenets of character and morality."

The Hawk Attitude

The students and staff of Cedarwood operate by the Hawk Attitude, a list of 20 character tenets that exemplify the school's values. Every student has a printed copy of the Hawk Attitude, which they attach to their binders as regular reminders of the following tenets:

1. Do the right thing
2. Actions speak louder than words
3. Talk to adults and peers with respect
4. Always do your best work
5. Say please and thank you
6. No excuses
7. Always make eye-contact
8. Learn from watching
9. Clap for teammates
10. Have good posture
11. Pay attention in class
12. Be the best you can be
13. Don't cut corners
14. Don't worry, be happy
15. Play fair
16. Win with class, lose with dignity
17. Do your homework
18. Always be honest
19. No teasing/no bullying
20. Be organized

CENTER FOR ADVANCED RESEARCH AND TECHNOLOGY

By Linda Robertson

A mission in education

A unique school exists as part of the Clovis Unified School District. In fact, some might call it a mission in education.

The Center for Advanced Research and Technology, or CART, officially opened in August 2000 to serve junior and senior high school students from both the Fresno and Clovis unified school districts offering specialized areas of education, ranging from law to robotics to forensics to designing short films and music videos.

The school is a joint partnership between Clovis and Fresno unified school districts. Each district shares funding equally to staff and operate the school, notwithstanding enrollment from each district, with additional funding coming from Fresno County's Regional Occupational Program. An independent board of directors made up of representatives from the two school districts and the private and business sectors governs CART under the authority of a joint powers agreement. Members include the superintendents of both CUSD and FUSD; a governing board member from each district; and a business representative appointed by each district. When the school was still in the development stages, then-CUSD Superintendent Dr. Walt Buster, then-FUSD Superintendent Chuck McCully and former CUSD Governing Board member Richard P. Lake, C.P.A., suggested that a seventh board member be appointed by the Fresno Business Council. "If not approved by both school boards, CART would not exist today," said former CUSD Superintendent Terry Bradley, Ed.D.

CART combines rigorous academics with technical, design, process, entrepreneurial and critical thinking skills. Eleventh and twelfth grade students from Clovis and Fresno unified school districts are bused to CART where they attend half-day classes, five days a week, in one of the laboratories taught by teams of instructors from both education and business.

CART's goal for its students is for them to become better learners by creating education relevant to the workplace. CART's mission, in partnership with education, business and community agencies, is to educate students through interdisciplinary curriculum in a project-based environment that is rigorous, standards-based and facilitated through a business instructional model.

Students who elect to take a course at CART spend three hours a day at the school, either in the morning or afternoon session, with the remaining school-day hours spent at their home school. Students choose one course of study from specialized educational curriculum while also earning high school credit in English, science, social science or mathematics depending on their field of study at CART. Courses are built upon the California State Academics standards and are approved and designated as meeting the University of California core requirements.

Project-based academy

CART is not just a high school, charter school or magnet school; rather, it is an educational and career technical program, a project-based academy. CART students are exposed to technology and hands-on learning situations that encourage them to think and work at a higher level.

Designed with a high performance business atmosphere in mind, CART is organized around four career clusters: Professional Sciences, Advanced Communications, Global Dynamics, and Engineering and Design. Within each cluster are career-specific laboratories available to students.

The school design allows the career focus labs to evolve and change as the needs of the community and the work force changes.

ESTABLISHED: 2000
GRADES: 11-12
MOTTO: "Your Future Is at Stake – Failure Is Not an Option"
LOCATION: 2555 Clovis Avenue, Clovis
ACREAGE: 18.83

In the Professional Sciences cluster, students utilize scientific principles and methods to conduct research and develop solutions to medical, forensic and environmental issues that impact the community. Labs include Forensic Research, Biomedicine, Environmental Sciences and Field Research, and Psychology and Human Behavior.

In the Advanced Communications cluster, students explore and apply a spectrum of communication skills including satellite communications, wireless technology, network and Internet design, database fundamentals, electronic graphic design, Web broadcasting, and Web design. Labs include Interactive Game Design, Multimedia, both graphics and video, Network Management, Web Applications, and Computer Science.

In the Global Dynamics cluster, students conduct research and analyze information through the study of economics, finance, marketing, law and public policy. Labs include Economics and Finance, Marketing and Advertising, and Law and Order and Policy.

Labs in the Engineering and Design cluster are Architectural Design, Biomedical Engineering, Engineering and Product Development, and Robotics and Electronics. Students in this cluster create solutions to actual engineering problems faced by society.

Inside a typical lab

The Network and Database Design lab, in the professional sciences career cluster, serves as a good example to illustrate the varying benefits of a CART course. On the first day of class, students enrolled in the lab are given computer parts, sticks of RAM, DVD drives and flat-screen monitors, all waiting to be assembled. The students spend the first weeks in the lab building the computers they will use throughout the year.

Students gain technology knowledge, as well as receiving credit in science, math and English, which they earn through keeping detailed notes as they assemble the computer and eventually convert into a "how to" guide.

Entering the program

CART serves as an extension of CUSD's and FUSD's high schools in order to provide half-day instruction for interested students. Students must apply for entrance to CART, and in 2009-2010 the school reached its maximum capacity of 1,400 students enrolled. CART is unique in that students retain their privileges to all programs and activities provided by their home schools while enrolled at CART. They also remain eligible to join clubs and participate in extra-curricular activities, and earn diplomas from their home schools.

In order to participate in specific labs in the program, students are required to meet certain entrance requirements, including the completion of two years of English, biology or science 9 and 10, and algebra I. They must also maintain regular attendance in all classes, and gain permission from their high school counselors to attend the unique campus.

Approximately 65 percent of junior students return to take a second course at CART their senior year.

State-of-the-art facility

The land and holdings where CART sits, near Clovis and Santa Ana avenues, were previously owned by the Grundfos Pump Manufacturing Company. When CART obtained the structure in 1997, the former Grundfos Manufacturing building was leveled down to its footprint, removing all manufacturing equipment and meeting standards for public schools created by the Office of Public School Construction. Reconstruction of the CART facility was innovatively funded through the application for a federal Qualified Zone Academy Bond (QZAB). The first of its kind granted in Fresno County, the QZAB in effect provided 50 percent of the construction expenses at no cost to Fresno or Clovis unified school districts, with the remainder provided through local school facility funds.

This building was designed specifically for a project-based learning environment. It was anticipated that the CART model of teaching and learning would draw visitors from around the world. Wide hallways and windows to every classroom are design features that allow visitors to observe the classroom environment without interrupting the class activities.

Partnering with the community

CART is dedicated to partnering with education, business and community agencies. These partnerships enable students to engage in specific fields of study in a rigorous, project-based environment, facilitated through an instructional business framework. Their goal is to provide an education for students that prepares them for entry-level positions, based on CISCO standards, and/or qualifies them for admission to a university.

Educational partners include Clovis Unified School District, Fresno Unified School District, Fresno County Office of Education, State Center Community College District, California State University, Fresno, the University of California, National Association of Secondary Principals and DeVry University. These partners provide a connection for students to the business world they are preparing to enter.

> ### Recognized Excellence
>
> CART has received:
> >> Title of Microsoft Center of Excellence (2003) for innovative use of technology in the classroom
> >> California School Boards Association's Golden Bell Award (2004)
> >> ConnectEd's Model Site in California Award (2008)

CART's teachers and business partners create an exciting and innovative educational environment by teaching students to solve problems faced by local businesses, industries and public agencies. Working in teams, the students gain valuable experience in developing personal relationships and teamwork skills that they can use in the workforce.

Today, key business partners include Wells Fargo, Kaiser Permanente, Grundfos Pumps, McCormick Barstow LLP, Community Medical Centers, Microsoft Corporation, Children's Hospital of Central California, Saint Agnes Medical Center, Pacific Gas & Electric, VS Visual Statement Inc., AT&T, The California Endowment, Fresno Business Council, Economic Development Corporation of Fresno and of Clovis, and the Greater Fresno Area and Clovis chambers of commerce. These companies and organizations provide leadership and fiscal support, and collaborate as instructors and mentors. Students and businesses find mutual benefits by participating in research and development, enhancing learning, and directly contributing to their community.

CISCO Academy

CART is a CISCO Academy. CISCO is a company that certifies students as being proficient to work on computer networks. This indicates to an employer that the student has the skills necessary for employment. Certification is usually the result of attending a trade or technical school or attending a two-year college program. CART prepares high school students to pass this "industry standard" test.

Faculty and staff

Jane Hammaker was CART's first principal, serving from 2000 to 2001. Steve Ward took over in 2001 and stayed until 2004. Susan Fisher became the chief operating officer in 2004 and held that position until her retirement in 2010 when Devin Blizzard assumed the role.

Fifty percent of CART teachers are from Fresno Unified and 50 percent are from Clovis Unified, maintaining the salary schedules and benefits of their respective districts. CART staff members are available between the hours of 10:30 A.M. and 12:30 P.M., and after 3:30 P.M. each day for informal meetings with parents to discuss any factor regarding a student's welfare at the school. Teachers also hold open lab nights for students to get extra help on Thursday evenings.

GOT MILK?

In 2008, Marketing and Advertising Learning Lab students won a campaign-development contest held in celebration of California Milk Processor Board (CMPB)'s 15th anniversary of its successful GOT MILK? advertising campaign. CMPB partnered with Junior Achievement, a non-profit organization that brings the real world to students through hands-on curriculum, to challenge Junior Achievement students in northern, central and southern California to create a concept for the GOT MILK? campaign. CART was only one of three schools chosen statewide to participate in the unique program.

The CART team of five juniors and seniors had six weeks to prepare three ideas for TV spots for a GOT MILK? campaign that they would eventually present to a panel of 12 ad executives at the Bay Area agency that handles the high-profile milk account. The five students made the actual presentation but they did not work alone to get to that point; in total, more than 80 students from CART's finance, advertising and marketing, and graphics classes came together to research and create the campaign that ultimately won the CMPB contest.

International recognition

In 2007, a camera crew from the Japan Broadcasting Company came to CART to shoot footage for a special program being produced in Japan, in which CART served as an example of a cutting-edge model in education that prepares students for the emerging knowledge-led society. The film team was interested in students working on projects relevant to their community and to society as a whole.

In 2009, CART hosted visitors from Sri Lanka, China and Singapore who wanted to view the school and learn from its staff some of the unique and forward-thinking teaching methods to implement into their own schools when they returned to their home countries.

SHOWCASE

Every January, all students enrolled in CART participate in the day-long SHOWCASE event in which they prepare to be an "expert" in their particular lab's course of study. Students display presentations, project boards, reports and highlights of the work they have completed up to that point in the school year. The public is invited, with an average of 2,000 visitors attending to view the innovative work of the accomplished students. Visitors and event judges ask the students about their projects and the research they conducted to put them together.

SHOWCASE requires students to synthesize, organize, and think on their feet as they demonstrate what they have learned so far that year.

CENTURY ELEMENTARY SCHOOL

By Carole Grosch

Millennium school

Student growth at neighboring schools in northeast Clovis was the major reason for the building of what was to quickly become one of the most populous of the district's elementary schools, and the only new school to open for the 2000-01 school year. Marking the beginning of the millennium, the working name of the school was "New Century Elementary," to be officially shortened to Century Elementary in the spring of 2000.

The campus, located on 15 acres, consists of 36 classrooms, housed in seven permanent and eight portable buildings.

Before the school opened, students from Garfield and Dry Creek elementary schools who were to attend Century had the opportunity to vote for their choice of the new school's mascot and colors. Suggested mascots included colts, longhorns, stallions, tigers and titans. Students ultimately chose their mascot to be the "tigers" and their school colors to be black and gold.

Century Elementary, located on Sunnyside Avenue between Alluvial and Nees avenues, opened August 21, 2000, with 29 teachers and 641 students. "The day we opened, we were full," said Scott Steele, the school's first principal. "Our unofficial motto is that our school has a 'calm sense of purpose.' We have goals and expectations, but we let our teachers teach, and we've been pretty successful."

Enrollment increased in the school's first years with portable units added to the campus to accommodate the growing student population. Student enrollment reached a peak in the 2004-05 school year with 911 students, but declined the next year with the opening of nearby

Woods Elementary, which alleviated the overcrowding of Century and Garfield elementary schools.

Early intervention program

Century houses the Clovis Infant Toddler Intervention (CITI) program, familiarly known as "CITI Kids," which is an Early Start program aiding children with special needs from birth through 3 years of age. Early Start is a state and federal program, and provides early intervention services to infants and toddlers with disabilities, as well as supporting their families through a coordinated, family-centered network.

CITI Kids provides assessment for preschoolers who may qualify for special services. Home visits by teachers are provided to children up to 18 months of age. Receiving funding through a direct grant from the State of California as well as from Central Valley Regional Center, which helps individuals with developmental disabilities as well as at-risk children reach their goals, Century is now the permanent site of the district's Early Start program. CUSD's program originally began at a school of portables located on the east side of the Clovis High campus, and then moved to Reyburn Intermediate while Century was being built. Early Start is now housed in several portables on the Century campus.

ESTABLISHED: 2000
GRADES: K-6
MASCOT: Tigers
COLORS: Black and gold
MOTTO: "Building Pride in Every Way"
LOCATION: 965 N. Sunnyside, Clovis
ACREAGE: 15

Also part of Early Start is the Family Resource Center, which is staffed by parents with experience in raising developmentally delayed children. The Center's goal is to provide optimal early childhood education, as well as being an informational and supportive source for parents.

A Preschool Assessment Team assesses children in the program when they are getting ready to leave Early Start as well as assesses other children throughout the district who may be in need of established and developing intensive preschool special education programs.

"Our newest program is an intensive behavioral program for children who may be on the autism spectrum; the program reaches the needs of qualifying children ages twelve to eighteen months old and can continue until they are six years old," said Shirley Feasel, CUSD psychologist and program specialist. "We work in the home with parents to help them learn to manage the child's behavior and to provide behavioral interventions that are based upon behavioral analysis principles."

Chess, anyone?

A recent and popular addition to student activities is Century's Chess Club led by music teacher Peter Gaffney. The club meets twice a week during lunch and Gaffney notes that it is the district's largest elementary chess club.

Another popular activity is the K-Kids Club, which works in conjunction with Kiwanis Club members. The community service project-based club was first brought to Century by the Old Town Clovis Kiwanis Club and is now overseen by Kiwanis Club of Clovis. Some of K-Kids' recent efforts have been car washes benefitting the Make-a-Wish Foundation, school beautification by planting flowers or plants on campus, making holiday cards for seniors at nursing facilities, plastic bag recycling drives and planting trees on a bike trail.

Students have their pick of co-curricular activities such as instrumental music, chorus, art, dance, drama and oral interpretation. A wide variety of sports from wrestling to track are also available, and all students are encouraged to get involved in an activity of their interest.

Staff and community

According to current Principal Gary Comstock, who became principal after Ruth DiSanto had served in the role from 2004 to 2009, two of Century's greatest strengths are its staff and community. "Staff is fully committed and dedicated to making each student's experience at Century a positive experience they will never forget," he said. "We are committed to creating opportunities for each student and each family to connect to Century Elementary School."

The Century staff and community celebrated a major milestone for the school in 2009 when the students' score surpassed the 900 mark on the state's Academic Performance Index. "That has been a goal Century had been working toward over the last four years," said DiSanto.

Recognized Excellence

Century Elementary has received:

>> State Distinguished School Award (2008)
>> California Business for Education Excellence Foundation's Scholar Schools Award (2009)

CHESTER A. NELSON ELEMENTARY SCHOOL

By Earlene Holguin

Post-World War II growth in Pinedale brought the need to build a second elementary school in the close-knit Pinedale School District. Out of this need, Chester A. Nelson Elementary School was born.

The school was necessary to accommodate the increasing population of nearby Pinedale Elementary School.

Building Pinedale's second elementary school

Chester A. Nelson Elementary School opened to students for the 1957-58 school year. The school joined the Pinedale School District, of which Pinedale Elementary was already a member.

Located at 1336 West Spruce Avenue in the community of Pinedale, Nelson Elementary was originally built to accommodate the overflow from Pinedale Elementary School, located one mile away. When Nelson first opened, it served approximately 300 students on its small 12-classroom campus, with one of the classrooms housing the library, nurse's station and administration office. Meals made at Pinedale Elementary were transported daily to Nelson's "cafeteria" — two rooms separated by a sliding door where students would eat their lunches.

The school's initial student population was composed of students in fourth through sixth grades, with Pinedale Elementary serving grades kindergarten through third, and also seventh and eighth grades (until these two grades were transferred to Clark Intermediate upon its opening in 1969).

Origins of a name

In January 1956, the new school was dedicated to lifelong Pinedale resident Albert Chester Nelson, who most commonly went by Chester A. Nelson, or "Chet," as family and friends called him.

Born to parents Albert and Laura Nelson on December 18, 1905, in Fresno, Nelson grew up in the community of Pinedale, and later became one of Pinedale's most active and notable citizens. On August 28, 1937, Nelson married Helen Keogh, and they soon established a home in the Pinedale community.

Championing the community's interests, Nelson was instrumental in the progression and much of the success in the building of both the Pinedale community and Nelson Elementary School. As a community activist, Nelson served on the board of trustees for the Pinedale School District from 1943 through 1955, serving as clerk for the board from 1946 through 1954. He was also chairman of the Pinedale Chamber of Commerce, chief of the Pinedale Fire Department, secretary-treasurer of the Pinedale Property Owner's Association, president of the Lion's Club, president of Fresno Native Sons of the Golden West, a Pinedale constable, president of the Fresno Rifle and Pistol Club, and active in the Pinedale Teenagers' Club. Additionally, he served the Pinedale Water District as ditch tender and later on the board of the Pinedale Water District.

On March 23, 1979, Nelson died at 74 years of age.

Chester A. Nelson
Photo Courtesy of Nelson Elementary School

Through the years

Not long after Nelson opened, changes were underway. In 1960, the Pinedale School District, comprised of Nelson and Pinedale elementary schools, was one of seven districts that unified to create Clovis Unified School District.

Transition issues for the community remained complicated and difficult. While the majority of community members supported unification, one of the obstacles they faced was the distance from Pinedale to Clovis, which their high school-age students were initially required to travel. Because of the distance, families believed that neither schools nor the services they provided were readily available to their children.

The building of nearby Clovis West High School in 1976 and Kastner Intermediate School in 1980 eased some of the transportation and growth issues both Pinedale and Nelson elementary schools faced.

In the late 1970s, Nelson, which was still serving only fourth- through sixth-graders, had doubled its enrollment and its facilities, adding more classrooms including one for kindergarten, an office, a multipurpose room and a library. As of 1976, Nelson was primed and ready to serve a full complement of kindergarten through sixth grade students. By 1977, when construction was completed by Palmo Construction Company, all of the community's students were consolidated into one school, attending Nelson Elementary until Pinedale reverted back to serving its own students again in 1990-91.

In 2001, the school again increased its capacity by adding a library media center, computer lab, teacher workroom and parking lot, and expanded the administration building.

Despite the renovations and additions, Nelson's history is not lost; the original 1957 school facilities still serve as the first three building wings on the east end of the campus.

Principals who have served at the helm of Nelson Elementary have included Clyde Willis, Mel Milton, Carl Campbell, Tony Petersen, Linda Hauser, Isabel Facio, Rich Smith, Mary Bass and Chuck Sandoval who became principal in 2008, a role he holds today.

BEEP-BEEP

With school colors of forest green and gold, the school also promotes student pride with the acronym "BEEP," which represents: Best school, Exemplary, Extraordinary and Perseverance. It's no coincidence that BEEP is also the signature sound of the school's mascot, the Roadrunner.

> **ESTABLISHED:** 1957
> **GRADES:** K-6
> **MASCOT:** Roadrunners
> **COLORS:** Forest green and gold
> **MOTTO:** "BEEP" which represents: Best school, Exemplary, Extraordinary, and Perseverance
> **LOCATION:** 1336 W. Spruce Avenue, Pinedale
> **ACREAGE:** 15

Interfacing with world history:
A view of the Japanese Internment Center

Duane Barker, local historian and former Clovis Unified School District administrator, was an early Nelson Elementary School educator, teaching at the school from 1971 through 1975.

During his tenure at Nelson School, Barker recalled one of the most unusual things about the location. While the school was built after Pinedale Elementary School was established, the residual effects of both the Japanese Internment Center and the Army military camp once located in the neighborhood were apparent, as portions of those buildings and barracks still existed, and were plainly visible on a daily basis, by both faculty and students at Nelson, he said.

After the start of WWII, the United States Army acquired the former Sugar Pine Lumber Company mill area for the purpose of building a temporary internment camp for housing Japanese-Americans who had been ordered to the camps for the duration of the war under Executive Order 9066, a declaration issued by President Franklin D. Roosevelt. Acquired in March of 1942, the site housed approximately 4,382 internees from May to July 1942.

Following the transfer of the Japanese-Americans to more permanent sites, the United States Army utilized the area for a training center. The area was known as Camp Pinedale and became the training location for several military units which included the aviation, wing and radio intelligence signal companies, and included the signal construction battalions and mobile radio squadrons. Camp Pinedale was relocated in 1945, after which the property reverted to its owner Pinedale Compress and Warehouse Company.

Student resources, support

As part of the community of Pinedale, Nelson students benefit from services provided in Pinedale such as the community health center, a library and the Neighborhood Resource Center operated by Clovis Unified.

An ACES (After-school Co-curricular Education and Safety) program also is offered at the school, in alignment with Nelson's mission statement, to assure that each student achieves at his or her highest social and academic levels. Funded through a state grant, the after- school program is open to students from kindergarten through sixth grades and offers homework assistance, organized recreation, academic enrichment taught by CSUF teaching fellows and safe, constructive opportunities from the time school is out until 6 P.M. each day of the school year.

Through the generations

Recognized Excellence

Nelson Elementary has received:
>> National Blue Ribbon School Award (1992, 2006)
>> State Distinguished School Award (1998, 2004, 2006)
>> California Blue Ribbon Nominee (1992)
>> Title I Academic Achievement Award (2006)
>> California Business for Education Excellence Foundation's Star Schools Award (2009)
>> CSU Fresno's Bonner Center Character for Education's Virtues and Character Education Award (2000, 2002, 2004)

Nelson shares a unique feature with its surrounding community — pride and love of local neighborhoods. Many parents now sending their children to the school are second- or third-generation residents, many of whom attended Nelson Elementary as children themselves and went on to purchase their parents' houses. These families have truly found a home in their neighborhood school and in the community.

Nelson has one of the most balanced socioeconomically diverse populations in the Clovis West Area. Bluff residents and Title I populations combine in a greater community that richly benefits from its diversity at Nelson

CLOVIS ADULT EDUCATION

By Janice Stevens

Establishing the adult school

Everett G. "Bud" Rank, Jr., the first official president of the Clovis Unified School Board, formed in 1960, recalled the need for a school outside the perimeters of a traditional high school. "It started because there was more demand," Rank said. "People [were] getting out of high school and not getting a degree or wanting to move into a different or another position, or they needed further education or a high school diploma that they never got. The school started very small. It has really grown to be one of the finer things the district did."

When Clovis Unified School District began offering adult education courses in 1960, classes were held in the original 1920 Clovis High School on Fifth Street in Old Town Clovis. In 1967, the adult program had grown significantly and qualified to be recognized as an adult school. In the early 1970s, the adult school shared the building with Gateway Continuation School until 1975, when Gateway relocated two miles east to its new campus on Herndon Avenue. The adult school was then once again the sole occupant of the 1920 high school building, which by this time was owned by the City of Clovis and leased back to the district. Space was still tight, however, so in 1977, the adult school's nursing program was housed at Pinedale Elementary School.

In 1995, Clovis Adult School required more space and relocated adjacent to CUSD's District Office campus on the southeast corner of Herndon and Sunnyside avenues, which is where it remains today. The school's entrance is located just off of Sunnyside Avenue on David E.

Cook Way, named in honor of David E. Cook, a former CUSD deputy superintendent and business administrator. Cook was valued for the important role he played in developing the district's financially responsible business practices, setting the tone and standards that are still in place throughout the district today including careful stewardship of taxpayers' dollars and providing high-quality and well-maintained buildings for students. Cook also created camaraderie among classified and plant operations employees. He knew every one of the classified employees who worked in the district and helped them understand that their role was vital to the education of students. It was appropriate then that the street named for him houses most of the district service buildings out of which many of the employees he so strongly supported are based.

When the adult school moved to its new location at 1452 David E. Cook Way, the campus had 35 classrooms to accommodate its students, who also enjoyed their new student lounge and bookstore, while staff was pleased with the increased office space.

Evolving

Clovis Adult School's physical location wasn't the only part of the school that has evolved over time. From a scant few course offerings in the late 1960s, the adult school has become a powerful educational force, today offering 450 classes and serving more than 15,000 students 18 years of age and older in the Clovis and surrounding areas.

Even the school's name has evolved from Clovis Adult School to Clovis Adult and Vocational Education in the early 1980s to its current official name, Clovis Adult Education, or CAE, in 1993. At that time, the district created the self-contained Regional Occupational Program (ROP), a vocational program for high school students, and the adult school condensed its name to Clovis Adult Education (CAE).

Principals

In the adult school's 50-year history, only four principals have overseen the program. Jack Howard was the first principal, serving from 1960 to 1964; Charles Peterson served as the school's principal/director for nearly 30 years, from 1965 until 1993; Dave Lennon served as principal from 1993 to 2000; and current CAE Director John Ballinger has been at the helm since 2001.

Standards

According to CAE's mission statement, the purpose of Clovis Adult Education is to offer lifelong educational opportunities and services which address the unique needs of the diverse community by providing the means to become productive community members and workers, effective family members and lifelong learners.

CAE has adopted five "Expected School-wide Learning Results," or ESLRs, with the expectation that during their time at the school, students will become active problem solvers; goal setters and achievers; effective communicators; quality producers; and involved community members.

Through the ESLRs, when students graduate from the adult school they are expected to apply critical thinking skills and problem-solving processes, utilize technology on the job and in day-to-day life, establish and accomplish constructive short- and long-term goals, use spoken and written communication competently and confidently, use technology creatively and ethi-cally, demonstrate a strong work ethic, strive for excellence, work well independently and with others, respect the rights of others, and make a positive contribution to their family, school, workplace and community.

Programs

Clovis Adult Education offers a vast array of programs.

Academic courses at CAE include classes to earn a high school diploma, General Educational Development (GED) test preparation, and the Adult Basic Education program which teaches reading, writing and math.

The English as a second language, or ESL, program offers lessons not only in learning the English language, but also in citi-zenship, pronunciation, idioms and conversation.

Clovis Family Literacy program offers free classes to quali-fying families. Over the years, this program has been funded through CBET (California Basic Education Test), Even Start and First 5 grants. The purpose of the multiple programs that comprise the Clovis Family Literacy component is to empower parents in becoming their child's first teacher through active and involved parenting. Programs include: Community Based English Tutoring, Even Start, Family Strengthening, Let's Read Together and Student Intervention Program.

> **ESTABLISHED:** 1968
> **AGES SERVED:** 18 to older adult
> **MASCOT:** Peacock
> **COLORS:** Blue and green
> **MOTTO:** "Proud as a Peacock," "Educating with Pride"
> **LOCATION:** 1452 David E. Cook Way, Clovis
> **ACREAGE:** 3.9

The state-approved Nurse Education Program prepares students to successfully pass exams required for licensure in the field of health care. Offerings include licensed vocational nurse pre-requisite classes, activity leader training, and certified nurse assistant and IV therapy certi-fication. All curriculum and training are designed to meet current and future needs of an ever-changing health care delivery system.

Under the Career Technical Education category, CAE offers vocational certification pro-grams and classes for computer businesses, trades and medical assistants.

More than 1,000 older adults, ages 50 years and up, participate in CAE's fee-based Older Adult Program consisting of courses in health and fitness, literacy, family, world, the arts, com-munications, and technology.

The Community Education program includes more than 250 fee-based self-enrichment classes for community members of all ages. A wide variety of courses are offered including travel, conversational foreign languages, cooking, computers, crafts, music, dancing, exercise, Notary Public certification and much more. One of the highlights of Community Education is "Summer Fun," a six-week enrichment program held each summer that provides children ages 3 through 18 from the Fresno/Clovis area the opportunity to be active and creative during their summer break through a variety of classes in the arts, academics and athletics.

Until its closure in 2010, CAE operated its Community Technology Center (CTC) in southeast Fresno which provided relevant, up-to-date computer instruction to enhance partici-pants' opportunities for employment. CTC classes included computer concepts, e-mail, basic keyboarding and Windows operating systems. Also offered were two levels of Auto Computer Aided Design (CAD) Fundamentals in which drafting students learned to generate three-dimensional wire frame modeling, assemblies, detailed drawings and renderings.

Breaking precedence: adult school mascot

Long before official school approval, the Peacock flaunted its colors at Clovis Adult Education. Unofficially adopted by the faculty, miscellaneous memorabilia of cups, screen savers, paintings, wall hangings, tee shirts and a peacock-shaped lamp all carried the image of the proud bird.

A large banner used as a backdrop to the 2004 high school graduation ceremonies drew the attention of viewers, including Clovis Unified administration, who reminded then-Principal John Ballinger that all school mascots required official approval from the governing board.

Undaunted, Ballinger approached the board, received approval and thus included the Peacock into the officially noted school mascot roster. Typically, adult schools do not boast mascots, but CAE's staff, faculty and students have an unusual bond to their school, and they believed the "Proud as a Peacock" motto was especially suitable. Ballinger, a former activities director at Clovis High School, used his talent for inspiring others to rally student and staff enthusiasm and school spirit to continue their support of the Peacock.

Taking it one step further, Kathy Adolph, school registrar, remembers an artist's rendering of a peacock adorning a garish lime green shirt. She said in a *Clovis Independent* article, "Instead of just blending into the crowd and people saying, 'Oh, there's the adult school,' people really noticed us and said, 'Wow! There is the adult school!'"

CLOVIS EAST HIGH SCHOOL

By Edna Herstein

In the late 1990s, the population in southeast Clovis was booming, with people arriving on the previously undeveloped agricultural land as fast as new subdivisions could accommodate them. Clovis Unified administration was acutely aware of the need for new schools in the area as growth was expected to continue. At the top of the list of needs were a new intermediate school and a new high school.

Reagan Educational Center

Based on the success of the district's Buchanan Educational Center, which houses three schools on one parcel of land, came the idea to recreate a similar complex in southeast Clovis.

Clovis Unified purchased 160 acres of bare land bordered by DeWolf, Gettysburg, Leonard and Ashlan avenues; across the street stood a pecan orchard. The expansive land would be used to house CUSD's second complex, Reagan Educational Center, or REC. The three schools that would occupy the land would be: Clovis East High School (opened in 2000), Reyburn Intermediate School (opened in 1999) and Reagan Elementary School (opened in 2006).

A key advantage to housing the three schools in close proximity was the ability to provide students a seamless transition from kindergarten through twelfth grade. Additionally, the three schools would have the advantage of being able to share facilities and grounds.

Attendance boundaries were redrawn to shift the district's existing high school boundaries to accommodate the southeast campus. Students who would have attended Clark Intermediate and Clovis High School or Alta Sierra Intermediate and Buchanan High now attended the REC secondary schools.

Clark and Alta Sierra intermediate students slated to attend the new schools were asked to choose the school colors and mascot. Their selections were school colors of hunter green, navy blue and silver, and a mascot of the Timberwolves. Their choices were approved by the governing board, and it was decided that all three Reagan Educational Center schools would share the same colors and mascot in order to ensure an all-inclusive feel.

Reyburn Intermediate was the first REC school to be completed on the $90 million site and opened to students in the 1999-2000 school year. At the time Reyburn opened, Clovis East was yet to be finished and adjoining Reagan Elementary yet to be built. In the first year the intermediate school was open, Clovis East ninth-graders shared the new campus with Reyburn's seventh and eighth grade students.

The Clovis East campus opened to ninth- and tenth-graders for the 2000-01 school year. One grade level per year was added until a full complement of ninth- through twelfth-graders attended the school in 2003-04.

Charter school

Early in the planning process, the district applied to the state for REC to become a charter school which would have helped facilitate opportunities for innovation. However, because the charter school movement in California was still evolving, it was decided not to go forward with the application and designation at that time.

"The charter school movement was just evolving," said Lyn Snauffer, who served as the first assistant superintendent over the new schools. "Staying with what we knew best seemed the best course to take at the time so we later decided to withdraw our application. CUSD provided tremendous opportunities for future innovation at the Center."

Clovis Colony

Clovis East High School, so named for its geographical location within CUSD's boundaries, was not always going to be "Clovis East." The name Clovis Colony High School was initially approved by CUSD's Governing Board for the first new high school the district had built in 10 years.

The idea for the "Colony" name was a tribute to a time when, in the late 1800s, various small area schools annexed themselves into larger ones to form schools which became known as colonies. Early local colonies included Temperance Colony, Garfield Colony, Jefferson Colony, Kutner Colony and Nees Colony.

Despite its basis in the historical shaping of what would eventually become Clovis Unified School District, the Colony name met with significant community concerns that its modern connotation didn't accurately reflect the positive environment hoped for the new campus. With school spirit wear and signage already on order, the governing board responded to the concerns by selecting the alternative recommendation of Clovis East High School as the new name.

Feel the Love

When Clovis East opened, Jeff Eben was the school's principal. He created a unique identity for the school based on hope, community and love, with a focus on alternatives to the negative.

Eben encouraged his staff to focus on the positive both in their classrooms and offices, and began every staff meeting by asking, "How many wins have you had today?"

Another defining element of the school's early culture was Eben's implementation of the motto, "Feel the Love." "There are always reasons to be mad, frustrated, discouraged, whatever. Rather than get swallowed up in that, take the time to celebrate each day and always 'Feel the Love,'" Eben said.

The Feel the Love culture was never more evident than on September 14, 2001. Along with the entire world, the Clovis East campus was in shock following the tragic terrorist attacks on the World Trade Center and Pentagon on September 11, 2001. Moved to do something different on the Friday three days after the attacks, Eben announced to the campus, "I will be sitting outside at noon in the amphitheater and observing 25 minutes of silence. Anyone who wants can join me."

Within five minutes, nearly the entire student body of 1,500 students silently joined Eben. "Eventually, one girl came forward and got on her knees," Eben said. "Soon hundreds were linked arm-in-arm on their knees in complete silence. It was a very powerful moment of reverence which defined us as a culture. That was the proudest moment of my professional career."

Another of the many CEHS "Feel the Love" moments came on February 16, 2005, in the Clovis East gym during a boys' basketball game between CEHS and Buchanan High.

Clovis East senior Ryan "Ryno" Bellflower, a special education student, had been devoted to both the girls' and boys' basketball teams all four years of his high school career, serving as a manager and an indispensable help to the coaches, and never missing a game.

ESTABLISHED: 2000
GRADES: 9-12
MASCOT: Timberwolves
COLORS: Navy blue, hunter green and silver
ADDRESS: 2940 Leonard Avenue, Clovis
ACREAGE: Part of the 160-acre Reagan Educational Center

Suddenly, in the fourth quarter of the February 16 Senior Night Game, the CEHS student section rose in unison and began chanting "We want Ryno!" With just over three minutes to play, the coach motioned Ryno, widely known for his dedication and heart, onto the floor and the crowd erupted. With the clock ticking, everyone in the gym was rooting for him to score. After missing two shots, Ryno once again found the ball in his hands as he stood just behind the three point line with the final buzzer of the game ringing. Ryno attempted his final shot, sinking a three-pointer just in time and setting off a wild celebration.

Students, parents and staff charged the court, mobbing Ryno. "The Buchanan fans were right there in the mix, and at that moment, no one seemed to care who won or lost," said Eben. "Ryno wasn't able to walk off the court because he was being carried on the shoulders of his peers. There wasn't a dry eye in the building for several minutes, and I think we all knew we had witnessed the very best part of sports and of our youth."

Continuing philosophies

When Eben left his position of principal at Clovis East in 2006 to work at Clovis Adult Education while pursuing a public speaking career, Steve Martinez took the reins. Martinez implemented the theme "Don't Stop Believin'." "It is important for us to continue believing that Clovis East can obtain success in everything we do," he said at the time. "With opportunities in top academic programs, coupled with a strong co-curricular program (including elective offerings, clubs and organizations, performing arts, academic competitive teams, and athletic teams), there is something of interest for every student at Clovis East." Upon Martinez' departure in 2009, Darin Tockey took over as CEHS' principal, a role he still holds today. He and his staff adhere to the district's core beliefs of high standards and expectations; putting students first and treating them with respect; teamwork and trust; and providing a quality education for all students.

Agriculture program

Unique to Clovis East is the McFarlane-Coffman Ag Center, a comprehensive, state-of-the-art facility offering students real-world hands-on experiences in animal science, plant science, agricultural engineering and environmental/natural resources.

CEHS students who participate in the school's agriculture program can choose from courses in the five career certificate programs offered which are derived from the basic core and advanced clusters. These certificate programs include Agricultural Engineering, Animal Science, Environmental Science/Natural Resources, General Agricultural Science and Plant Science/Ornamental Horticulture.

The Clovis FFA chapter is also based out of the McFarlane-Coffman Ag Center. Complementing the agriculture program, FFA enables agriculture students to compete against other high school students to show the quality of their crops and livestock.

Smart-wired students

Another unique program offered at Clovis East is the Virtual Enterprise (VE) class which was established in 2005. Striving to prepare students for the workplace, California Virtual Enterprise was established in 1998 as a nonprofit business simulation organization. Clovis East's class draws on the foundation of the statewide organization that has expanded internationally. Students in the VE course earn college credit.

Every VE class operates its own virtual business. The class is responsible for marketing, human resources, bookkeeping, e-commerce and most other daily operations of running a business. The program is designed to be as realistic as possible; students are required to attend job interviews with district administrators in order to be accepted into the class, and are awarded salaries based on their responsibilities. They also "purchase" and "sell" products to and from other VE classes across the state and country.

Since the program began, Clovis East's VE students have won awards at both state and national Virtual Enterprise competitions.

Honors

The Reagan Educational Center was the recipient of the 2000 Governor's Book Fund School Library Enrichment Grant.

The school's instrumental music programs have earned multiple honors. Clovis East's Winter Percussion was named World Champions in Dayton, Ohio, in 2003. The same week, Clovis East's Choir won a gold medal for their performance at the Lincoln Center. In 2006, the Beginning Band, Symphonic Band and Wind Ensemble were selected to play at the World Projects Wind Band Festival, featuring high school and college wind bands from throughout the United States, at the Kennedy Center in Washington, D.C. In addition, the Clovis East High School Wind Ensemble was the Featured Wind Band at the California Music Educators Association State Convention 2009.

Athletics

In athletics, girls' team Tri-River Athletic Conference (TRAC) champions have included cross country in 2002; water polo in 2003; tennis in 2003 and 2007; soccer in 2003; badminton in 2009. Boys' team TRAC champions have included cross country in 2002; soccer in 2002; football in 2002, 2003, 2005, 2006, 2007; track and field in 2003, 2004 and 2008; and basketball in 2009 and 2010.

CIF central section valley champions have included girls' cross country in 2001 and 2003; football in 2003 and 2006; boys' track and field in 2007 and 2009; and boys' basketball in 2007, 2008 and 2010; boys' golf in 2007; and girls' badminton in 2009. Boys' track and field won the CIF State Championship in 2009.

Football is a significant part of the Clovis East culture. In 2005, the *Fresno Bee* deemed that year's CEHS varsity football program "the most successful new school the valley had seen." In 2007, it called the T-wolves "the most dominant football program in the valley this decade." In Clovis East's first six years, the varsity football team claimed four league championships; two valley championships; two state top 10 rankings; one top 25 national ranking; four Central Valley powerlifting championships; 28 city/county all-star game players; nine all-valley players; two all-state players; and more than 30 all-league players.

> ### Recognized Excellence
> Clovis East High has received:
> >> National Blue Ribbon Award (2008)
> >> State Distinguished School Award (2007)
> >> Governor's Book Fund School Library Enrichment Grant (2000)

CLOVIS ELEMENTARY SCHOOL

By Monica Stevens

The first Clovis Elementary

In the early 1890s, lumbering, farming and mining drew many to settle in Clovis. But there was no school, and children had to be sent to outlying areas to get an education. To provide a local school, Clovis citizens petitioned and received authorization from Fresno County Schools Superintendent T. J. Kirk for a school, and on March 5, 1895, the Clovis Elementary District was formed.

Trustees Clovis M. Cole, H. A. Foulke and J. A. Ferguson held a bond election for the funds to build a school. The bond was for $5,000 at a 7 percent interest rate. It passed August 10, 1895, without a single negative vote.

On September 19, 1895, Clovis Grammar School, or Clovis Elementary School as it was also called, opened in a temporary location in the warehouse of the Southern Pacific Railroad at Fifth Street and Dewitt Avenue in Clovis. The first teacher, Elizabeth Kanstrup, taught nine grades for a salary of $65 per month. A single-room wooden school was soon built for the 14 Clovis Grammar students and was located on the northeast corner of Third Street and Dewitt Avenue.

The school attained a permanent home in 1897, when an austere wooden two-story building was constructed at Second Street and Pollasky Avenue. Mr. Troutwine was the only faculty member, overseeing the education of all his students ranging from grades one through nine. The school featured four classrooms, a storeroom, a principal's office, a washbasin, an indoor drinking fountain, a wood stove, electric lighting in the classrooms and two "Doolies," or restrooms, at the back of the schoolyard.

A stable was available on the grounds to house the horses and mules the students rode to school.

Every morning, the bell in the belfry rang first at 8:30 A.M., then a second and final time at 9 A.M. to signify the official beginning of classes. School continued each day until 4 P.M. except for students in grades one and two whose school day ended at 2:30 P.M.

On June 27, 1899, Clovis District was one of seven participating elementary school districts in the area to unite with Clovis High School to form Clovis Union High School District. The elementary districts still retained their status as separate districts.

Clovis High School used the top floor of the Clovis Grammar School building from 1899 to 1903 until the school's nearby permanent home was completed, located between Fourth and Fifth streets in Clovis.

Due to increasing enrollment, a primary building with four rooms and a small library was eventually added just east of the school. Charles Edgecomb was principal.

In 1918, a one-story brick building replaced the old two-story school. Ernest J. Kump, Sr., a prominent local architect noted for designing schools across the valley, designed the building that was built by contractor E. P. Smith. Enrollment at the newly constructed school was 307 fourth- through eighth-graders.

Additional land was purchased from Arthur Frame in 1939 giving the school the entire block on the west side of Pollasky Avenue and a half block on the east side of the street.

Enrollment continued to increase. To accommodate the influx of students, temporary buildings were moved onto the campus. Planners turned to Hammer Field, previously the Fresno Air Field and Municipal Airport at Fresno, to acquire available facilities. The old mess hall was used as a classroom and kitchen. The quartermaster corps office building became two classrooms and an office for the school nurse.

In 1952, the one-story brick building was condemned following the discovery of major structural cracks. Two new schools had recently been completed in the Clovis Elementary District to accommodate the growing community, and to replace the aging Clovis Grammar School; so following the school's closure, students found new homes at either Sierra Vista or Weldon.

ORIGINALLY ESTABLISHED: 1895

RE-ESTABLISHED: 1999 in portables, 2000 in its permanent facility

GRADES: K-6

MASCOT: Jaguars

COLORS: Navy blue and Vegas gold

MOTTO: "Learning Today, Leading Tomorrow"

LOCATION: 1100 Armstrong Avenue, Clovis

ACREAGE: 15

The frame buildings of Clovis Elementary were sold; the brick building was torn down; materials from the building were salvaged; and the land where the school once sat was cleared and sold.

Soon after, Clovis Elementary District was one of the seven districts that elected to join to form Clovis Unified School District in 1960.

A new beginning

Even though the original Clovis Elementary School was condemned in 1952 and subsequently demolished, Clovis had not seen the last of its namesake elementary.

In the late 1990s, Jefferson, Red Bank and Weldon elementary schools in the central Clovis area were overcrowded, creating the need for a new school. The district first tried to secure farmland near Peach and Sierra avenues as the site on which to build the school. However, the landowner and CUSD could not agree to terms of a sale so the decision was made to build on open land that was already owned by the district. The new school would be built on the corner of Armstrong and Barstow avenues, adjacent to Clovis High School.

In December 1998, Bob Hansen, who was serving as the principal of nearby Jefferson Elementary School at that time, was named principal of the not-yet-constructed school. The early appointment enabled Hansen to select the educational team well in advance and thoroughly prepare for the opening of a new school.

New attendance areas were drawn with students coming from Jefferson, Red Bank and Weldon elementary schools to form Clovis Elementary's student body.

Prior to the opening of the new school, Hansen held meetings with parents, sometimes as small groups in neighborhood homes, to begin creating the school's culture. He met regularly with students at each of the three feeder schools to select school colors of navy blue and Vegas gold, the Jaguar mascot and athletic uniforms. A committee was formed consisting of parents and community members to recommend a school name to the CUSD Governing Board. Several names were considered. One name, Pendergrass Elementary, was suggested to honor the well-respected Clovis Pendergrass family and Dr. Clayton Pendergrass, the town of Clovis' beloved physician for many years. Two others were Pioneer Elementary or Pioneer Academy, suggested to recognize the "pioneers" of Clovis Unified — the governing board members involved in the district's unification in 1960. Ultimately, the governing board selected the name Clovis Elementary at a March 1999 board meeting.

"It seemed appropriate to bring back 'Clovis Elementary School,' given that more than half of our student population comes from the Weldon attendance area, the same area that once served students for the first Clovis Elementary," said Hansen.

Work began on the new school on July 5, 1999. While their permanent school was being built, Clovis Elementary School students began the 1999-2000 school year at a temporary home of portable classrooms on the Clovis High campus. Students and staff were able to watch the construction of their new school as the site was just several hundred feet to the north of the portables.

The new facilities opened to students for the 2000-01 school year.

"Seeing students and parents from three distinct school communities come together as one was extremely gratifying," Hansen said. "Watching an amazing team of educators work together to ensure that the process went smoothly was impressive. Our goal as a staff was to create a 'school of choice' environment. Simply, this meant that if parents could choose their child's school, we wanted them to choose Clovis Elementary. Starting with that mindset, other things tend to fall into place. It was an honor to be part of the experience."

Tradition of excellence continues

Principal Isabel Herrera-Facio arrived in Jaguar Country in 2003, stepping into the role left by Hansen when he became principal at nearby Dry Creek Elementary. Herrera-Facio remains at the helm today.

"Clovis Elementary is unique in that, currently, we have one hundred English language learners, and fifty percent of our families are socio-economically disadvantaged," she said. "Our diverse population brings a wide variety of experiences that contribute to making Clovis Elementary the great school it is today."

Clovis Elementary features seven special education classrooms which include two resource specialists, three intervention classes and two special day classrooms.

Herrera-Facio attributes students' success to a variety of factors.

"The teachers and staff who serve Clovis kids are incredibly talented and constantly search for new ways to get students to achieve and attain their goals," she said. "The entire staff, student body and community are very accepting of all kids and are sensitive to individual student needs. Clovis Elementary School is truly a family; where everyone is accepted and supported. I am blessed to be a part of this exemplary educational institution."

> **Recognized Excellence**
>
> Clovis Elementary has received:
> >> Title I Academic Achievement Award (2007, 2010)
> >> California Business for Education Excellence Foundation's Star Schools Award (2009)
> >> CSU Fresno's Bonner Center Character for Education's Virtues and Character Education Award (2002)

Herrera-Facio emphasizes that Clovis Elementary's greatest strengths lie in the passion and determination of its teachers.

"Teachers are relentless in their effort to make sure all students learn while providing a nurturing environment. Clovis Elementary will continue to cultivate a 'kids first' atmosphere, celebrate our diversity and foster an institution where all students can and will learn," she said.

CES' core values

Clovis Elementary's core values were written by the staff and drive instruction, decisions and routines on the Jaguar campus. These core values are: kids first; high standards; develop the mind, body and spirit; teamwork; character development; and competition.

CLOVIS HIGH SCHOOL

By Kathleen Lund Coates

Clovis High School is "the original," the first high school built in the Clovis Unified School District, and it is defined by its historic past even today. The loyalty runs deep among students, alumni, faculty and administrators at the school, dating back to its opening in September 1899. "Once a Cougar, always a Cougar" isn't just a saying; it's a way of life.

The beginning

Before 1899, the year Clovis High School was founded, students in the small mill town of Clovis who attended area elementary school districts and wanted to earn a high school diploma had to apply to go to Fresno High School. If you were a young man, you could also choose to travel to Stockton, Sacramento or the Bay Area. Girls went to San Jose, if they went at all.

Attempts to form a high school district began in 1889, and were finally successful on June 27, 1899, when Lee Beall, a Jefferson Colony farmer, and John Rutledge, a Clovis mill man, organized seven school districts — Red Banks, Jefferson, Garfield, Mississippi, Wolters Colony, Temperance and Clovis — to form Clovis Union High School District, with each elementary district agreeing to send its ninth-graders to Clovis Union High School. Each district elected one trustee to the board of the new Clovis Union High School.

Enrollment included 17 students that first year, and the average attendance was 12. The school operated out of two rooms rented for $100 per year on the second floor of the Clovis Grammar School on the west side of Pollasky Avenue between First and Second streets. The building had electric lights and running water but outhouses were located behind the school and heating was provided by cast-iron wood stoves. Instead of walking, some lucky students rode their horses to school, and the animals were sheltered by a shed south of the school yard.

Louis K. Webb was the first principal and teacher; he was paid $120 per month. In 1900, Estelle Kellogg was added to the staff.

Just two students made up the first graduating class of 1902: Emory Reyburn and Robert Lee Brown. According to a scrapbook from that time belonging to Mary Martin, a prominent Clovis resident, "the low percentage of graduates in this class cannot be attributed to dullness on the part of the students. No one at that time had to go to school over the age of 14. These boys and girls fell out because in most cases they had to go to work. And another thing, lots of parents did not 'hold to too much education,' especially for women."

The school emphasized training for entrance to college, qualifying students to attend the University of California at Berkeley.

A school of its own

The first Clovis Union High School campus, on the corner of Fifth and Osmun streets, was financed by a school bond in 1902. The new wooden building opened in 1903. A handbook from Clovis Union High School in 1904-05 listed the school colors as gold and white and the motto as "Excelsior," meaning ever onward and upward.

By 1907, the graduating class was up to 11 students. An article from that year's Clovis Union High School commencement program listed the class colors as scarlet and white, and the class motto as "Never Say Fail." Circa 1910, the growing enrollment led to the construction of an additional rectangular clapboard Arts and Crafts Building behind the school. A was added in 1912-13 to house vocational classes.

Clovis Union High's second campus, built in 1920.

In 1915, the district purchased and moved onto the campus a civic auditorium that was modified for use as the high school's first gymnasium.

By 1916, more than 150 students were enrolled and the board called for a $60,000 bond election in April 1917. Some residents opposed the bond, claiming they were bearing too heavy a tax burden. In addition, residents were concerned about a recent congressional declaration of war against Germany. "Facing war and the high taxes and prices for everything," the *Clovis Tribune* noted, "the people are in no mood for issuing bonds."

Another new home

The bond issue was defeated by a sizeable margin, and high school district trustees did not propose another bond until well after the end of World War I. In June 1919, they called for a special election for a $100,000 bond issue for the construction of a new high school.

The bond carried overwhelmingly, despite opposition from local newspapers, and construction of a "Mediterranean-style" building began in January 1920. General contractors were Del Favio and Rosari. The school, located in the same location as the 1903 school, was designed by noted San Francisco architect William Weeks. A 1981 report by California State University, Fresno history professor Ephraim Smith, and architectural historian John Powell noted the historical and architectural significance of the 1920 Clovis Union High School building, calling the proportions of the building "near-perfect." Weeks has been credited as one of the architects who helped develop the state's regional architectural heritage. The report also mentions that it is believed that the 1920 building is the only one in Fresno County designed by Weeks and concludes that "the building was and continues to be the most elegant public and historic structure in the City of Clovis."

ESTABLISHED: 1899
GRADES: 9-12
MASCOT: Cougar
COLORS: Blue and gold
MOTTO: "A Tradition of Excellence in Education"
LOCATION: 1055 Fowler Avenue, Clovis
ACREAGE: 80

Clovis Union's previous wood building was demolished with the construction of the new school. Only the doors and window frames were kept and used on a house at Fourth and Osmun streets.

The new school, which opened in September 1920, was a two-story building made of reinforced concrete. It had a flat roof and brick stairs leading up to two entry doors. Inside, concrete ramps led to the second floor and rear exits. The largest room was the auditorium, which could seat up to 400 people. The building was described as "handsome, modern and up to date."

The new campus would serve as "the focal point of the community, particularly in the early years," according to George Kastner, a 1937 graduate and a Clovis Unified School District administrator. Early principals included H. Rode (1920-1922); E. C. McKesson (1922-1924) and Fordyce Stewart (1924-1925). Paul Andrews was superintendent of the high school district from 1925 to 1946 and also served as principal from 1925 to 1935.

Enrollment increased along with the growth of the town, and by 1937, there were 500 students attending classes at the 5.2-acre campus. The school offered football, basketball, baseball, track and girls' volleyball programs.

Facility expansion also got a boost through funding provided by the federal Work Projects Administration (WPA) program started in 1935 to employ millions of Americans in public works projects. In 1941, for example, $66,170 of the total $92,000 cost to build a new CHS science building was covered by a WPA grant; the remainder was paid for by school bonds. Clovis High's theater was built in 1942 also made possible by a WPA grant. The theater remains today on the Clark Intermediate campus, serving the community since as a desirable performing arts location due to its spacious elegance. It has hosted performances of plays, musicals, dance, music, choral and more. It was named in 1982 in honor of Mercedes Edwards who served for 28 years in Clovis Unified as a music teacher and as Clovis High's choir director.

A cafeteria was built in 1948, and, as enrollment continued to grow, an auditorium complex was constructed in 1953, and in 1956, additional classrooms, a gym, a music building and a shop were built.

The school yearbook, "The Argus" later, in 1937, known as "The Cavalcade," reflected the times during which the students were living. For example, an Argus from 1921 featured serious senior portraits of students with names like Pearl and Vivian with playful sayings alongside. Advertisements were sold to businesses including the Clovis-Fresno Stage Co. and the Clovis Cash Grocery.

Fort Washington joined the Clovis district April 5, 1926, followed by Dry Creek December 13, 1929. Pinedale students had their choice of attending Fresno or Clovis high schools until the Clovis facility could no longer accommodate them in 1932. The Pinedale District re-joined with Clovis July 26, 1935.

Everett G. "Bud" Rank, Jr., the first official president of the Clovis Unified Board of Trustees, graduated from Clovis Union High School in 1940. He recalled with fondness his time in agricultural classes and Future Farmers of America. Since his family lived on a farm and there were no school buses, if he wanted to stay afterward for sports practice, he had to walk nine miles if he couldn't catch a ride.

"Teachers were tough back then," he recalled. "We had one teacher who taught math; he had a pistol he kept in his drawer, with no shells. He would sit in the back of the room, and if you talked, he would throw a piece of chalk at your head."

During the 1940s, the school colors changed to blue and white and then morphed again into blue and gold.

The Cavalcade from 1945 set aside a page "In Memoriam" to students who had died defending their country and an ad by John E. Good & Co. encouraging readers to buy war bonds and stamps. "If liberty is worth fighting for, it is worth paying for," read the advertisement.

Peg Bos, president of the Clovis Historical Society, graduated in 1948. She, her mother and her son all attended Clovis High in the 1920 building, which was just three blocks from the home in which she was raised.

"My grandparents had a shop nearby. Students could walk downtown and get their lunch," she recalled. "The teachers were good people; you saw them at church and at all the community functions."

One standout student was Daryle Lamonica, 1959 graduate and class president and football, basketball, baseball and track champion. He went on to play at the University of Notre Dame and played professionally from 1963 to 1974, first as the quarterback for the Buffalo Bills, then for the Oakland Raiders where he earned the nickname "The Mad Bomber." When the current CHS facility was built in 1969 on Fowler Avenue, the school's football stadium was dedicated to him in 1970.

Another standout was Lloyd Merriman, class of 1942, who was an All-American fullback at Stanford University, a Marine fighter pilot in World War II, and was drafted to play professional football by the Chicago Bears and the Los Angeles Dons. Instead however, he chose to pursue professional baseball, signing a contract with the Cincinnati Reds in 1949 and later with the Chicago White Sox. He took a leave from baseball to fight in the Korean War, returning to Clovis after his service to open an insurance agency. The Clovis High varsity baseball field was dedicated in his honor in 1993.

Unification

By 1959, attendance was more than 1,800 and the Clovis Union High School District's valuation was more than $38 million. At one point, district boundaries stretched all the way to Blackstone and Shields avenues, covering both Fresno Unified's McLane and Hoover high schools as well as part of Bullard High's attendance areas. However, bit by bit, the larger, adjacent Fresno Unified School District nibbled away at Clovis' territory. Fresno Unified had annexed more than 40 percent of the assessed valuation of the Clovis Union High School District in a single year. The law at the time allowed any land annexed into the City of Fresno to come under the jurisdiction of Fresno Unified. Existing small school districts, if their enrollment was under 901 students, were dissolved into the larger Fresno district.

On December 22, 1959, district officials recognized the need to protect their territory and proposed a vote to create the Clovis Unified School District. The community members of the various elementary districts voted to form one large district, effective July 1, 1960. Proponents of unification knew that by creating a single, large district with enrollment well over the 901-student threshold, they would be protected should the City of Fresno continue to grow. Even so, some smaller districts voted to stay with Fresno Unified or remain independent.

"It was a major deal," recalled Tom Wright, who was on the staff of the Clovis High newspaper, "Cougar Growl," at the time, which covered the community divide. "Parents got real involved. The community was ready for it."

He said when unification was approved there was "a lot of animosity between Clovis and McLane High students, who were considered traitors or whatever. We were always considered second fiddle to Fresno Unified, but things have changed," he added.

A new high school campus

In 1960, the first year of unification, the Clovis High principal was a crew cut-wearing George Kastner; horn-rimmed glasses and page boy hairdos were all the rage; and school clubs included the Future Homemakers of America and the Future Nurses Club. There were 69 certificated personnel onsite and 1,429 students. The Cavalcade was dedicated that year to band director Harley Freeman, who led the Golden Cougar Band to participation in the All Western Band Revue in Long Beach.

Businesses were squarely behind Clovis High, taking out ads in the Cavalcade, the Cougar's Growl and various school programs, a tradition that continues today. Many put students to work during the summer sweeping the floors or minding the soda fountain. It was common for students to work picking or packing apricots, peaches or other crops.

During the 1960s, Clovis Unified attendance grew an average of nearly 5 percent every year. Over time, the campus spread south, across Fifth Street into buildings that would later become Clark Intermediate School. According to students who attended the school at the height of enrollment, Fifth Street would become a mass of high school students rushing to and from class during passing periods. Any motorist unlucky enough to be headed down Fifth Street when a passing bell rang would typically be stuck until student foot traffic cleared six minutes later before they could continue their journey.

A plan was formed by the late 1960s to establish a new, larger high school campus. The plan to move the high school was also in response to the transportation issues facing the Fifth Street campus.

"They had the buses back behind the math and science building and by the gym," said then-Superintendent Dr. Floyd B. "Doc" Buchanan. "There were twenty-two buses running, and the kids going across the street and stuff. And finally, I walked out, and I was standing on the curb, and this little girl ran out across the street. I think she was a freshman, and the bus came, and she stopped. The driver didn't see her, and when she finished, she had dirt on her rump and her chest. I said to the board, 'We're going to get that school out of here; we're going to move the high school. We can't take a chance we're going to lose a kid.'"

The new high school would be built at Fowler and Barstow avenues to accommodate current and future students.

Former district teacher, administrator and historian Duane Barker recalled the controversy surrounding the selection of the Fowler site for the new school. "Everybody kind of got upset and asked, 'Why are you building that school so far out in the country?' Cause it was. I mean, it was. There was a lot of vacant land between the city limits of Clovis and Clovis High School," he said. "Barstow Avenue didn't even run through. Even after Lamonica Stadium had been built, Barstow still didn't go through. But then, there wasn't much traffic out there. I have a picture that was taken from the press box of the stadium and there is not a house in that picture. You can see all the way past Shaw, and there's not one house over there either."

Barker would pull out the photo years later after homes had been built nearby and neighbors of the stadium complained about the noise from Friday night football games. "I'd say, 'Oh, gee, where's your home in this picture? The stadium was there before your home was. How can you complain?'" Barker said.

Another controversy surrounding the new Barstow and Fowler school involved the fence, or lack thereof, according to Buchanan. "When we built Clovis High School, people got real excited when they came to the school board and they said, 'There's no fence around the school.' There was a fence around the playground, and finally the board president came in and said, 'Maybe you'd like to let people question you how you are going to protect the school?' I said, 'Well, first, I'd have to ask these people who have questions that I need to know whether I'm in the business of education or incarceration? Once I know the answer to that, I'll know what to do with the fence.' Everybody got up and left," Buchanan said.

The new school campus would be 60 acres and include 74 classrooms, a multipurpose building, a swimming pool, kitchen and administrative offices. It would cost $4.1 million, with the state paying $2 million. A library, 2,200-capacity gymnasium and cafeteria were added for $883,000, with the state picking up all but $4,000 of the cost. The school was designed by architects Edwin S. Darden, Allen Y. Lew and James J. Nargis.

The 1968-69 Cavalcade depicted students studying on the lawn of the Fifth Street campus and intoned: "…we take a long last look at the walls which have captivated the anxieties and youth of many generations. We leave behind us memories of yesterday and look anew to tomorrow…"

The former Clovis High building on Fifth Street was used to house continuation and adult school classes, and the second high school campus, located across Fifth Street, became the district's first intermediate school for seventh- and eighth-graders. The school would open in 1969 as Clark Intermediate School with Ralph Lockwood as principal.

The new Clovis High School opened in 1969 with Peter G. Mehas as principal. The 1969-70 Cavalcade includes construction photos of the new school with the message: "Our main goal has been, as we have entered our new school, to make our old family at home in our new house. … This is our Renaissance. May it be a strong foundation on which future generations may build."

The new freshman class was considered "out of sight," girls with long hair abounded and "the diversity of talents and abilities" of individual students was lauded in that year's Cavalcade. "Perhaps the attitude of the student body is best described by Dr. Floyd Buchanan's motto, 'sic 'em!'" said the Cavalcade in 1969-70.

1920 campus saved

Alumni opposition was vociferous in 1973-74 when it appeared that the graceful, historic building erected in 1920 would be demolished by the City of Clovis to build a new civic center. Wrote Malcolm Johnson in the *Clovis News*: "I cannot see destroying one of Clovis' finest and oldest landmarks in the name of progress."

The Fifth Street building was "the hub, the landmark, the thing we all came through and recognized," said Tom Wright, the alumni association president.

By mid-March three alumni groups were discussing the problem. Shortly afterward, the city and the district came to an agreement allowing the old high school to escape the wrecking ball. The city acquired property to the rear of the school for its civic center and leased the school to the district. Today, the school building houses the San Joaquin College of Law.

Teacher Candace Lane began her teaching career at Clovis High in 1974 and still teaches there today. Her career reflects the changing times from the 1970s to the 2000s.

When she was hired to teach home economics the school curriculum was chock-full of electives such as child development, sociology and nutrition. In those days, there were five home economics teachers to instruct the burgeoning student body. Classes like jewelry making, film studies and auto shop were popular. Clovis was the only high school and it was getting crowded.

"The year I was hired [the school] was on a 10-period day," said Lane, whose name then was Candace Russell. "The freshmen came to school at 11 A.M. and stayed until 5 P.M. The last three periods of the day were only freshmen, and there were three lunch periods."

The school boasts many longtime teachers like Lane, who have taught at the school, perhaps leaving for short periods to teach at other schools in the district, only to return.

During the 1970s, the student body was less diverse. Many were of a country-western bent and came from rural homes built on a couple of acres. A band of local boys who were CHS alumni called Double Gauge was popular at school dances. That would change over the years.

As more emphasis was placed on core subjects and academic results, electives went by the wayside. And a new high school, Clovis West, opened in 1976. Football games between the two were intensely competitive, Lane said.

Commemorative plaques

The class of 1926 started a unique tradition that would continue until 1969. The 1926 class, along with the support of Principal Paul Andrews, decided they would like to commemorate their class in stone at Clovis High. Members of the Clovis community who were stone cutters at the Academy Granite Quarry just northeast of Clovis in Academy were eager to help with the project and also provided the granite. Stones were engraved with the names of all graduating students, class officers, faculty and trustees. The first class plaque was located on the sidewalk outside the southwest door of the main school building. Subsequent classes kept the tradition alive, each year creating its own class stone and placing time capsules underneath. The tradition lasted until in 1969 when the new Clovis High campus opened at Fowler and Barstow avenues.

The class of 1936 decided the classes from 1902 to 1925 should also be immortalized. A large rectangular stone containing all of the graduates' names, listed by class year, was dedicated in the spring of 1936. The stone is engraved with two quotes: "There is past which is gone forever, but there is a future which is still our own" and "Alumni reunion in the spring of 1936 and every decade thereafter."

Since then, there has been an organized all-school reunion every year that ends with a "6" for graduates of all classes, in addition to the 10 to 12 individual class reunions every year. The last 10-year reunion was in 2006. Some 15,000 alumni returned to their alma mater coming from nearby towns and from throughout the United States and the world. The celebration included a parade through downtown Clovis, a dinner, a car show, two dances, a golf tournament, a breakfast and a memorial service. The alumni choir sang and they all joined in on the school anthem. An excerpt: "Sing, we now, to Clovis High, sons and daughters true. Raise our colors to the sky, cheer the gold and blue."

At the Clovis High All-School Reunion in the spring of 1996, the 1902 to 1969 class plaques were moved and rededicated at their new Alumni Walk location between the 1920 Clovis High building (now the San Joaquin College of Law) and the Clovis Veterans Memorial Building.

President of the Clovis High School Alumni Association Tom Wright describes a humorous incident involving the plaques when they were dug up in 1996: "Each stone had a time capsule below it; when the stones were being moved and capsules were being dug up, some guys from the class of 1932 were watching the digging process with interest. When they got to their stone, they got excited and ran over there, but what they wanted wasn't in there. Turns out [the men] had dug it up and put a bottle of scotch in there in 1932, but after that time, someone else had dug it up and toasted their classmates."

Then and now

Advances in technology and changes in the general moral climate have caused changes in students' lives.

Back then, students registered by visiting teachers at tables set up at the school instead of by computer. Today, parents are able to view their children's homework assignments and test results online.

Clovis High then and now has always maintained a strict dress code. In the 1960s, boys were not allowed to have long hair and very short skirts were outlawed by the governing board in the 1970s. Now boys are not allowed to wear saggy pants and girls can't have spaghetti-strap tank tops and short skirts are still taboo. The girls in the 1960s had to wear dresses to school except for two days when pants were allowed: Rodeo day and Sadie Hawkins day.

Back then, Lane used to love chaperoning dances and going on student trips to Disneyland. "We used to go to the prom and dance as much as the kids," she said. Now, chaperones have a whole new set of student safety issues to be vigilant about to ensure the safety of students.

For Lane and her teaching career, home economics gave way to child development, which gave way to science, which gave way to teaching Regional Occupational Program classes as student needs evolved.

Clovis High has become more diverse and students come from all social and economic classes. There is an emphasis on encouraging students to get involved in extracurricular activities such as sports and music. The school offers a range of Advanced Placement courses and has many co-curricular activities, including Academic Decathlon, Mock Trial, the Ecology Club and Young Successful Latinas.

A 2009 state Career and Technical Education grant and matching district funds were used to establish a new Careers in Construction Pathway. This hands-on program integrates math, English and science coursework while training students in building trades.

Recognized Excellence

Clovis High has received:

>> National Exemplary School Award (1987)

>> National Blue Ribbon School Award (1993)

>> State Distinguished School Award (1986, 1999, 2003)

>> California Blue Ribbon Nominee (1993)

A majority of the current crop of students understands and appreciates the tradition that is Clovis High. Natalie Nax, who was a member of the school color guard and graduated in 2010, said she swelled with pride when her school was introduced at competitions. "They say 'Clovis High, the original,' and that's a point of pride. People are really into the aspects of multi-generation and tradition," she said.

Alumni consider Cougars, young and old, to be colleagues. "Once a Cougar, always a Cougar," as the saying goes.

The appearance of the 1969 school has changed over time with multiple additions and remodeling projects. Tennis courts, a ceramic studio, an aquatics center, baseball and softball fields, a library media center, choir room, lecture halls and a small theater are just some of the many additions. Biology teacher Bobbie Bass recalled a time in the 1998-99 school year when several academic buildings were being remodeled: "During the 'D' building remodeling, the teachers had to teach in portables in the faculty parking lot. Once their building was remodeled, then the teachers in the 'C' building taught out in the parking lot. The administration gave everyone flashlights because one time, when it got dark, the science department learning director fell into one of the trenches from the construction and had to dig her way out."

Athletics

Athletics at Clovis High was part of Clovis Union High's co-curricular activities from about 1906. Before that time, the school did not have a large enough student body to field teams. Basketball, both boys and girls, and baseball were the first organized sports. Clovis was not a part of any organized leagues until 1908 when girls' basketball was classified into a quasi-league, with Fowler, Selma and Clovis. The first mention of a boys' baseball league was in 1910. Clovis track competitions featured a county championship meet as early as 1909, but no leagues and no mention of league competition until 1923. Track competition was reported very rarely until about 1934 and sparingly until about 1947. Football and tennis were not mentioned until 1923. Swimming was started in the mid-1930s.

In its history, Clovis High athletics has won more than 230 league championships, eight Fresno County titles, more than 90 valley titles and 10 state titles in sports including baseball, basketball, cross-country, football, golf, gymnastics, soccer, softball, swimming, tennis, track, volleyball, water polo and wrestling. The school's pep and cheer squads have won seven major titles.

Athletics have long been a source of pride for Clovis High School, and the school continues to have a large fan base, even when the football team is going through a slump. Clovis High always has one of the largest student sections at games. Football championships have included Northern Fresno County 1923; Shasta League 1941 and 1946; North Sequoia 1956 (co-champions); North Yosemite League 1970, 1974, 1979,1980, 1984, 1987 (co-champions), 1988, 1990 (co-champions) and 1991; North East Yosemite League 1989 and 1994; Tri-River Athletic Conference 1996 and co-champions in 1999, 2001 and 2002; and valley champions in 1970, 1974, 1979, 1984, 1991, 1997, 1999 and 2002.

CHS' alumni who have gone on to play professional athletics include:
- Johnny Estrada, all-star pro baseball
- Zack Follet, football
- Mark Gardner, baseball
- Daryle Lamonica, football
- Chad McCarty, pro soccer player, Olympian
- Lloyd Merriman, baseball
- Keith Poole, football
- Stephen Spach, football

CLOVIS M. COLE ELEMENTARY SCHOOL

By Carole Grosch

Need for a new school

Due to the population growth and expansion of the City of Clovis in the 1950s, a new school was needed. William Hastrup was chosen as its architect and the contractor was the Bob Long Construction Company. Funds derived from Clovis city bond issues financed the project.

The new school, named Clovis M. Cole Elementary, opened to students in the 1958-59 school year. The original school buildings at the time consisted of an office, seven classrooms, a kindergarten and multipurpose room. The red bulldog was chosen as the mascot of the school. Red and blue were selected as the school colors in honor of Fresno State College, the previous owners of the land on which Cole was built; the college also boasts the bulldog mascot and red and blue school colors.

Origins of a name

The past met the present when school trustees decided to name a new school after Clovis Marshall Cole.

Originally from Vevay, Indiana, Clovis Cole came to Fresno as a child with his parents in 1872. The family homesteaded 320 acres located 15 miles northeast of Fresno. His father, Stephen Cole, was elected Fresno's mayor in 1891.

In 1880, Clovis Cole bought 480 acres of land for $4 an acre in what is now the town of Clovis. By 1884, Clovis Cole was farming 40,000 acres from Centerville to Madera County.

In order to harvest the large amount of wheat produced, he and his uncle, Jacob Cole, were the first in Fresno County to purchase a combined header and thresher that cut, threshed and stacked wheat in one operation. The per-acre profit was one dollar, which was unequaled. It was no surprise Clovis Cole became known as the "Wheat King of the Nation."

For $4,000 gold coin, Cole sold 480 acres of land east of Clovis Avenue to Marcus Pollasky for the San Joaquin Valley Railroad branch line. The depot was named Clovis and was incorporated as the City of Clovis in 1912.

Cole was married to Elizabeth Reynolds. They had two children: a son, Glen, who died in his twenties, and a daughter, Ida. Their home ranch was located near Baron Street north of Third Street. The home can be seen today north of Third Street, on the east side of Osmun Street.

As a civic-minded citizen, Cole was one of three men serving on the first board of trustees for the Clovis Elementary School District when it was organized March 5, 1895.

Clovis M. Cole
Photo Courtesy of Clovis-Big Dry Creek Historical Society

Cole quit farming after the drought year of 1897-98 when his crop failed. He opened a machinery repair shop for farmers, which specialized in Holt combine harvester repair. The shop was on the northeast corner of the depot at Clovis Avenue and Fourth Street. It was during this time his wife managed the Clovis Hotel at the northwest corner of Clovis Avenue and Fourth Street.

Clovis Cole died on November 14, 1939, two weeks after his 83rd birthday.

The school named for Cole was dedicated on March 17, 1958. His daughter, Ida Cole Beal, was the honored guest at the dedication ceremony. Cole Elementary joined the Clovis Elementary School District, the same district for which Clovis Cole had served as a trustee.

A quick change

In 1960, just two short years after the opening of Cole Elementary, seven school districts combined to form Clovis Unified School District. The Clovis Elementary District, of which Cole Elementary was a part, was one of these seven original districts. But reportedly because Cole was so new, it was not much affected by the tumultuousness caused by the unification.

Progress and pain

Cole Elementary was destined to undergo many changes throughout its history reflecting the changing community it serves. The student body was originally comprised of kindergarten through eighth grade students until the end of the 1969 school year, when Clark Intermediate School opened, educating all of Clovis Unified's seventh-and eighth-graders. After that time, Cole became a kindergarten through sixth grade school. Due to overcrowding at other schools, students were bused to Cole from nearby schools. Tarpey Elementary bused third-graders to Cole from 1965 to 1969, and Sierra Vista bused some of its seventh- and eighth-graders during the last school year Cole accommodated those grade levels.

In 1992, the district changed the operating schedule from a traditional calendar year to a year-round schedule at selected elementary schools: Cole, Gettysburg, Miramonte, Tarpey and Weldon. It was a difficult and trying time for parents, students and school personnel. The decision to try this change was due to growth; overcrowding; obtaining construction funds from the state that required 30 percent of a district's kindergarten through sixth grade students to be enrolled in year-round education; and a need for a bond measure to pass in order to build a new school.

> **ESTABLISHED:** 1958
> **GRADES:** K-6
> **MASCOT:** Bulldogs
> **COLORS:** Red and blue
> **MOTTO:** "Positive Attitudes Work"
> **LOCATION:** 615 W. Stuart, Clovis
> **ACREAGE:** 15 acres

The year-round experiment lasted two years. Under pressure from dissatisfied parents and the community, the school board voted to return to the traditional schedule. At that time, a school comprised solely of portables opened on the southeast grounds of Clovis High as a site that would temporarily accommodate overcrowding.

Throughout the years, changes were made to the 15-acre campus. Classrooms were updated, enlarged and remodeled. Portable buildings were added. A north wing was built in the early 1990s that created some logistical issues such as keeping children safely out of the construction area. In the case of the kindergarten rooms' construction, which was taking place at the same time as the year-round schedule was implemented, students and teachers were moving in and out of the portables on the far side of the campus, which was lacking a play yard. In the long run, the inconveniences were well worth the improvements.

In 1997-98 school year, the school was wired for Internet access as well as a modernization of the 23 permanent classrooms. Cole was a forerunner in giving sixth-graders laptop computers. The library media center was equipped with wireless technology to make it the academic center of the school.

Unique to Cole

In 1966, Cole was the only Clovis school to offer French as a foreign language. Terry Allen, Ed.D., who was later to serve as Cole's principal from 1986 to 1994, taught the language to fifth- through eighth-graders. The reason French was taught was that Allen had just returned from French-speaking Senegal, West Africa, as a Peace Corps volunteer. At the time, he was the only staff member fluent in a foreign language.

In 1996, the district started an Early Literacy Intervention (ELI) program at Title I schools, of which Cole was a member. The program provided teachers with methods to assist at-risk first-graders with their reading skills. Then-Superintendent Walt Buster and administrator Linda Hauser spearheaded the program at Cole over a period of six years, during the principalships of Debra Parra and Edwin Javis. According to teacher Kim Judd, who was actively involved in the program, "There were three literary specialists who trained the first grade teachers in teaching techniques to improve students' reading skills. We had 'behind the glass room' sessions with modeled lessons showing teachers' classroom practices."

Clovis M. Cole Elementary is home to P.A.W. Pride — Positive Attitudes Work. It is the belief that through hard work and having a positive attitude, students will be academically successful.

Close community

"Cole is an unusual school in its diversity, its family support and involvement, and its feeling as 'the right place to be.' It sits in a quiet neighborhood of singular residences and apartments that cushion it from the wild world of Bullard Avenue," said Allen.

Another former Cole principal, Ruth DiSanto, characterized Cole as "a close-knit community that is important to the neighborhood. People watch out for you."

Second and third generation students at Cole are not unusual. Mary Enos, who has taught at Cole for 20 years, knows something about this. She had two pupils just last year who were children of former students.

Though families at Cole come from varied socioeconomic backgrounds, they have a commitment to the school as well as a strong sense of community. They come together to help those in need within their own community, the Fresno area and the nation, as the need arises.

Current Cole Principal Annette Bitter said, "One of the characteristics of which we are most proud is the student, staff and parent commitment to community service opportunities. The Cole community frequently chooses non-profit groups for which they raise funds. For instance, Cole students have given their snack bar money to fire victims, canned food drives, Coats for Kids, etc. The generosity of the students and parents is pretty amazing."

> **Recognized Excellence**
> Cole Elementary has received:
> >> State Distinguished School Award (1998, 2002, 2006)
> >> CSU Fresno's Bonner Center Character for Education's Virtues and Character Education Award (1996, 1998, 2004)

The community came together to celebrate the choir having been chosen in the early 1990s to perform at New York's famous Carnegie Hall. "It was a wonderful accomplishment and honor for the students," said Allen.

"It's Nifty to Be Fifty!"

In 2008, the school celebrated its fiftieth year with an "It's Nifty to Be Fifty!" celebration to honor the students, staff and community of Cole Elementary. To take part in the celebration, a group of former students and staff members flew in from the Midwest; the group had created a Cole Facebook site to help spread the word about the event. It was estimated that about 250 alumni and past staff attended. Former principals were introduced and picture boards were displayed depicting past years at Cole. Students, past and present, enjoyed snack booths, game areas and a bounce house — a mixture of carnival and nostalgia. Parents and their children shared a common bond.

CLOVIS NORTH EDUCATIONAL CENTER

By Robyn Young Stafford

The turn of the new century occurred in the midst of a housing boom in northeast Fresno and Clovis. And, new houses meant new students for Clovis Unified, with enrollment reaching an all-time high. Enrollment projections continued to climb. The district purchased 80 acres of agricultural land bordered by International, Willow, Maple and Copper avenues from farmer Pat V. Ricchiuti, Jr., with 20 more acres purchased from the adjoining lot.

With the land secured, and financing in place through 2001 and 2004 bond measures, plans were set into motion for a new secondary campus that would contain not only one, but two schools.

Darden Architects was hired to design the new school, which would include a single, expansive academic building housing both intermediate and high school classrooms, a large pool complex, and the district's first performing arts center, which included a small black box theater and a concert hall.

At that time, the district already had two educational centers in place — Buchanan Educational Center and Reagan Educational Center. Both BEC and REC house students in grades kindergarten through 12 but within three separate schools — one at the elementary level, one at the intermediate level and one at the high school level, all in close proximity through sharing a large plot of land. The new Center would feature a single complex to house grades from seven to 12, but still exist as an intermediate and high school.

Before ground was broken on the district's northernmost secondary campus, ideas for naming the new high and middle school were requested from the community. Names such as Clovis

International and Granite were suggested, along with Clovis North. Governing board members ultimately selected Clovis North Educational Center with the schools comprising the Center to be named Clovis North High School and Granite Ridge Intermediate. With Clovis Unified's reputation across the state for having outstanding academic and co-curricular programs, the decision to keep "Clovis" in the name motivated the board's decision to select Clovis North as its newest educational center.

ESTABLISHED: 2007	
GRADES: 7-12	
MASCOT: Broncos	
COLORS: Columbia blue, black and silver	
MOTTO: "Unity, Courage, and Commitment"	
LOCATION: 2770 E. International Avenue, Fresno	
ACREAGE: 101.9	

Ground breaking

In 2005, construction crews managed by Harris Construction broke ground at 2770 East International Avenue in Fresno. The school's main academic facility houses classrooms, a library media center, a nurse's office and administrative offices, and, at 275,000-square feet, is one of the largest single academic buildings in the western United States. The campus also includes an individual music building, three air conditioned gymnasiums, two technology labs, a tennis arena, two 50-meter swimming pools, soccer fields, baseball and softball stadiums, track field, football fields, and a state-of-the-art performing arts center.

Opening day

Driven by large enrollment jumps, for the first time in CUSD history three new schools opened on one day. The August 20, 2007, milestone saw the opening of Granite Ridge and Clovis North as well as Bud Rank Elementary School, located six miles east of CNEC in Clovis. Like the secondary schools, Bud Rank was built to accommodate growth in the northeast part of the Fresno/Clovis area. Students from Bud Rank feed into Granite Ridge and Clovis North.

Granite Ridge Intermediate School.

At CNEC, the first of group of students that opened the school was comprised of seventh-through ninth-graders, and from there, one grade level per year was added until a full complement of seventh- through twelfth-graders attended the school in 2010-2011.

Unique opportunities for students

The main academic building accommodates 147 classrooms. As of the 2009-10 school year, the enrollment had reached 2,240 students.

CNEC is governed by one principal, a role Norm Anderson has held since the school's inception. Curriculum and staff are blended seventh through twelfth grade with only a social separation of the students. The Center accommodates the intermediate students' social hub on the east side, while the high school students congregate on the west side of the campus, each with age and grade appropriate social activities. Positive and appropriate interaction among the intermediate and high school students includes academic and co-curricular environments, as well as peer tutoring opportunities

A unique educational opportunity for Clovis North High students to experience college is easily acquired through the neighboring State Center Community College District's (SCCCD) Willow International campus, located across the street from the Clovis North Educational Center. Due to proximity and cooperation between CNEC and SCCCD, eleventh and twelfth grade students are provided the opportunity to enroll in junior college classes, for which they can receive college credit.

A 2009 state Career and Technical Education grant and matching district funds were used to establish a Therapeutic Services Pathway program at CNEC. This hands-on program integrates math, English and science coursework while training students in health science and medical technology.

Go Broncos!

Both Clovis North and Granite Ridge share the campus in every way. Sports are no exception, including three section championships and a league championship, all without a senior class yet to attend the school.

The Bronco mascot represents all grades, the colors of Columbia blue (called Bronco blue by the CNEC community), black and silver wave proudly for both schools. Individually, however, they compete for championships within their own intermediate and high school leagues.

The Performing Arts Center

An exquisite addition to CNEC was the state-of-the-art Clovis Unified Performing Arts Center (PAC), the last major building to be completed on the new campus. Long desired by the community, the PAC was first included in plans for the Buchanan Educational Center, but had to be put on hold until additional funding could be found. The $20 million facility was constructed to fulfill the community's vision of providing exceptional facilities for music, drama, dance and musical theater for all performance groups within CUSD, with funding specifically designated in the 2004 facility bond measure approved by voters.

The PAC is comprised of two performing arts venues. Just inside the front doors is the Dan Pessano Black Box Theater. With flex seating to hold 150 to 250 spectators depending on the design of the set and seating configuration, the stage sits at ground level, surrounded on three sides with upward stair-step rows of cushioned seats. This setup allows the acoustics to rise to the audience, and gives the performance a "theater in the round" effect in which the perspective of the audience is enjoyed from three sides.

Through an adjoining lobby, which houses a rotating display of student artwork, the Paul Shaghoian Concert Hall was carefully crafted to showcase choral and instrumental performances. To enhance acoustics, there are no flat surfaces in the hall, which is lined with convex parquet walls, as well as an ethereal ceiling soaring six stories high.

The 750-seat concert hall incorporates a reverberation chamber that wraps around the upper half of the performance area. Drapery hangs at the sides of the hall and at the back of the stage. Not only does it lend a dramatic appearance to the concert hall — it is also functional; depending on whether the drapes are open or closed, the room's reverberation can be increased or decreased by up to two seconds. The hall's adjustable acoustic tiles positioned above the stage can be raised, lowered or tilted to enhance the sound quality of different types of ensembles. Exactingly crafted wall coverings and panels have curved surfaces to reflect rather than absorb sound. With the ability to control the reverberation and acoustics with such precision, the sound can be fine tuned to suit each performance.

In conjunction with Harris Construction, Darden Architects and consultations with the firms of Dohn & Associates for the acoustics, Rosen, Goldberg, Der and Lewitz for the audiovisual, and Landry & Bogan for the layout and design, "The Paul Shaghoian Concert Hall has received excellent reviews and stated as the 'best in the western U.S.,'" said Anderson.

The PAC received a 2008 "Impact on Learning Award" from *School Planning & Management* magazine. The award is given to new construction and/or renovation school projects throughout the United States. The Performing Arts Center was recognized for "solving realworld problems through innovative design, engineering and technology solutions." Since its opening in April 2008, the concert hall has hosted performances by every CUSD choir and band, as well as internationally known amateur and professional groups.

Clovis North Educational Center provides a unique learning environment that offers students stepping stones to enable them to reach for the highest capacity in their secondary educational career, inspiring them to maximize their lives in mind, body and spirit.

CLOVIS WEST HIGH SCHOOL

By Susan Sawyer Wise

When Clovis West High School opened in 1976, it sent waves rippling through the Clovis Unified community. Clovis High School had been the only school that had served ninth through twelfth grade students since it first opened in 1899. But, after 77 years, and a significant population growth within the CUSD boundaries, a second high school was needed.

"Many of the parents and students who would be attending Clovis West were excited, but, on the other hand, there were those who wanted to be part of Clovis High's already established programs and teams," said Roger Oraze, who served as a learning director when the school opened and as principal from 1979 to 1984. "In the beginning, the ninth-graders who first started at Clovis West were basically seniors all four years, there wasn't a 'varsity' anything and the band was just being formed. In that sense, some students thrived on getting things started while others were a little disappointed that they didn't have access to the opportunities available at Clovis High."

Many of the teaching staff was hired from Clovis High and Clark Intermediate. The transition was made even easier for those coming from Clark who had already worked with Clovis West's first principal, Bill Noli (1976-79), when he was principal at Clark and had liked his leadership, Oraze said.

"The staff was really excited," said Oraze. "From their point of view, being part of Clovis West was a unique opportunity. We could start new programs; the new school was full of possibilities."

On January 22, 1975, ground was broken at Millbrook and Teague avenues, the future site of Clovis West High School. The 60 acres that would be used to create the new campus were once farmland previously owned by the Mesple and Hotchkiss families. Clovis West was designed by Darden Architects and built by Robert G. Fisher Co. for $7 million, and included 65 classrooms to house the approximately 1,400 students who attended the school in its inaugural year.

In its first year, 1976-77, Clovis West opened its doors to seventh-, eighth- and ninth-graders who would have otherwise attended Clark Intermediate then Clovis High. The campus served all students residing north of Herndon Avenue plus students coming from Cole and Tarpey elementary schools. The following year, Clovis West taught seventh though tenth grade students, and the 1978-79 school year was comprised of seventh- through eleventh-graders. By 1979-80, the school taught a full complement of ninth through twelfth grade students, while that same year, Kastner Intermediate opened in portable buildings on the Clovis West campus to serve the seventh- and eighth-graders who feed into Clovis West. Meanwhile, Kastner's permanent home was being built one mile away and would open in spring 1980.

Clovis West's first graduates were the Class of 1980.

Principals following Noli and Oraze have included Dan Kaiser (1984-1986), Jerry MacDonald (1986-1994), Gary Giannoni (1994-2001), Carlo Prandini (2001-2005), Jeanne Hatfield (2005-2008) and Ben Drati (2008-present).

Facilities

Only 65 classrooms and an administration building were completed in time for students to attend their first year at Clovis West in September 1976. Over the next several years, additions were made including a science building and other additional classrooms, a multipurpose room, gym, tennis courts, and an Olympic-sized pool and diving complex.

"[Then-Superintendent Dr. Floyd B.] 'Doc' Buchanan and the governing board wanted to create facilities and programs unique to Clovis West, just as Clovis High was known for its football stadium and an ag program," said Oraze. "Since Clovis High had a small pool, Doc and the board wanted to build a facility on the Clovis West campus that would attract quality swim and diving meets beyond the district. The complex has gone on to host national swim meets including many that were broadcast on national television."

The school's academic buildings were built with moveable partitions instead of fixed walls. At the time, this style was in line with the educational philosophy at the state-level of creating open space. However, teachers and students soon found that the open classrooms were loud and a disturbance to learning. To try to solve the noise problem, Plexiglas and acoustic panels were installed. However, it would take a complete redesign (which did not occur until 1997) to solve the problem and enclose classrooms. While the remodel was taking place, a new technology infrastructure was also installed.

In the 1990s, a wing for science labs and math classrooms was added, as was a second gymnasium and new band facilities.

ESTABLISHED: 1976
GRADES: 9-12
MASCOT: Golden Eagle
COLORS: Cardinal and gold
LOCATION: 1070 E. Teague, Fresno
ACREAGE: 60

Organizations

In addition to classrooms, each Clovis West academic building originally contained office space for a learning director, counselor and secretary in order to create "clusters" within each building. Each cluster served as a school-within-a-school with students assigned to one of four clusters. "Using the cluster concept, students were far less likely to slip through the cracks," said Hatfield.

The four cluster names, correlating with Clovis West having been founded as the "School of Olympic Spirit," were Athens, Delphi, Olympus and Sparta. Those are still the names of the academic buildings on campus even as the "cluster" concept has given way to centralizing services in a more efficient reorganization plan.

Clovis West was reorganized in 2002 under Principal Carlo Prandini. Efficiency and effectiveness in streamlining services drove the reorganization. Three service centers were created in the reorganization: a counseling center, a student services office and a Freshman Academy office. Academic learning directors, no longer responsible for discipline, could focus on teaching and learning. This organizational structure is still in place at Clovis West today. "Streamlining services and consistency in delivery have improved with this model," said Hatfield.

Dedication

On December 10, 1976, Clovis West's dedication and cornerstone laying ceremony was held. In an act of goodwill, the Clovis High School student body gave a check for $2,500 to Clovis West's student body who had not yet built up funds for activities in its short three-month history. Clovis High's gift was followed that day by an additional check for $1,238 given on behalf of the students from Clark Intermediate School. The generous donations exemplified the mutual camaraderie and support behind the rivalries that existed between the schools from day one.

Immediately following the school's official dedication, the cornerstone ceremony was conducted by the California Free and Accepted Masons grand master with the help of grand lodge officers and members of Clovis' Masonic lodge. Inside the time capsule placed in the cornerstone the students included a school newspaper, coins and a two dollar bill, and a "Jimmy Carter for President" pin, among other items.

Early notable events

One of the first challenges at the new school was creating its own identity under the long shadow of the well-established Clovis High School.

"Clovis West, being the second high school in Clovis Unified, had to fight to earn a place in the community," said Hatfield. "It took time for the Clovis West community to emerge and for our students to find an identity."

Several key events helped put Clovis West on the map.

In the fall of 1977, Clovis West won the title of "Most Popular High School" in a Central Valley contest sponsored by a local radio station. Despite having students only up to tenth grade that year, CWHS earned the most signatures on its petition. The students worked hard to win the contest and make a statement. For their win, the students received a free dance.

Another moment of school pride also took place in the fall of 1977 when Clovis West's boys' cross country team won the school's first-ever Central Sequoia League championship, before CWHS even had seniors. Three years later, Clovis West was able to win its first Central

Section championship in the spring of 1980 in girls' track and field. Following these championships, Clovis West prided itself on having a balanced athletic program excelling in all the sports offered at the school.

The students also identified themselves through the pride of their school colors and mascot. The Golden Eagle mascot was recommended to the board for being majestic, yet predatory and smart, while the colors were recommended to counteract Clovis High's colors of blue and gold. "It was a parallel to the rivalry between UCLA and its blue and gold colors and USC's cardinal and gold colors. It seemed like a natural choice," said Oraze. The CUSD Governing Board approved both the Golden Eagle mascot, and cardinal and gold colors.

The Clovis West spirit demonstrated at the first Clovis West vs. Clovis High football game in November 1979 was also significant, according to Hatfield. Prior to the game, a Clovis West banner was hung prominently across Clovis Avenue, right in the middle of Clovis High country. At the game, the school pulled out all the stops bringing in a hot air balloon, while a sea of cardinal and gold fans who never sat down filled the stands and the song "We Are Family" blared on loud speakers. A fired-up group of athletes knew it was their night to prove themselves.

"The Clovis West community came together for the first time that night," Hatfield said. "Even though the team went on to lose, it was a huge victory for the school in many ways."

Early in Clovis West's development was the inclusion of and emphasis on Advanced Placement (AP) courses. Teachers and administration recognized the challenges and opportunities the courses could provide students. "AP classes can stretch learning and create a bridge between high school and college," said Oraze.

"This was the beginning of the juggernaut that would take off with CW's commitment to the AP program, one that would later earn the school national recognition in prominent magazines and school rating publications as a top AP school in America," added Hatfield.

Eagles of Honor Pledge

Today, Clovis West has more than 50 clubs and organizations from which students may choose to get involved. Involvement is a key component to the principles of "Olympic spirit" on which the school was founded. In the 2007-08 school year, Clovis West kicked off its Eagles of Honor Pledge campaign, the first of its kind in the district. The pledge drive was initiated by the school's leadership students to encourage Clovis West students to make good choices, and to let them know that they are not alone when they do the right thing.

Students who sign the pledge agree to the following: "I do solemnly pledge that as long as I am a student at Clovis West High School, I will faithfully uphold its principles, guard its traditions, respect its values and abide by the Code of Ethics. I make this pledge to my fellow students, teammates, faculty and parents, which signifies our mutual trust and resolve to keep our honor forever sacred."

Environmental Club Pond

In 1998, Clovis West High School Environmental Club and science department members envisioned a unique addition to their campus: an aquatic field studies pond that would be operated through a solar-driven pump.

Through a variety of grants, public donations and various fundraisers, the dream became a reality when, on May 19, 2007, the CWHS Environmental Club Pond and Outdoor School was officially unveiled. Nestled among a grouping of redwood trees, an 80-foot-long stream leads into a 25-foot-diameter solar pond surrounded entirely by river rock. Not only does the pond provide serenity, it offers renewable energy resource education and ecosystem studies to nearly 700 students per year in biology, general sciences and Advanced Placement environmental science classes, as well as environmental lessons for students who visit from nearby Fort Washington and Valley Oak elementary schools.

Automotive Technology program

Unique to Clovis West is its well-established automotive program which provides students with theory, hands-on mechanical experience and an opportunity to train in a soon-to-be National Automotive Technicians Education Foundation (NATEF)-certified facility. This training will allow those who have successfully completed the program to enter the workforce as entry-level technicians, or to pursue additional training in automotive technology at a post-secondary school.

The auto program received a big boost through a recent career technical grant from the state. Clovis West's automotive department received $530,808, plus the same amount from CUSD's bond measure, to expand and update its facilities and equipment. The program will soon have the facilities and equipment needed to meet standards required for certification by both the NATEF and Automotive Youth Education Systems. With these certifications, seniors in the program will be able to intern at local dealerships and independent service facilities. In addition, expansion of the program allowed freshman students to enroll in the automotive technology academy. By the time ninth-graders in the academy graduate, they will know the math, science and English standards required for successful completion of the NATEF program.

Athletics

Clovis West has won 23 of the last 26 Athletic Supremacy awards given to the top high school in each CIF league. The ability to succeed in a wide range of sports has also benefited Clovis West at the state level. Three times — in 1993-94, 1998-99 and 2004-05 — Clovis West has been named the California Athletic High School of the Year by Cal-Hi Sports. During the 2009-10 school year, Cal-Hi named Clovis West girls' athletic program the top in the state.

Since 1976, Clovis West High School has won 298 league, 166 central section, two southern section, seven state and 14 national championships.

The school's wrestling teams have been state champions three times — in 1983-84, 1984-85 and 1989-90.

On the national level, boys' soccer has won a national title, and between the pep and cheer teams, 13 national titles have been earned.

Along with great team success, Clovis West has also produced many outstanding student athletes that went on to successful professional careers.

In basketball: Adrian Williams was the 21st overall pick by the Phoenix Mercury in the 2000 WNBA and played with the Sacramento Monarchs until the franchise closed in 2009.

In football: 1994 graduate Damien Richardson was drafted 1998 by the Carolina Panthers and completed seven successful NFL seasons with the Panthers. Paul Green played for the Denver Broncos. George Petersen played for the Kansas City Chiefs. Bill Volek played for the Tennessee Titans from 2000 to 2006 and has played for the San Diego Chargers since 2006.

In baseball: 1994 graduate McKay Christensen was the sixth overall pick in the 1994 Major League Baseball draft by the Anaheim Angels. He completed four years in the major leagues with a career batting average of .250.

The school has also produced two Olympians. Dan Klatt was a 1996 graduate who was selected to play on the 2004 Olympic Water Polo Team in Athens, Greece. Alumnae Ruth Lawanson was a member of the 1992 bronze-medal winning U.S. Olympic volleyball team in Barcelona, Spain. Lawanson also played Major League Volleyball (1987-89) with the Dallas Belles and Minnesota Monarchs and was the 1988 league MVP.

Recognized Excellence

>> National Blue Ribbon School Award (1989, 2000)
>> State Distinguished School Award (1988, 1994, 2003)
>> California Business for Education Excellence Foundation's Scholar Schools Award (2009)
>> *Newsweek* magazine's Top 100 Schools in the Nation (2005)

COPPER HILLS ELEMENTARY SCHOOL

By Monica Stevens

With a name like Copper Hills Elementary School, the mascot "Miners" is especially appropriate. And living up to the wealth suggested in the name, Copper Hills Elementary School has high expectations for its students. "It's the key to students becoming the best they can be in mind, body and spirit," said Christine Archer, who has served the school as its principal since 2005.

Copper Hills Elementary School was named for the first copper mine in the area, located near Armstrong and Copper avenues just 6.4 miles from the school, and the nearby beautiful rolling hills. The school was built for $9 million in 1996 by contractor David A. Bush Inc., and designed by Temple Andersen Moore Architects.

Twin ground breaking ceremonies

The rapid growth of Clovis in the mid-1990s led to twin ground breaking ceremonies on October 6, 1995 — one at 9 A.M. and the other at 10:30 A.M. — for two new Clovis Unified elementary schools: Cedarwood, built to accommodate the students east of central Clovis, and Copper Hills, built to house students to the northeast of Clovis. There were several similarities between the two campuses. Both school sites covered about 15 acres, and had the same square footage and number of classrooms. Both were scheduled to begin serving their student populations in September 1996.

Once built, Copper Hills Elementary had 20 classrooms, two kindergarten rooms, three special education rooms, a library, a multipurpose room and offices in 47,195-square feet. Located in north Fresno, Copper Hills' students feed into the Clovis North Educational Center schools, Granite Ridge Intermediate and Clovis North High.

Ginger Thomas was the first principal when the school opened on September 3, 1996. Devin Blizzard served as the school's second principal from 2002 to 2005, followed by Archer who remains at the helm today.

When the school first opened to students for the 1996-97 school year, attendance areas had been redrawn and students who would have attended Garfield, Liberty and Maple Creek elementary schools now comprised the Copper Hills student body of approximately 300 students.

"When Copper Hills opened, it was at a time of soft real estate, with a lot of projected housing developments that didn't end up happening so our enrollment was lower than expected," said Thomas. "We had a beautiful new school and we thought we were going to have extra empty classrooms to use. However, things changed when we learned that we would be receiving students from Cole's second grade and Garfield's third grade in our first year. A twenty-to-one student/teacher ratio had just been instated and schools needed space. Copper Hills had space so it made sense to house these students on our campus."

When the 1996-97 school year started, Copper Hill's inaugural year, 573 students filled the campus, nearly 270 from outside Copper Hills' boundaries.

Soon, the economy was changing, enrollment was rapidly growing and Copper Hills was running out of space to house its own students, let alone other schools' students. At one point, Copper Hills had to send its first-graders to nearby Liberty Elementary for lack of room. After just a couple of years, Cole's second grade and Garfield's third grade students were returned to their home schools, but it wasn't until 2002 when Riverview opened just over a half mile away that relief came to Copper Hills when some of its students were rerouted to the new school.

ESTABLISHED: 1996
GRADES: K-6
MASCOT: Miners
COLORS: Navy blue, maroon, grey and white
MOTTO: "Try Hard, Do Your Best and Never Give Up!"
LOCATION: 1881 E. Plymouth Avenue, Fresno
ACREAGE: 15

Positive attitudes foster outstanding success

Copper Hills follows the belief that the best way to achieve academic excellence, promote mutual respect and enforce a consistent behavior plan is to teach students to communicate their own expectations and goals. The school motto, "Try hard, do your best, and never give up!" is a daily message heard by all students and staff.

Copper Hills' stakeholders are encouraged to attend meetings to share information and address concerns. "Together," Archer said, "we actively share a common vision and responsibility as we prepare students to meet the challenges of the future as competent, committed members of a global community."

The positive attitude toward a culture of high academic standards, exceptional behavioral expectations and co-curricular involvement is contagious on the Miners campus, and is reflected by the partnership between the school and the community through multi-generational family involvement and generous business support.

High academic standards

Copper Hills has implemented a strategic academic plan that includes a well-defined standards-based curricular program and ongoing assessment. The result is a high promotion rate and overall academic success.

Co-curricular activities are also part of the equation at Copper Hills.

The annual Dessert Theater Production, hosted by students in the Drama Club and Student Council, is the highlight of the year for many students and parents. On the three straight "sold out" evenings each year, drama students put on a Broadway-worthy production while Student Council students serve dessert and beverages to the full house.

Copper Hills' athletic program is continually at the apex in athletics in the area. The school's faculty and staff are dedicated to maintaining a high-quality athletic program with caring, nurturing coaches who understand that "mind, body and spirit" are not just words, but a way of life at Copper Hills. "We always win with character and lose with dignity," Archer said.

Students benefit from a state-of-the-art library media center and computer lab, and all play areas have been built to accommodate school athletic activities as well as community organized athletic leagues.

The Copper Hills community

The students, parents, staff and community surrounding Copper Hills share a common vision and responsibility to prepare students to meet the challenges of the future. The skilled, caring staff and enthusiastic, dedicated students, parents and community of CH have established and continue to maintain an environment and culture that fosters the outstanding success of the school.

In 2006, Copper Hills Elementary celebrated its 10th anniversary with the dedication of a bronze sculpture by renowned local artist Clement Renzi called "Children Learning." Current and former students, parents and employees of the school were on hand to witness the dedication of the sculpture. It has become a daily reminder of the importance of education by students, staff and families.

The Miners' philosophy is reflected in the success the students have achieved. "CH believes that the best way to achieve academic excellence, promote mutual respect and enforce a consistent behavior plan is to teach students to communicate their own expectations and goals," said Archer.

Central Valley Robotics

In 2002, Principal Devin Blizzard brought Robotics to Copper Hills, and in a short time, its popularity spread throughout the Central Valley. In its first year in Clovis, six teams from Copper Hills participated in the FIRST (For Inspiration and Recognition of Science and Technology) LEGO League, a multinational non-profit organization started in New Hampshire in 1989 that aims to inspire children around the world to work together, use their creativity, and engage in real world problems and opportunities.

Early in Robotics, Blizzard unified local Robotics participants by starting the Central Valley Robotics, or CVRobotics, organization in which valley communities, businesses, schools, educators, students, parents and volunteers come together to advance student opportunities in the fields of science and technology.

The second year of Robotics in Clovis, participation significantly increased with 30 teams in Clovis Unified and 50 in the Central Valley participating. Today, more than 90 valley teams participate.

In Robotics, student teams build operational robots from a common kit of parts provided by FIRST. The robots then compete against each other in tournaments in a series of challenges. High school students participate in FIRST Robotics Competition (FRC) teams, while fourth-through eighth-graders participate in FIRST LEGO League (FLL) teams.

Valley tournaments are held annually in December at Alta Sierra Intermediate; from there, top winners advance to the state tournament. Those who place first in the state advance to Global Finals, in which teams from all over the world converge to compete for international titles.

Recognized Excellence

Copper Hills Elementary has received:
>> State Distinguished School Award (2000)
>> California Business for Education Excellence Foundation's Scholar Schools Award (2009)

DRY CREEK ELEMENTARY SCHOOL

By Linda Hayward

Dry Creek District – One of the first

On June 12, 1866, the Dry Creek District was established, making it one of the first eight school districts in Fresno County. Initially, it was formed to accommodate the children of the Dry Creek settlement, nine miles northeast of present-day Dry Creek Elementary's location at Nees and Armstrong avenues in Clovis. The school was petitioned by 10 Dry Creek settlement families to educate their combined 12 children.

In the beginning, the school was held in a private home and was named Dry Creek, after the area where the majority of voting residents lived. As noted in the board of supervisors' minutes, the Dry Creek District was "bounded and defined as follows: Commencing at the crossing of Fancher's creek on the Visalia and Millerton Road, and running up said creek to its head, thence, a southeast course to the mouth of Sycamore Gulch; then on a northwest line to the head of little Dry Creek, then down said creek to the crossing of Visalia and Millerton Road, thence following said road south to the point of the beginning."

Miss Elizabeth Ellis was the settlement's first teacher, and as a teacher, she benefitted from receiving room, board and a monthly compensation of $30. Approximately 40 students were enrolled at the time. Early records were kept by teachers using dipped quill pens and delicate penmanship to record their daily attendance and student progress. The first school year lasted only three months due to the harvest season.

During the years from 1870 to 1890, available funds did not cover school operating expenses; therefore, families of the area donated land, built schoolhouses, and even hired, paid, and housed their teachers.

Dry Creek Academy Corporation

The Dry Creek Academy Corporation was formed in 1872 to provide for the building and to maintain a private educational system for the Dry Creek settlement. The Academy was incorporated for a capital stock of $50,000 for 50 years at a cost of $50 dollars per share. Andrew D. Firebaugh purchased the first 30 shares according to his great-great-granddaughter, Brenda Burnett Preston.

The Dry Creek Academy, or "The Academy," schoolhouse was rated one of the best in the county and was built in 1872 near the banks of Dog Creek, which in current terms, places it north of Tollhouse Road between Madsen and Mendocino avenues.

The schoolhouse had four rooms: a study room and library, which housed an outstanding selection of books, a recitation room, and two anterooms where coats and lunchboxes might be found. Separate entrances into the schoolhouse were provided, one for boys and one for girls, as were outhouses, or "Doolies."

James Darwin "J. D." Collins was the Academy's first teacher, and would remain at the school until 1876 when he was elected to the state legislature. He was later elected sheriff and served from 1898-1906. Subsequent teachers were W. A. Sanders and Frank W. Blackman.

Dry Creek School, built in 1920 in Academy, California.

By 1877, enrollment at the school had grown to 50 students.

On August 4, 1914, the Dry Creek District annexed part of the Fancher District and continued to expand in 1916 when the nearby Letcher District was annexed as of August 8 of that year. The Academy building, still in use as Dry Creek School, remained open until it was demolished in 1920. A new Dry Creek School, complete with a front porch and bell tower, was opened that same year and was located north of Tollhouse Road near Academy post office.

On December 13, 1929, Dry Creek District united with the Clovis Union High School District until 1945 when Dry Creek District was suspended.

Dry Creek Union District

The Dry Creek District was suspended on July 1, 1945, due to declining enrollment. Two years later, on May 16, 1947, the Dry Creek District and Nees Colony would join to form Dry Creek Union District, giving the school district a new life. Two months later on July 1, 1947, Dry Creek Union District was reinstated and used Nees Colony's school at Nees and Armstrong avenues to educate its students. May Mathews was principal of the school with an average attendance of 122 students.

On September 10, 1952, voters approved by a vote of 53 to six to annex the Garfield School District into Dry Creek Union District. It soon became apparent that a new and larger schoolhouse was needed because of the addition of the extra districts, increased enrollment and the deterioration of the old Nees Colony School.

The new school, located at the same Nees and Armstrong avenues site, was comprised of two classroom wings and a facing of bricks salvaged from the old Nees Colony building. It opened to students in September 1954, costing the voters an approved bond issue of $116,000 for the first phase of the new school. In 1956, a multipurpose building and kindergarten were added.

On December 22, 1959, changes were once again occurring as Dry Creek Union District joined the six other school districts aligned with Clovis Union High School District to form Clovis Unified School District.

ORIGINALLY ESTABLISHED: 1866
RE-ESTABLISHED: 1947
GRADES: K-6
MASCOT: Panthers
COLORS: Royal blue and white
LOCATION: 1273 N. Armstrong, Clovis
ACRES: 17

The changing face of Dry Creek

The modern Dry Creek campus is a far cry from its humble beginnings nestled in a grove of oak trees on a dry knoll in Academy.

The 1920 Dry Creek schoolhouse remained on the new Dry Creek Elementary campus until 1970, when it was purchased for one dollar by Emil J. Prudek, a long-time Clovis barber, and moved back to Academy. Reports stated that Prudek died before seeing his dream of relocating the schoolhouse come true. It was hoped the old school house would one day be renewed to its former state and be given a new life where it would serve as a reminder of Dry Creek's meager beginnings. Instead, it has stood deteriorating in the midst of rubble at its original site on Madsen Avenue where it still stands today.

All that remains of the past on the current school campus are some of the brick facing and the original school bell from the Nees Colony campus displayed in front of the Dry Creek administrative office where it stands as a reminder of the school's beginnings. Another reminder of the past, an old cedar tree from the original Nees Colony, stood on school grounds until 2006.

Dry Creek underwent significant additions in the early 1970s with 10 classrooms, a library and an office added in 1972-73. Alberta Brown was the school's principal at the time of these additions.

The school's library media center was modernized in 1999 and dedicated to James "Mr. C" Countois, a 16-year volunteer at the school. Mr. C volunteered 20 hours a week, even after celebrating his 90th birthday, to help and encourage the children he loved so much. The library media center now houses a substantial book collection and new computer lab consisting of 34 Thin Client work stations, which are solid state (no moving parts like hard drives and fans), inexpensive and energy-efficient computers that run all of their applications off a server.

Recognized Excellence

Dry Creek Elementary has received:
>> National Blue Ribbon School Award (1994)
>> State Distinguished School Award (1993, 2008)
>> California Blue Ribbon Nominee (1994)
>> California Business for Education Excellence Foundation's Scholar Schools Award (2007, 2008, 2009)

Today, the school supports 21 classrooms and 22 portables, and at times has housed up to 1,040 students. A new multipurpose room was completed in the summer of 2007 to replace the one built in 1956.

The "Panther Express," named after the school's mascot, is a weekly publication sent home on Fridays to communicate the weekly calendar and to list any events that might be of interest to parents and students during the next week. The school's mascot was not always the Panther. In the 1980s, the school's mascot was changed from the Blue Devils to the Panthers in response to some parent concern over having their children referred to as "Devils."

Dry Creek, the first of all current CUSD schools to be established in name, has come along way from serving 12 students in a private home in 1866 to the 2010-11 school year when the school served nearly 800 students on its 17-acre expansive campus. While there are many more students in attendance today than there were 145 years ago, the personal touch is not lost as each teacher and staff member makes it his or her priority to look after the needs of each individual student and to teach the students to be their best in mind, body and spirit.

EVERETT "BUD" RANK ELEMENTARY SCHOOL

By Charlotte Hutchison

By 2006, necessity dictated that Clovis Unified build another elementary school to accommodate the new growth in the district, and to ease the overcrowded conditions in the Dry Creek Elementary area.

On May 10, 2006, the CUSD Governing Board voted unanimously to name the district's thirty-second elementary school for Clovis native and favorite son, Everett G. "Bud" Rank, Jr.

From an orange grove

Everett "Bud" Rank Elementary School was built in a former orange grove on a portion of a farming area known as Harlan Ranch, owned by Greg Harlan, and was centered in the new Harlan Ranch master-planned community housing development.

Principal Sylvia Borges was brought onboard early during the planning stages of the school. Her 30 years of experience in the district as a teacher, learning director, vice-principal and principal proved to be invaluable.

The new school was designed by S. I. M. Architects and built by Harris Construction.

The developers worked with the district to incorporate features in the school that reflected the style of the homes, and financed these special features, including a fence with stone pillars, tile roof, painting scheme and additional skylights inside the building's hallways.

The school's Parent Teacher Club sold Founder's Bricks to families who were part of the new school. The bricks were installed near the flagpole on campus, with the funds used to purchase a marquee system to announce school events.

The attendance area for the school reaches from east of Academy Avenue, west to Locan Avenue, to Clovis Unified's northernmost borders and south to Herndon Avenue. This includes more than the children living in the Harlan Ranch development. Two-thirds of the 350 students attending Bud Rank Elementary the first year had previously attended Dry Creek Elementary or other district schools and one-third came from outside of the district.

Students from the new elementary school feed into Granite Ridge Intermediate School and Clovis North High School.

Official ceremonies

Bud Rank was the guest of honor at the October 24, 2006, official ground breaking ceremony for the new school, and again on August 16, 2007, during the official grand opening. At this event, the school's new students enjoyed a scavenger hunt which was designed to introduce them to their new campus. One of the stops on their search was meeting Rank.

On August 20, 2007, the first day of the 2007-08 school year, Rank attended the opening day rally on the new campus. Afterward, he visited every classroom and talked with each child. All students were given the opportunity to meet the man whose perseverance and community service helped to define a town, two school districts and a nation.

The Clovis country boy

When the doors to Everett "Bud" Rank Elementary School first opened to students on August 20, 2007, its namesake, Everett "Bud" Rank, Jr., was still living with his wife, Evelyn, in the ranch house on Old Friant Road where he was born in 1921. He attended Fort Washington Elementary School and graduated from Clovis High School in 1940.

As a student at Clovis High School, he helped organize the Clovis chapter of the Future Farmers of America and served as its president during his senior year.

After graduation, Rank worked for the Bureau of Engineers at Millerton Lake until he heard Pearl Harbor had been bombed. On December 8, 1941, he enlisted in the Navy. During World War II, he served aboard the *USS Monongahela,* and was involved in numerous naval engagements in the South Pacific, including the Allied invasions at Guadalcanal, Okinawa, Iwo Jima and the Leyte campaign. After the war, young Rank returned to the family ranch near Clovis.

In 1952, Rank was elected as a trustee on the Fort Washington Elementary District School Board. He served in that capacity until the seven small Clovis school districts united in 1960 to form Clovis Unified School District. When the new district became an operational entity on July 1, 1960, Rank was elected as the trustee from the Fort Washington District. As a member of the new Clovis Unified School Board, he was instrumental in selecting Dr. Floyd B. "Doc" Buchanan as the first superintendent of the new district. During his 13 years on the board, Rank served three terms as president. Her resigned from the board in 1973 to accept a Presidential appointment to the U.S. Department of Agriculture. In 1982,

Everett G. "Bud" Rank, Jr.

he accepted the position of chairman of the World Cotton Commission, a post he held for five years.

When he returned home from Washington, D.C., Rank continued his many community service endeavors, including mentoring troubled inner-city boys. In recognition of his copious contributions to the community and the nation, the Clovis-Big Dry Creek Historical Society selected him as the 2004 Clovis Living Legend. Three years later, on June 15, 2007, he was honored again when he was presented the Friend of Youth Award by the Clovis Chamber of Commerce.

ESTABLISHED: 2007
GRADES: K-6
MASCOT: Ravens
COLORS: Navy blue and Columbia blue
MOTTO: "Ravens Rise above the Rest"
LOCATION: 3650 Powers, Clovis
ACREAGE: 15

A family affair

Rank's father, Everett G. Rank, Sr., served on Fort Washington's Board of Trustees from 1925-1953. He encouraged his son to follow in his footsteps. "My dad said to me, 'Son, it's time for you to take over,'" Rank said. "I ran for his position, and got elected to the Clovis Fort Washington school board. That's how I started."

Continuing the Rank family tradition of serving on the Board of Trustees, Rank's daughter, Ginny L. Hovsepian, has served on Clovis Unified's Governing Board since November 1991.

"Bud Rank came to watch us play!"

Judy Rank is one of the original third grade teachers on the staff of the school named for her father. In a 2009 interview, she told the following story about the school's first football game that demonstrates the admiration and high regard the students had for their school's namesake:

> [At] our first football game, Dad came out to watch the kids play football. Our Bud Rank Ravens have the ball. The kids are running. Suddenly they stop. I mean they are not too far from the goal and they stop. They said, "Look Bud Rank came to watch us play! He came to watch us play football!"
>
> The coaches are on the sidelines, and they are yelling. "RUN! RUN!"
>
> "But wait, Bud Rank came to watch us play!"
>
> "Run! Run! You've got the ball, run!"
>
> "Bud Rank came to watch us! There's Bud Rank!"
>
> Finally, the coaches convinced the kids to run for the goal and they made the touchdown. After the game, all of the students ran over to visit with "Mr. Bud Rank."

Rank continues to be a visible part of everyday life at Bud Rank Elementary, said Borges: "He attends sports events on campus and even travels with the team. His wife Evelyn is often with him. He is a popular figure on the BR campus."

Ravens rise above the rest

After the end of the school's first term, the California Department of Education released the Academic Performance Index (API) scores in 2009. Bud Rank Elementary exceeded the state's goal of 800. With an API growth score of 913 and a base score of 891, it appeared the Bud Rank Ravens were indeed rising above the rest.

FANCHER CREEK ELEMENTARY SCHOOL

By Naoma Hayes

On May 4, 1869, the Fancher District was organized in the foothills northeast of Fresno whose local residents primarily raised cattle and hogs, and whose children needed a place of education.

Origins of a name

Fancher Creek, which runs on the southeast side of Fresno, was named for cattleman John Fancher whose ranch, located at that time in Tulare County, was later broken up into several different counties, one of which was Fresno. The former John Fancher ranch is now, in modern terms, near the intersections of McKinley and Del Rey avenues, in southeast Fresno. The creek named after Fancher runs through the ranch property.

Fancher Creek, once also known as Fancy Creek on Round Mountain, was the inspiration for the naming of the original Fancher District and Fancher School, as well as the new Fancher Creek Elementary School, opened in 1989.

The Fancher name is prominent in local and national history because of a tragic incident involving John Fancher's brother, Alexander Fancher, who served as the captain of an emigrant wagon train headed from Arkansas to California. Alexander was reportedly bound for John's ranch where he was to join his brother in the cattle business. However, Alexander would never make it to Tulare County. On September 11, 1857, as he led the 140 members of the wagon train through southern Utah, they were attacked by a local Mormon militia group, with the help of local Paiute Indians; historians agree the emigrants, innocent victims of high tension from years of Mormon persecution, did not provoke the attack. More than 120 emigrants were killed with only 17 young children surviving what was to be known as the Mountain Meadows Massacre.

The first Fancher

A schoolhouse, once located at Watts Valley and Pittman Hill roads, is assumed to be the original Fancher School, but it is uncertain when the school was first constructed.

Several publications, including the *Fresno Weekly Expositor*, describe the original Fancher School as being a comfortable building that was well-stocked with desks for up to 40 students, a terrestrial globe, a Webster's Unabridged Dictionary, a complete set of Cornell's Outline Maps mounted to the walls and McGuffey's Reading Charts.

The school's unique blackboard was made from a sapwood pine cut nearly four-feet wide and three-feet long. Timber cuts, at a minimum of three-feet wide, were also used to make countertops and tabletops.

In 1877, the *Expositor* reported that "the school in the charge of Mr. A. H. Day is in excellent condition." Day served as the school's first teacher.

County records cite local rancher John G. Crump as the first clerk of the Fancher board of trustees.

Early teachers spanning from 1900 to 1905 included Mattie Kelsey (1900-01), Ruth Killiam (1901-02), Georgie Johnson (1902-03), Mrs. Mary Haedin (1903-04) and Mrs. Helen Kirch (1904-05).

ORIGINALLY
ESTABLISHED: 1869
RE-ESTABLISHED: 1989 in portables, 1990 in its permanent facility
GRADES: K-6
MASCOT: Falcons
COLORS: Red, white and blue
LOCATION: 5948 E. Tulare Avenue, Fresno
ACREAGE: 15

In 1904, Fancher School's attendance averaged nine students, and by August 4, 1914, attendance had fallen so low that the district lapsed and was annexed in part to the Round Mountain School District in the Sanger area and to the Dry Creek District in an area northeast of Clovis. Documentation of the fate of the original Fancher School building has been lost over time. Following the dissolution of the original Fancher District, memories of the rural farming community faded.

Fancher resurrected

It wasn't until the late 1980s that the Fancher Creek name was resurrected. A new Clovis Unified campus opened in 1990 at 5948 Tulare Avenue in Fresno, on the southwest corner of Tulare and Fowler avenues, to accommodate the growth in Fresno's southeast neighborhoods. The enrollment at nearby Temperance-Kutner Elementary School had grown by leaps and bounds and a new school was needed to relieve crowded conditions. The new student body at Fancher Creek came primarily from T-K, along with a handful of students from Miramonte Elementary.

Snaking just six miles from the new school is Fancher Creek. As an homage to the original Fancher School, located 21 miles northeast of the new campus and to the nearby waterway itself, it was decided that Clovis Unified's new school would be named Fancher Creek Elementary School.

Sue Van Doren, Ed.D., the first principal of the new Fancher Creek Elementary School, recalled that a committee of parents and staff recommended to the governing board the colors of red, white and blue as no other school in the district boasted these same school colors at the time. The committee also suggested that the school's mascot be the falcon, a meaningful symbol to the community for multiple reasons. The falcon represented the wildlife in the rural part of Fresno where Fancher Creek was located; the "Fancher Creek Falcons" alliteration was appealing; and it was part of a vision that teachers Gayle Peck and Charley Ford had for creating a refuge and rehabilitation sanctuary for injured birds of prey, a vision that was ultimately realized at Red Bank Elementary School.

Fancher Creek, built on land previously used as a plum orchard owned by John Garabedian, was designed by Darden Architects and built by Palmo Construction Company for $9 million. The 41,683-square foot facility included 24 classrooms, an administration office, a library media center and a multipurpose room.

One year prior to the 1990-91 school year opening of the new school, Fancher Creek's 650 students were housed at a temporary school of portable classrooms located on the east side of the Clovis High campus that served as home while their new school was being built.

Van Doren served as Fancher Creek Elementary School's first principal followed by Pete Reyes, Rosie Rivera-Borjas and the current principal, Kevin Kerney.

Promoting good health

California Governor Arnold Schwarzenegger visited Fancher Creek Elementary on December 20, 2007. The stop was part of a statewide tour to encourage healthy living and to promote a healthcare reform plan approved by the state assembly. Supporters of the plan, including Fresno Mayor Alan Autry, California assembly members, and healthcare, labor and education officials, participated in the Fancher Creek rally where the governor received an enthusiastic welcome from about 100 students gathered in the school's multipurpose room. Schwarzenegger said he wanted to stress the importance of health care for children and asked the students to promise to exercise every day.

Unique to Fancher Creek is that it is home to one of only three CUSD Children's Health Centers, which is located on the school's grounds and serves the local community. Services offered include immunizations, tuberculosis skin tests, sports screenings, preschool and first grade physicals, and is a safety net for underinsured and uninsured children. In addition, there is no charge to Medi-Cal patients for sick visits, complete physical examinations and immunizations.

CUSD's three busy health centers on the campuses of Fancher Creek, Pinedale and Tarpey elementary schools are considered models throughout the state. District officials estimate the district would have an average of more than 2,000 more student sick days per year without treatment provided by the centers.

Recognized Excellence

Fancher Creek Elementary has received:

>> State Distinguished School Award (1997, 2006)

>> Title I Academic Achievement Award (2007, 2010)

>> CSU Fresno's Bonner Center Character for Education's Virtues and Character Education Award (1998, 2006)

FLOYD B. BUCHANAN HIGH SCHOOL

By Linda Robertson

One hundred sixty acres of land, situated between Nees and Teague avenues, is the site where dreams came true. Dr. Floyd B. "Doc" Buchanan, Clovis Unified's superintendent from 1960 to 1991, had envisioned three schools serving grades kindergarten through 12 on a single site. The complex would function as one with students, teachers, administrators, parents and community members working together, creating new opportunities, overcoming barriers, mentoring one another and sharing resources to achieve the common goal of all students fulfilling their personal potential.

When completed, the educational complex housed three schools, Buchanan High, Alta Sierra Intermediate and Garfield Elementary; extensive athletic facilities, including nine shared full-sized soccer/football fields, a softball complex and a football stadium; and a unique Medical Therapy Unit on Garfield's campus, all located on one plot of land making it the first of its kind in the state.

The land where the schools was to be built was purchased by Clovis Unified from farmer Pat V. Ricchiuti, Jr., and plans were soon developed to build the first school of the complex, Alta Sierra Intermediate (ASI), which opened to eighth- and ninth-graders in 1991. In the 1992-93 school year, ASI housed eighth, ninth and tenth grades. When Buchanan High School, which was designed by Darden Architects and constructed by Lewis C. Nelson and Sons, opened in 1993, these three classes, comprised of 1,600 students, moved into the new school as freshman, sophomores and juniors. That same year, the intermediate school began serving seventh and eighth grades.

With the opening of Garfield Elementary in 1994, the district's first educational center was complete. And, by 1995, Buchanan was celebrating its first graduating class of 469 students.

The school's principals include Randy Rowe (1993-2001), who opened the school, Cheryl McKinney (2001-2005), Don Ulrich (2005-2008) and Ricci Ulrich (no relation to Don), who has held the position since 2008.

A sense of identity

Originally, consideration was given to naming all three schools Buchanan, but a governing board majority voted that each school deserved its own name, designating "Buchanan" as the official name of the high school, as well as the identifier of the entire complex, which would be called the Buchanan Educational Center.

Buchanan High's school colors are Air Force blue, red and white, chosen through a vote by all incoming eighth and ninth grade students for the colors at both Buchanan and Alta Sierra. The governing board approved this choice of school colors.

Dr. Floyd B. "Doc" Buchanan,
CUSD Superintendent 1960-1991
Clovis Unified School District Archives

Dr. Buchanan chose the style of BHS' first band uniforms after watching a marching band celebrating the bicentennial year; he was moved not only by their performance, but also their extremely tailored and colorful uniforms.

Buchanan High School's mascot is a Bear, another tribute to Doc Buchanan, whose alma mater is UC Berkeley, home of the Golden Bears. Again, each of the three schools on the campus has similar, but unique, mascots. The elementary school was given the name Garfield Cubs, and the intermediate school chose Alta Sierra Bruins. "We were thinking this way, but on the back of one of the votes for school colors was written 'Bears, Bruins and Cubs.' It fit Doc and Cal so we used them," said Rowe.

In celebration of Buchanan High's mascot, two special Bear mascots were introduced in 2005 named "Doc" and "Molly," in honor of Buchanan's wife.

Cutting edge

Since its opening, Buchanan High and the educational center have been on the cutting edge of technology.

Alta Sierra and Buchanan were the first CUSD schools to have all staff members on e-mail. Additionally, Buchanan was the first to give all its teachers their own computers in their classrooms and the first to go completely wireless. While these technological firsts sometimes meant that the schools were the first to experience the challenges that come with maintaining a technology infrastructure, they were also the first to reap the benefits that came from rapid communication and on-the-go computing.

The school's library media center was the first school on the West Coast to have networked CD-ROMs. Stations in the library were designed to facilitate technology, another district first.

Excellence for all

The school's vision — the expectation for excellence in everything it does — was established by the original staff and remains in place at BHS today. "It is evident that the original staff's vision was to do well in everything a comprehensive high school has to offer with all activities getting the same level of support from the math team to academic achievement to the varsity football team," said former Principal Don Ulrich.

Providing leadership

The leadership classes at Buchanan are very guidance-oriented, supported by a community service-based program.

Buchanan's annual blood drive was first started in 1995 by then-Activities Director Matt Mueller who, as a past blood recipient, knew the importance of blood donation. The annual student-organized blood drive was renamed the Matt Mueller Memorial Blood Drive in 2001 following Mueller's untimely death. Shortly after leaving the school to serve as a principal in a nearby school district, Mueller died suddenly in the midst of a school day.

ESTABLISHED: 1993
GRADES: 9-12
MASCOT: Bears
MOTTO: "Building Unity, Committed to Success"
COLORS: Red, white and Air Force blue
LOCATION: 1560 N. Minnewawa, Clovis
ACREAGE: Part of the 160-acre Buchanan Educational Center

Through the efforts of leadership students at Buchanan, the yearly blood drive, which continues today, has grown to be one of the largest in the Central Valley. In 2003, Buchanan received a National High School Community Service Award from America's Blood Centers given to the school's leadership students for chairing such a large blood drive and for sharing the importance of blood donation by peer-to-peer instruction, the first program in the valley to do this type of teaching. The 2010 drive achieved a school and Central Valley high school drive record of 1,040 pints of blood collected.

The leadership classes work with their teachers and mentors to raise money for a variety of charities, including holding powderpuff football games to raise funds for the Multiple Sclerosis Society and the annual Ambiance Fashion Show organized by leadership students benefitting Children's Hospital of Central California. Over its 12 year run, the show has brought in more than $115,000 through donations, ticket sales and a special VIP night silent auction. The students not only earn money to provide for the hospital, they also spend time with the children who are patients in the hospital, and provide mentorship to the sick children.

For their efforts on the Ambiance Fashion Show, Buchanan's leadership students received a 2009 Outstanding Youth in Philanthropy Award from the Association of Fundraising Professionals of the San Joaquin Valley.

Fallen heroes

Over a period of three years, Buchanan lost six alumni turned soldiers who were killed serving in Iraq and Afghanistan between 2004 and 2007. The school and entire community were devastated; in response, six senior Buchanan leadership students decided to develop a lasting tribute to their memory that would be located at the high school flag pole. The memorial garden was dedicated June 4, 2007. Just over three years later, the Buchanan community was once again jarred by the death of 2001 graduate Army Sgt. Brian Piercy, killed while serving in Afghanistan, followed less than six months later by former BHS student Marine Sgt. Matthew Abbate, 26, who also died in Afghanistan.

Buchanan's fallen heroes are Jeremiah Baro, December 1, 1982-November 4, 2004; Jared Hubbard, October 29, 1982-November 4, 2004; Anthony "Tony" Butterfield, May 4, 1987-July 29, 2006; Rowan Walter, July 12, 1981-February 23, 2007; Nathan Hubbard (brother to Jared), December 16, 1985-August 22, 2007; Nicholas Eischen, July 6, 1983-December 24, 2007 (who died while serving on active duty); Brian Piercy, March 11, 1983-July 19, 2010; and Matthew Abbate, September 10, 1984-December 2, 2010.

The memories of these brave men live on in the Fallen Soldier Memorial Garden, which surrounds the campus' flagpole. The garden honors the military losses with plaques located below the flag. Each plaque includes the name, birth date, date of death and graduation year of Buchanan's fallen soldier alumni who gave their lives for their country. The garden also honors those in the Armed Forces who continue to defend freedom.

Closure

The 2000-01 school year was tumultuous for the young Buchanan community. In September, shortly after the school year started, potentially hazardous mold was discovered contained within the walls of several offices on the campus. This was the result of construction defects that allowed water to penetrate the buildings during rainstorms. Immediately upon receiving word of the presence of this health hazard, it was decided to close the school until a complete environmental study could be conducted, and the safety of the campus ensured.

Within one afternoon, the school community was notified of the temporary closure, and additional testing was begun. After extensive study by toxicologists and mold experts, it was determined that only several offices in the main administration building were affected by the mold, there was no health risk to students and staff, and that classes could be resumed, though repairs to the offices were needed.

Seven days after the abrupt closure of the school, classes were back in session. The temporary closure was the only one of its kind in the district's 50-year history. To make up for instructional time lost during the seven-day closure, the school's break and lunchtime minutes were adjusted to allow for 14 additional instructional minutes during the school day.

Repairs to the campus to stop any leaks and remove any and all damaged building materials contained within walls were completed in 2003. With careful planning, and close communication with the community, the school remained opening during the months of reconstruction. Contractors with specific expertise in eliminating possibly hazardous materials were hired, and buildings and rooms were closed as needed during the repairs.

Following the incident, the district was praised for its swift response and decisions that were entirely based on protecting the health and safety of students and employees. The Buchanan community became even more closely knit by the shared experience.

The academies

Buchanan is home to two unique academies, the Energy Academy and the Fine Arts Academy. The academies are Career and Technical Education (CTE) programs in which students are able to finish high school with qualifications for an entry level job and the technical skills to continue in the field of their study.

The unique Energy Academy serves students in all four grades, and is made possible by state grants and local bond funds for developing CTE programs. The primary purpose of the academy is to learn science with an energy emphasis. Ninth-graders study earth science, incorporating English 9 and algebra 1, and examine major energy sources throughout the year. Tenth-graders study biology, with links to English 10 and geometry. Eleventh-graders take the course, "Energy Technology with Industry Applications." Students receive hands-on experience with electrical concepts and delve into local energy resources. Seniors in the program take appropriate coursework depending on their areas of interest: physics for the engineering track, AP Environmental Science for the environmental track, and specialized courses for those who want to go to technical school or straight to a job in the business world.

Recognized Excellence

Buchanan High School has received:

>> National Blue Ribbon School Award (1998)

>> State Distinguished School Award (1996, 2005, 2009)

>> California Exemplary School Award in Physical Education and Health Education (1998)

The Energy Academy is housed in a state-of-the-art renewable energy building that also serves as a tool to teach students about environmental careers. The building itself is a showcase of renewable energy and green building standards, and includes radiant heat flooring, a rooftop garden and innovative recycled building products.

Buchanan's Fine Arts Academy includes instruction for all four years of high school and enables students to focus their elective studies in the fine arts and visual and performing arts, and prepares them for college, conservatories or careers in the fine arts. Students in the academy have additional exposure to arts professionals who are regular guest speakers in their "Life in the Arts" course. Advanced courses in the arts are being developed for Buchanan, including additional music theory and history classes, technical theater arts, design for theater, projects in production for drama, Advanced Placement (AP) art history, and AP studio art.

Athletics

Buchanan athletics has also received numerous titles and awards since the school's inception to date, including 136 conference championship titles; 66 valley championships; state titles in girls' cross country (1994-95) and wrestling (2005-06); and a No. 1 state ranking for softball in 1997-98. Buchanan has developed dominant girls' volleyball and soccer teams that have been nationally ranked. The school has earned five Supremacy Awards: two in the East Sequoia League in 1992-93 and 1993-94; one in the North East Yosemite League in 1994-95; and two in the Tri-River Athletic Conference in 2000-01 and 2005-06. One of the most significant moments in BHS' athletics was being named the State School of the Year in 2006 by Cal-Hi Sports.

FORT WASHINGTON ELEMENTARY SCHOOL

By Naoma Hayes and Susan Sawyer Wise

The Fort Washington District, located northeast of Fresno, is the only district in what would later become Clovis Unified to have not just one but two initial organization dates.

The first organization was June 6, 1874; the second was July 20, 1875. According to County Superintendent Dr. Thomas O. Ellis, Jr., the second organization was necessary because Fort Washington District did not operate a school within four months from the time the board of supervisors formed it into a district and as a result, state and county funds were withheld. The district was revived by an order from the Supervisors' Court, reorganized and promptly started a school.

The first trustees were Van Buren Cobb, J. M. Carrick, and B. S. Birkhead.

The first Fort Washington School was built in 1875 on the Van Buren Cobb homestead, called Old Fort Washington Ranch, located on Old Friant Road below the river bluffs. Cobb's 1875 tax records show a donation of $500 which may have been used to build the school.

Miss Ellen Wren was the teacher at the new 24-foot-long and 15-foot-wide school that featured six-inch-wide siding and tall windows with 12 panes. Black and valley oaks surrounded the building. Wren's salary was reported to be $65 per month.

Records do not indicate all teachers but those on record include Annie J. Hopkins who served as Fort Washington's teacher from 1884 to 1886; Isabell Gray, 1900-01; William Clark, 1901-02; Beatrice Jamison, 1902-03; W. W. Poole, 1903-05; and Emma Bercaw, 1905-06.

In 1903-04, enrollment was 25 students.

A new school

In 1906, a site at present-day Copper Avenue and Friant Road above the river bluffs was donated by J. W. Sherwood for a new Fort Washington School to replace the 1875 school, one mile southeast of the original site.

The single-room building featured a large belfry bordered at each corner by three pillars and a flagpole on top. A windmill, stable and tank house were also on the grounds.

Former Fort Washington District Board and CUSD Governing Board trustee Everett G. "Bud" Rank, Jr. attended Fort Washington from 1927 to 1936, and served on the Fort Washington-Lincoln Union Board from 1953 to 1960. His mother, Evelyn Dawson, also attended the school. His father, Everett G. Rank, Sr., later served as a trustee on the Fort Washington District Board from 1925 to 1953.

Bud Rank, Jr. fondly recalled his years attending Fort Washington: "I attended Fort Washington School when it was a one room school with one teacher. Between eight to 11 children made up the eight grades. My dad was a trustee, and every year they thought seriously about closing the school because there were not enough kids. Then another family would move in and solve the problem. Some kids rode a horse or donkey to school, and some had to walk. I lived about a mile from the school, and rode my donkey named Si. I took the saddle and bridle off and turned him loose in the schoolyard."

Si had plenty of company, with most students riding a donkey or horse to school.

Rank also recalled that starting in fifth grade he served as the school's janitor along with his older sister. "My sister and I made seven dollars a month to share," he said. "We had the only set of keys for the school. We would stay after school and bring in coal, clear the blackboards and clean. Then it was just me serving as janitor and I got the seven dollars for myself. That was good money."

ORIGINALLY
ESTABLISHED: 1874
GRADES: K-6
MASCOT: Patriots
COLORS: Navy blue and gold
MOTTO: "Whatever the Challenge, Whatever the Test, Whatever You're Striving for, Give It Your Best"
LOCATION: 960 E. Teague, Fresno
ACREAGE: 15

The school facility was the social hub of the community, playing host to card games, picnics and parties for families living in the rural area surrounding the schoolhouse.

Fort Washington united with the Clovis Union High School District on April 5, 1926. In doing so, all students who completed eighth grade were eligible to attend Clovis Union High School for grades nine through 12. This arrangement was advantageous to the Fort Washington community for multiple reasons. Clovis was closer to Fort Washington than the Fresno high schools open at that time, Fresno High and Edison High. This was a significant factor considering students had to provide their own transportation to and from school. Even though Clovis

Union High was closer, it was still a trek, according to Rank, who often had to find his way home on foot when he stayed after school and no bus transportation was available.

"We didn't have buses for the sports program, so when I played baseball for Clovis High after school I'd have to walk home at night," he said. "It was about nine miles. Other boys were walking with us and we would get rides once in a while. You had to be really dedicated to play any sports or be in any after-school programs in those days."

In addition, the children of the farming community of Fort Washington related more comfortably to the rural Clovis Union High School than the urban Fresno schools. At Clovis, students could also benefit from the school's offerings of agriculture-related programs.

Lincoln fire

Mrs. Alta Polson taught an average of 11 students in 1944, Fort Washington District's last year of operation as its own district. An electrical fire on October 29, 1944, at Lincoln Elementary School, located a little more than four miles southeast of Fort Washington School, changed the course of the two schools' histories.

Following the destruction of Lincoln, children of the Lincoln District were transported to the Fort Washington School where the new students were enthusiastically welcomed. The two districts merged, becoming the Fort Washington-Lincoln Union School District, on March 23, 1945.

All 45 students in the new district attended school at the 1906 Fort Washington School facility. Additional space was needed so the old Pollasky District schoolhouse in Friant, which had closed in 1944, and barracks from a World War II Pinedale army camp were moved to the site of the Fort Washington School to accommodate the new students.

The Fort Washington-Lincoln School facility did not meet the approval of everyone. It was deemed primitive by some community members who urged the purchasing of land on which to build a new school. A minor divide was created between the district's older and newer residents by the issue.

The debate continued until 1956 when district voters approved a bond measure for the development of a new school at Teague and Millbrook avenues, four miles from the Copper Avenue and Friant Road facility.

School on Teague Avenue

For a cost of $193,000, William Hastrup designed, and Walker and Walker built the new Fort Washington-Lincoln School at 960 East Teague Avenue. Daniel Langpaap was the principal of the school.

Students started at the new Fort Washington-Lincoln School in the 1958-59 school year. Sometime during the weekend of January 9-11, 1959, the bell that was transferred from the old Fort Washington-Lincoln School was stolen from its place in the new bell tower. The bell was of sentimental value to the people of the district, who had planned to mount it on the new school. In addition, the bell that had once rung at the original Lincoln School had been stored away since the school fire in 1944 and forgotten, leaving the new Fort Washington-Lincoln campus without a bell.

Unification

On December 22, 1959, Fort Washington-Lincoln was one of seven districts to unify to become the Clovis Unified School District. At that time Fort Washington-Lincoln had about 100 students enrolled in grades one through eight.

The decision to unify was not a popular one with voters of the Fort Washington-Lincoln District with 23 voters in the district voting for unification, and 85 against. However, with unification approved by the majority of voters in the other voting areas, Fort Washington-Lincoln became part of the new Clovis Unified School District. Those opposed to unification were concerned that they would incur costs with their area's children going to a big school district. Their concerns proved unnecessary as the community did not have to pay any additional expenses associated with being part of Clovis Unified School District, said Everett G. "Bud" Rank, who served as trustee of the newly unified district.

With the opening of Clark Intermediate in 1969, Fort Washington-Lincoln's seventh- and eighth-graders attended the new school, leaving the elementary school to serve grades kindergarten through sixth, as it still does today.

Expansion

During the 1976-77 school year, additions were made to the school, following the addition of five acres to the site, bringing the grounds to a total of 15 acres. Thirteen new classrooms and a new kindergarten room were added as well as a multipurpose room, library media center, teachers' lunchroom, administrative offices, an outdoor amphitheater and tennis court. While construction was taking place at Fort Washington, the two pods of classrooms that housed the students were surrounded with a fence for the children's safety, which meant that the only place for students to play or eat their lunches was in the small space between the two pods.

Meanwhile, construction was underway across the street at Clovis West High School, which opened to seventh- through ninth-graders in the 1976-77 school year but still required significant additions. The student parking lot, however, was already complete, but with no student yet of driving age the lot sat unused.

The Fort Washington students were invited to use the parking lot as their playground. Every recess found the students walking on planks to get to the Clovis West parking lot where they would play and eat. Volleyball courts were created with chalk and basketball hoops were attached to light posts. Aides monitoring the students would use walkie-talkies to report back to the staff on site at Fort Washington.

With the disruptive sounds of construction and jackhammers pounding outside the classrooms, the teachers and students still managed to be the first school in CUSD to attain 90 percent of students school-wide on grade level. The achievement was a monumental one on the campus, according to then-Principal Dick Sparks who credited the entire community with the success. "We were truly blessed with marvelous people; incredible people doing incredible things for the right reasons," he said.

On September 17, 1977, to celebrate the end of construction and the beginning of the newly renovated school, a rededication and cornerstone laying ceremony was held.

In June 1978, the school's library was dedicated to former Trustee Everett G. Rank, Sr. for his service on the Fort Washington District board and later, his year-long service as president of the Fort Washington-Lincoln District board in 1944-45. Though Mr. Rank had passed in

1969, his family was in attendance to accept the honor. In April 2003, Rank's entire family was honored at Fort Washington's library media center for their longtime support of the school. Matriarch Evelyn (Dawson) Rank attended the school as did her four children. One of her sons, Everett G. "Bud" Rank, Jr., later served as a trustee for the school just as his father had. In addition, Bud Rank's three daughters and two grandchildren attended Fort Washington. Upholding the family's tradition of service to local schools, Bud Rank's daughter, Ginny L. Hovsepian, won a seat on the Clovis Unified Governing Board in 1991. A third generation trustee, she still serves on the board today.

A singular identity

By the late 1970s, Fort Washington-Lincoln was overcrowded, creating the need for an additional school. Plans were underway as of 1977 to build a new Lincoln Elementary School 1.3 miles south of Fort Washington Elementary as it was singularly known at that time.

The new school's student body was drawn from Fort Washington-Lincoln and was organized in 1979 with Dr. Tom Lutton serving as principal. The more than 400 Lincoln students were temporarily housed at Pinedale School, 1.5 miles away, from September 1979 until June 1983.

Lincoln Elementary School officially opened in 1983 at its permanent site at 774 East Alluvial Avenue in Fresno.

Sparks was Fort Washington's principal at that time followed by Janet Young, Joe Farkas, Jeff Eben, Debbie Parra, Marcy Guthrie and the current principal, Ann Kalashian.

Transition

When, after serving as principal for 16 years, Dick Sparks left to open Valley Oak Elementary in 1989, the Fort Washington community was in turmoil. Boundaries were redrawn and those Fort students living north of Shepherd Avenue were slated to attend Valley Oak when it opened for the 1989-90 school year. Janet Young was hired to serve as Fort Washington's new principal.

"It was an emotional time for the community," Young said. "Dick was the patriarch of the community, highly respected. He had such a wealth of experience and his leaving was hard, plus nine or ten teachers went with him to open Valley Oak. During this period of unrest, we had to build the school again. Beginning teachers were hired to serve alongside the veteran teachers who stayed. In the summer leading up to the 1989-90 school year, the community was uneasy about the new teachers, the new principal and the new staff they didn't know."

From the beginning, Young and her staff focused on student achievement, team building, and nurturing parent and community involvement through an active Parent Teacher Club and School Assessment Review Team. "Parents, staff, the community, everyone came together to do what needed to be done to maintain Fort Washington's excellence, to ensure the students' and school's success," Young said.

Through the support of the parent club and its fundraisers, Fort Washington became the first elementary school in the district to develop a computer lab. Guidance Instructional Specialist Rick Gold spearheaded the computer movement, while Brenda Smith, the first library media teacher in the district, incorporated technology-based lessons and research studies into the curriculum.

The lab, which consisted of Macintosh computers, was given a boost when the school won a contest sponsored by supermarket chain Vons called "Apples for Students," in which the school received additional Apple Macintosh computers.

"The CEO of Vons came to Fort Washington to congratulate the students for winning," said Young. "It was a very big deal and it really put us on the cutting edge."

The computer lab proved an invaluable tool in enhancing student education, as was reflected in the school's receiving the prestigious National Blue Ribbon Award in 1991-92. "The school had won the award the first time in 1985-86," said Young. "To win it again, we had to show that we were sustaining excellence and demonstrating improvement over time, which is the basis of the award. To do that again in just six years was not easy, but the computer lab played a big role in that."

Strong parent and community support and a family-like atmosphere have long been the norm at Fort Washington, a tradition that continues today. "Our community is action oriented and generous with time and resources, getting involved through our parent club, the Mac-N-Kids diversity club, School Assessment Review Team, Inter-cultural Diversity and Advisory Council, School Site Council, volunteering to help in classrooms, and on fieldtrips," said current Principal Ann Kalashian. "We are fortunate to have a community committed to doing whatever it takes to provide the highest quality of education to each of our students."

Recognized Excellence

Fort Washington Elementary has received:

>> National Exemplary School Award (1986)
>> National Blue Ribbon School Award (1992, 1999)
>> State Distinguished School Award (1987, 1997, 2004)
>> California Blue Ribbon Nominee (1992)
>> CSU Fresno's Bonner Center Character for Education's Virtues and Character Education Award (1996, 2000, 2002, 2004)
>> Phi Delta Kappa (a professional association for educators) Value and Character Education Award (1992)

FREEDOM ELEMENTARY SCHOOL

By Carol Lawson-Swezey

When Freedom Elementary opened in August 2002, it was fortunate to have one of Clovis Unified's most seasoned principals at its helm. Pete Reyes, who had served as a principal for 22 of his 43 years with the district, admitted he'd "been around the block at the district" when he transferred to Freedom from Fancher Creek Elementary where he had served as principal for 12 years. Reyes brought with him 12 teachers from that school as well as his office manager and head custodian.

"We hit the ground running," Reyes said. "We didn't have the disadvantage of breaking in new staff as a well as a new school."

The school first opened 1.7 miles from its permanent site in a portable campus on the grounds of the Reagan Educational Center, home to Clovis East High and Reyburn Intermediate schools, in August 2002, and moved to its permanent location at Gettysburg and Locan avenues the following January. "Our teachers had to open up their classrooms, not once that year, but twice," said Reyes.

The first day at the new permanent site was a memorable one including a visit from the Clovis Fire Department. In the middle of an all-school ceremony being held that day in the multipurpose room the piercing sound of the fire alarm suddenly broke through the welcoming speech being given onstage.

"It turned out that a sibling of one of the students was not being watched very well and found one of the pull stations along the wall," recalled then-plant supervisor David Martin. "I believe that the small person was in the arms of mom and, as kids do, just grabbed the pretty white handle. Needless to say those of us who were involved in the function scrambled. Clovis Fire showed up quite quickly, the station is just down the street. Within 20 seconds or so after a mad dash to the office the alarm was canceled, an announcement was made and the festivities continued."

The first year at Freedom also brought with it an unusual scent and unwelcome critters. When the school opened in 2002, it was surrounded by farmland and its neighbor was a defunct chicken farm across the street. The chickens were gone, but what remained were the remnants of the cages and buildings and a conspicuous smell.

ESTABLISHED: 2002
GRADES: K-6
MASCOT: Trailblazers
COLORS: Red, blue and white
MOTTO: "Blazing Trails of Excellence"
LOCATION: 2995 Gettysburg, Clovis
ACREAGE: 17

"There was a distinct aroma coming from there," said Chad Staebler, who was the evening custodian at the time. "It was particularly strong after the first winter rain."

Staebler, who is now plant supervisor at Century Elementary, remembered a lot of fun and excitement in those early days. Gopher snakes and lizards were commonplace in the undeveloped farmland and occasionally, baby lizards would scamper through the classroom, to the delight of the students and the horror of their teachers.

Staebler also had an opportunity to help kids make plaster castings of animal tracks with one of the Freedom teachers. "Our staff just seemed to gel well," he said. "Everybody seemed to have a good time."

Bees to a nest

The Freedom campus is comprised of five buildings with every three classrooms sharing a common conference area where teachers can send students to work quietly. The library has a carpeted staircase area used as a story corner where students can read privately or attend readings.

"The children congregated to that area," Reyes said. "They looked like a bunch of bees to a nest."

The school's mascot is the Trailblazers and its motto is "Blazing Trails of Excellence." School colors are red, white and blue, which, along with its name, are a reflection of the nation's surge of patriotism following the tragic terrorist attacks on the World Trade Center and Pentagon on September 11, 2001.

"The committee of staff, students and their families chose Freedom, from about 20 suggestions," Reyes said.

The community also stressed the importance of academics, a safe school and a strong opportunity for their children to flourish with programs like sports, arts, oral interpretation and multi-cultural education. The school has started its own unique traditions including a Halloween alternative called Literacy Day, in which students dress up as their favorite literary character.

Surviving the in and out transition

When Suzi Erickson took over as principal in 2005, she began a two-year period of transition. Freedom's enrollment swelled to more than 900 that first year. She had to hire nine additional teachers, move eight portables onto the campus and increase lunch periods to eight, at 20 minute intervals.

"Because of the portables, we became an overflow school for our area," Erickson said. "It presented a lot of logistical challenges."

The following school year presented another set of trials. Two hundred students were transferred to newly opened Reagan Elementary less than two miles away, nine positions had to be rerouted there, and multiple meetings with parents and students were scheduled.

"Those two years were definitely a whirlwind," Erickson said. "Just getting through them was a major accomplishment. Thankfully, we have transitioned nicely and are now a very well-oiled machine!"

Freedom's dedicated staff has played an integral role in the success of the school and its students. "We have had up to 200 English learner students at one time," Erickson said. "What makes us unique is that even though we are not designated as a Title I school, our staff still provides many of the same programs and opportunities. Our teachers volunteer their own time to do whatever it takes to get their students to academically advance to the next level."

In June 2009, the first batch of graduating high school seniors who had started at Freedom in sixth grade, stepped out into the world at the same time as Freedom's first beginning group of kindergartners graduated from sixth grade.

Paying it forward

In addition to Freedom's academic success, Erickson is most proud of the school's heart.

The spirit of community service is thriving on campus. They annually raise money for Children's Hospital of Central California and the Leukemia Lymphoma Cancer Society. The school also raised nearly $2,000 for the "Cents for Citrus" emergency freeze relief for local farmers. Truckloads of donated food are annually given by the Freedom community to the Poverello House, a nonprofit organization that serves the hungry, homeless and destitute of Fresno. The school's Build-a-Book program earned money for overseas orphans.

> **Recognized Excellence**
>
> Freedom Elementary has received:
> >> State Distinguished School Award (2008)
> >> California Business for Education Excellence Foundation's Scholar Schools Award (2009)

"Our kids know to give back to those less fortunate," Erickson said. "It's an important message to learn as individuals. Sometimes it's the neediest kids who bring that last can of something just to be able to contribute."

Freedom holds a special place in Erickson's heart. "Though I have loved every school I have worked at, Freedom has been the most giving, generous staff and school I've ever worked with," she said. "We are a family here and want to keep the right people on board and keep the students academically challenged. We hope to continue to be a school where people want to move here just to be part of the Freedom team."

FRIANT ELEMENTARY SCHOOL

By Charlotte Hutchison

A town of many names

To understand the unique school of Friant Elementary, it is first necessary to understand the evolution of the tiny community in which it is nestled.

The town of Friant has gone by many names and many guises. Located on the south bank of the San Joaquin River about 20 miles northeast of Fresno, Friant is one of the oldest settlements in Fresno County. When Charles Porter Converse and W. W. Worland established a ferry business on the banks of the San Joaquin, the settlement of Converse's Ferry was born. Their lucrative ferry business provided a convenient river crossing for people living in the mining camp of Millerton four miles upstream and for stagecoach travelers crossing the river. Converse was the sole owner of the ferry business in 1868 when he sold it to James Richardson Jones who owned a hotel and store on the river's north bank. After Jones purchased the ferry business, the name of the settlement was changed to Jonesville. When Jones died in 1877, his three businesses were leased to William R. Hampton.

Hampton bought land on the south side of the river, built a new hotel and store, and the name of the settlement was changed to Hamptonville.

The San Joaquin Valley Railroad Co.

The San Joaquin Valley Railroad Company was incorporated March 4, 1891, to build a railroad from Fresno to the Sierra Nevada timber belt. Speculator Marcus Pollasky was president of the new company. The tracks reached Hamptonville by the early fall of 1891. At that time, William Hampton sold all of his property in the small town that bore his name and moved to Fresno. The town's name changed December 16, 1891, to Pollasky.

After the sly Pollasky collected sizeable sums of money from his investors, he silently disappeared. On December 19, 1893, the San Joaquin Valley Railroad Company was bankrupt and the Southern Pacific Railroad assumed ownership. In 1909, the angry and disillusioned residents in Pollasky decided to change its name to Friant in honor of Thomas Friant, Jr., a longtime resident of the area, and a partner in the White-Friant Lumber Company. Thomas Friant died in 1927 and his name has remained attached to the little town.

Pollasky School District

On May 8, 1892, the first Pollasky School District was organized. Two years later on April 4, 1894, the first Pollasky District was annexed by the Millerton District.

The second Pollasky organization occurred on February 7, 1905, and was still located on Friant Road, 15 miles northeast of Fresno. Although the new district was larger than the first Pollasky organization, it included all of the territory covered by the first district. Seventeen students were enrolled during the first year and Lulu Evans was the teacher. The first trustees included J. K. Martin, G. W. Birmingham and John Shipp. Classes at Pollasky were suspended on August 1, 1944.

Even though both Pollasky organizations were located in the Sierra High School District, most of the students attended Clovis Union High School.

Friant School District

The Friant School District was organized on February 7, 1911, from a portion of the second Pollasky District. The one-room school building was built circa 1915, and located roughly 20 miles northeast of Fresno on the present Burroughs Road. The Friant School remained a one-room school for more than 20 years. In 1938, with 42 students enrolled, Friant added a second room to the building and a second teacher was hired.

Friant Dam

By 1934, when the Great Depression made it difficult for the State of California to sell enough bonds to complete the California Central Valley Project Act, state officials in Sacramento appealed to the federal government for assistance. In 1935, the U.S. Congress passed the Rivers and Harbors Act. That same year, President Franklin D. Roosevelt transferred $20 million from the Emergency Relief Act funds to the Department of Interior for the construction of Friant Dam. In California, the Central Valley Project Act was re-authorized as the Rivers and Harbors Act of 1937, and the contract to build the dam was awarded to the Griffith Company and the Bent Company of Los Angeles. Their successful contract bid was for $8.7 million.

Early on the morning of November 5, 1939, United States Secretary of Interior Harold Ickes, California Governor Culbert L. Olson, and more than 50,000 people arrived in Friant and gathered a mile downstream on the Madera County side of the river to dedicate the dam. Friant received national recognition when the NBC National Network arrived to record the celebration. Twenty-one 75mm cannons were brought in from an army base near Stockton, to give a 21-gun salute to the governor; a gigantic, symbolic dynamite blast was set off at the construction site; and the Clovis Union High School Band was one of 27 bands performing in Friant's gala event. When Secretary Ickes addressed the people, he compared the Friant Dam to the French Maginot Line as two structures standing to "preserve and enhance our civilization." The following day, a story appearing in the *San Francisco Chronicle* said, "Cannon boomed on America's Maginot Line."

An ADA explosion

Earlier in 1939, construction workers began arriving in the area. To house the sudden influx of people in 1938, the contractor built more than 50 houses and 48-man dormitories near the construction site. During the fall of 1939, average daily attendance (ADA) enrollment in Friant School increased to 129 students. Soon it was necessary for the Griffith and Bent companies to hastily build a new schoolhouse to accommodate the children arriving in the area.

The locals referred to the new expediently constructed building as the "Chicken Coop." One of its most noticeable flaws was the redwood floor that was laid directly on top of the bare ground with no foundation. The new building was located on the same site where the original Friant School had been. Additional teachers were provided by Fresno County to accommodate the influx of new students. At that time, Friant had six teachers on staff.

An ADA implosion

The Friant Dam was completed in 1942, the workers left, enrollment dropped and the temporary schoolhouse was in an extreme state of disrepair. During the 1944-45 school term, the district's final year of separate operation, only two teachers, Mary Browne and Birdie Bulfinch, were teaching at the school. On March 2, 1945, the Friant School District and the Pollasky School District merged to form the Friant Union School District.

Friant Union School District

In 1945, when the Friant Union District began operation, 64 students were enrolled, Mary Browne was principal and the district's three remaining teachers were still holding classes in the old "chicken coop" schoolhouse. The district continued to use the old school for several more years. It was later moved to 2140 North Cedar Avenue in Fresno where it served as a temporary building to house the Sacred Heart Church of Fresno. Afterward it was converted into a recreation hall, before being demolished in 1966.

In 1953, because the federal government owned a large portion of land adjacent to Friant Dam, federal money was made available to Friant to help pay the $225,000 cost of a new elementary school. The new building, designed by William Hastrup and built by Midstate Construction Company, had four classrooms, a multipurpose room, a kitchen and a principal's office. When classes began in the fall of 1953, Richard Herboldshimer was the school's new teaching principal.

During this time, the Friant Union District was still united to the Clovis Union High School District. On March 31, 1959, the Fresno County Board of Supervisors ordered it to be excluded from the Clovis District, and annexed by Sierra Union High School District at Tollhouse.

Twenty years after its organization in 1945, the district's area was about the same size, the ADA was down to 52 students, but the assessed value had tripled.

Struggle to survive

By the time another 20 years had passed, the Friant Elementary School was struggling for survival. In an article appearing in the December 24, 1986, issue of the *Mountain Press*, Friant's superintendent, Dr. Rowland King, described the Friant Elementary School's desperate struggle:

> We have lost a substantial block of ADA money. Our enrollment has been dropping for the last two years. We expected increases from the Ball Ranch and the Millerton New Town, but neither project has materialized.
>
> There is a lot of vacant housing and there are fewer children on our streets. The poor old town of Friant seems to be dying on the vine.
>
> The Friant district has already done almost everything they can do for themselves. The Superintendent has taken on the role of cafeteria manager and coach in addition to his main job. The cook is also working part-time as a custodian. The school has already laid off most of it non-teaching staff.
>
> The community is reluctant to put several grades into one classroom, but we don't have much choice, but to cut teaching staff. We are definitely facing elimination of the Superintendent's position.
>
> What keeps rubbing salt into our wounds is that our salaries are already the lowest in Fresno County.
>
> If the district stays on its own during the next school year it could only afford three teachers, one of whom would have to be an administrator/teacher. The County School's office would have to take up central office duties and the acting superintendent's role. There would still be the problem of funding the cafeteria.
>
> Facing these realities head-on, the Friant school board has contacted the three districts on its borders, Auberry, Spring Valley and Clovis, to ask if any of them are interested in unionization.

At that time, Superintendent King, Principal Herboldshimer and the Friant board members were still determined to keep the school open, and they were not willing to discuss closing down the Friant campus when they proposed annexation to their three neighboring districts.

Joining Clovis Unified School District

At the same time, Clovis Unified was growing rapidly. According to CUSD Superintendent Dr. Floyd Buchanan, families were moving to Clovis and the portion of Fresno in CUSD so their children could get "A private school education in a public school system." Buchanan and the CUSD Governing Board were aware their district would need room for future expansion, for without growth it would become difficult to finance the school system. The Friant District covered a vast area, stretching from Copper Avenue (the border shared with CUSD) and extending northeast to Millerton Lake. Knowing the annexation of Friant would assure continued growth for Clovis for the next 20 years, Buchanan responded favorably when the representatives from Friant approached him about a proposed merger.

On July 1, 1988, the Friant Elementary School was annexed to CUSD, but only after Buchanan and the governing board gave their guarantee to keep the Friant campus open for a minimum of five years. But, by this time, some parents in Friant District were already sending their children to Clovis Unified's Fort Washington and Dry Creek elementary schools, and, later to Liberty Elementary School, which opened in 1991.

Epilogue

The CUSD Governing Board kept its promise. The Friant School remained open for five years, but during that time classes continued to grow smaller and the cost of operation was more expensive. Since the five-acre site was landlocked by houses, it could not be expanded. On June 21, 1995, Clovis Unified closed Friant Elementary.

Herboldshimer served as Friant's principal from 1953 until 1988. Dave Derby, Marshall Doris and Bob Kampf, respectively, headed the school following Herboldshimer. For the majority of his 35 years at the elementary school, it was located in the Sierra Union High School District at Tollhouse, but in a letter written September 8, 2008, Herboldshimer explained one of the reasons why the people in Friant decided to leave the Sierra District and merge with CUSD: "One of the reasons the folks of the southern part of the district withdrew from the Sierra High District was the long distance to the school. Many of the children [in the southern part of the Sierra District] had interdistrict permits to attend Clovis Schools. They liked the small elementary school but not the long drive to Sierra High."

Principal Herboldshimer's fondness for Friant was evident when he wrote in an editorial in the July 21, 2006, issue of the *Fresno Bee* that "the school was the heart and spirit of the Friant community for more than 60 years...Those who lived in Friant and attended Friant School will long and fondly remember the glory days of the building."

After the closure of Friant, Clovis Unified still utilized the facility for professional development. From August 1996 through December 2003, the CUSD Curriculum Services and Innovations Department hosted lessons for second year teachers teaching grades one through six and their mentors. These lessons demonstrated current best practices and effective teaching strategies and techniques centered on appropriate academic content standards. Other professional development sessions held at Friant included workshops on math, science and writing, as well as other district meetings.

"Friant was the perfect place to have professional development sessions," said Carol Kilburn, coordinator of the Beginning Teacher Support Administration (BTSA) Induction and Peer Assistance and Review programs. "It was only a short drive from Clovis but far enough away so that people felt they had really left behind the worries of the work world and could immerse themselves in new learning. There were no bells or ringing phones to distract from concentrated study. In fact, cell phones didn't work up there! It was the perfect getaway!"

On September 13, 2006, the CUSD Governing Board voted to lease the building to Table Mountain Rancheria, which used the facility for employee training. Less than two years later, Table Mountain Rancheria bought the "Friant Learning Academy" for the appraised value of $950,000, which was deposited in the district Special Reserve Fund for Capital Projects, to be used only for capital facility projects within Clovis Unified.

GARFIELD ELEMENTARY SCHOOL

By Carol Lawson-Swezey

Garfield Elementary School has had two distinct lives and histories — first as a rural school-house that educated children of ranch families northeast of Clovis in the Garfield School District, to its present state-of-the-art facility as part of the Floyd B. Buchanan Educational Center, which was established in 1990.

Garfield School District

On May 14, 1883, the recently formed Garfield Colony, named for President James A. Garfield who had been assassinated in 1881, organized a school district.

Rancher Jeff Corrick donated one acre of his land to build the school in 1883 on the northwest corner of present-day Shepherd and Minnewawa avenues in northeast Clovis. In 1887, two more acres were purchased from Corrick for a reported $40 in gold coin. Local grower John Cadwallader was also a donor of land for the school. Cadwallader would later serve as a trustee of the Garfield District (1907-1915) and Clovis Union High School District (1899-1922).

On June 27, 1899, Garfield District, along with Red Banks, Jefferson, Mississippi, Wolters, Temperance and Clovis districts, joined the Clovis Union High School District.

By the 1900s, the landscape of the Garfield area had changed; gone were the fields of grain, replaced with orchards and vineyards.

In 1906, the original Garfield facility was replaced by a small wood schoolhouse built at the same location as the 1883 school. In 1912, a bond for $4,000 was approved to fund an additional facility to accommodate the growing number of students. It was built on the Shepherd and Minnewawa avenues site, with the 1906 school remaining intact and used for teaching first- and second-graders.

The new school facility, which included classrooms for students in third through eighth grades, was framed in wood, and had a brick veneer and a pronounced brick archway welcoming students through the front door. Water was available on the grounds between the two school buildings. Buggies and horses were housed in a shed behind the schools while class was in session.

Recollections of the school, as described in *Public Schools of Fresno County 1860–1998*, included:

> "…former students remember the walk to school, carrying a sack lunch or a tobacco can lunch pail. Sometimes the boys would roll cigarettes from dried horse manure behind the horse shed. Punishment might be a whack on the hand with a ruler or being sent to sit alone on the porch. Bad language might get your mouth washed out with soap. Most of the boys played soccer, basketball and softball. The girls played jacks, hopscotch and tether-ball."

On September 10, 1952, voters approved by a vote of 53 to six to annex the Garfield School District into Dry Creek Union District, with the 1952-53 school year being the last year the Garfield School was in operation.

The old 1912 building was purchased by the Clovis Grange in 1989 with the intention of renovating it as a meeting hall. On September 7, 1990, the building, which had just been designated an historic site on February 6, 1990, was burned to the ground, except for the brick archway and façade which remains on the northwest corner of Shepherd and Minnewawa today. Farmer Pat V. Ricchiuti, Jr., now owns the remains of the building.

Garfield schoolhouse built in 1912, located at Shepherd and Minnewawa avenues.

Then there were three

Construction of the district's first educational complex began in 1990 when the center, named after Clovis Unified's first superintendent, Dr. Floyd B. Buchanan, was still almost entirely surrounded by farmland. When completed four years later, it would be home to three separate schools — Garfield Elementary, Alta Sierra Intermediate School and Buchanan High School, all sharing one parcel of land. The vision in developing the Buchanan Educational Center was to create a community in which schools would share facilities, teachers and students. The schools share specialized learning centers including a large lecture hall, three media centers and small group instructional areas.

Alta Sierra, the first school to open on the complex, opened to eighth- and ninth-graders in 1991. In the 1992-93 school year, ASI housed eighth, ninth and tenth grades. When Buchanan High School opened in 1993, these three classes, comprised of 1,600 students, moved into the new school as freshman, sophomores, and juniors. That same year, the intermediate school began serving seventh and eighth grades. With the opening of Garfield Elementary in 1994, the district's first educational center was complete.

The three schools' mascots, Cubs (Garfield), Bruins (Alta Sierra) and Bears (Buchanan High) are members of the bear family, a tribute to Dr. Buchanan and Dr. Virginia Boris, the first Buchanan Area assistant superintendent. Both were graduates of the University of California at Berkeley whose mascot just happens to be the Golden Bears.

ESTABLISHED: 1994
GRADES: K-6
MASCOT: Cubs
COLORS: Royal blue, red and white
MOTTO: "Cub Pride"
LOCATION: 1315 N. Peach, Clovis
ACREAGE: Part of the 160-acre Buchanan Educational Center

Having a complex in which all three levels are in one location has many advantages, said current Garfield Principal Jessica Mele. "The Cubs always know they are going to be Bruins and then Bears," she said. "The children feel a part of the high school, which is a tremendous resource for both the intermediate and elementary schools."

Tracy Smith, Garfield's first principal at its current site, served for 11 years before transferring to open Harold L. Woods Elementary in 2005. She noted that the three-part integration from Garfield to Alta Sierra to Buchanan offered her students a "unique opportunity to get to know the other facilities and staff before they even got there."

Students from the intermediate and high schools can frequently be seen on the Garfield campus helping the younger students in a variety of ways. They provide assistance and mentoring to Garfield students participating in activities such as the science fair, Robotics team, in which students create working robots out of specialized LEGO building block kits, and the Destination ImagiNation team, which participates in creative problem-solving competitions where students work together to create answers to challenges given by judges.

Buchanan High supports Garfield academics with cross-age tutors in math, reading and physical education, and the high school students run intervention labs after school. Buchanan's peer counselors train Garfield peer counselors.

Garfield's 1912 schoolhouse, no longer occupied by students after Garfield School District was annexed into Dry Creek Union District in 1952, was nearly completely burned to the ground in September 1990.

Under construction

For the 1993-94 school year, while Garfield's construction was in progress, the elementary students attended a portable school located behind Clovis High School on Barstow Avenue in Clovis. Carl Tomlinson served as principal at that time.

A nod to the past

When Garfield Elementary commemorated its first full day at its new location in September 1994, it celebrated its future with a tribute to its past.

Among the dignitaries present were past alumni from the original fire-ravaged school including Clovis Unified administrator George W. Kastner, former Garfield School District and Dry Creek Union District trustees James Miyamoto and Earl Smittcamp (who also attended Garfield Elementary in the 1912 schoolhouse), and an early Garfield teacher who was over 100 years old at the time of the 1994 school opening.

Students show true patriotic colors

The school's colors are royal blue and red. There have been many opportunities for its students to show the school's solidarity and reflect its patriotic colors. Following the September 11, 2001, terrorist attacks on the World Trade Center and the Pentagon, the students created a chain of paper origami-style cranes to send its support to Washington.

A thousand cranes in red, white and blue, each containing a special message, were created by Garfield students. It is Japanese folklore that the power created by the collaborative creation of a thousand cranes can overcome any obstacle and grant any wish.

The cranes were symbolically linked in a ceremony at the school that September under a flag at half staff. For the first time since the school opened in 1994, each upper grade student was allowed to ring the school's bell, the same one that hung at the original Garfield school and remains in working order today.

As it was when the school sprang back from the ashes to begin anew in 1994, the crane ceremony offered new hope. "It was a show of tolerance for all cultures," Smith said. "It showed the importance of working together. It's something the kids will never forget."

Special education for special kids

Initially, Garfield offered a special education summer program on its campus, which was moved to Liberty and Riverview elementary schools. Medically fragile students were either home-schooled or sent to special classes at other schools. That all changed in 2005 when the district opened the Medical Therapy Unit (MTU) in conjunction with the Garfield Special Education Center. The state-of-the-art, 14,000-square-foot complex, located adjacent to the elementary school, houses medically fragile students from throughout the area and is the first of its kind for Clovis Unified.

The Garfield site was chosen because of its centralized location and convenient proximity to State Route 168. In addition, the Garfield campus "had extra green space compared to other schools," said Roger Oraze, then-assistant superintendent of facility services.

In one wing of the complex, the MTU offers medical therapy to clients ranging from infants through age 21 who live within the boundaries of Clovis Unified. The district owns the MTU facility but it is staffed by Fresno County employees. In another wing, the Garfield Center, comprised of four special education classrooms, serves Clovis Unified's medically fragile students. Jessica Mele oversees the operation of both wings.

Outside is a playground area with occupational and physical therapy equipment, play apparatus and a shade structure.

The center is both a medical therapy and an educational facility that focuses on sensory and motor skills as well as mobility activities. Curriculum is based on each student's intensity of needs.

Staffed by LVNs, RNs, special education teachers and instructional assistants, the school features many unique services. Key program components include utilization of a team approach in order to develop an individual education program that maximizes each student's abilities and level of independence.

Garfield Center students arrive at school daily just like the students at the elementary school. They are not ambulatory and require wheelchairs for transportation and mobility.

Teachers help the students learn to sit, stand and walk, as well as with other educational activities. The rooms are filled with bright colors and even feature a specially designed swing for the physically challenged students.

Instruction includes the Mobility Opportunities via Education, or MOVE, program that serves as a physical education component.

Activities within the MOVE program vary from student to student, depending on capabilities, needs and the goals of their Individualized Education Plan. For example, the program can help a student learn to sit up, blink his or her eyes for "yes" and "no," or stand or walk with the help of the specially designed equipment.

Mele considers opening the MTU and the Garfield Center as the highlight of her tenure at Garfield. "It's been an incredible partnership," she said. "All of the students in both facilities are part of this campus. We share assemblies, rallies. It's a really rewarding place for families whose only sense of normalcy might be at school. The collaboration has opened many people's eyes and hearts. The elementary kids work over at the center. It's a win-win situation for both Center kids and Garfield kids."

Ebb and flow of growth

Due to the area's burgeoning growth, Garfield's seams have been nearly bursting. The campus swelled to more than 1,100 students in 2000, when the school's entire third grade had to be bused to other schools. With the opening of Riverview Elementary the following year, and Woods Elementary in 2005, the school's growth was tempered.

The school prides itself on offering many extra-curricular programs and community outreaches. Environmental Club members grow flowers and produce in their own greenhouse on campus which they give away. The Recycling Club uses its proceeds to buy holiday gifts for Dakota House, a safe harbor house for students in Fresno County. Students volunteer at the Valley Animal Center and serve food at the Poverello House, a nonprofit organization that serves the hungry, homeless and destitute of Fresno.

Recognized Excellence

Garfield Elementary has received:

>> National Blue Ribbon School Award (1999)
>> State Distinguished School Award (1997, 2006)
>> California Business for Education Excellence Foundation's Scholar Schools Award (2006, 2007, 2008, 2009)
>> CSU Fresno's Bonner Center Character for Education's Virtues and Character Education Award (2008)

Then and now

In the fall of 2009, the campus commemorated its 15-year anniversary as part of the district's first educational complex. CUSD Superintendent Dave Cash, Ed.D., attended the event with other district dignitaries and many former alumni. A Bricks of Fame walkway was dedicated at that time. The bricks are inscribed with the names of those staff, students and their families from the past and present who have impacted the school and will always hold Garfield close to their hearts.

"Our school has a culture of inclusion," said Mele. "Everyone has a place and everyone feels important and validated — from the smallest kindergartner to parents who feel they have a wonderful voice."

GEORGE W. KASTNER INTERMEDIATE SCHOOL

By Susan Sawyer Wise

The ground breaking for Clovis Unified's second middle school, Kastner Intermediate, was held June 19, 1979, at the site of the new campus to be built on First Street between Nees and Alluvial avenues. Dr. James S. Fugman was present as the school's first principal to welcome students soon to attend the new school.

CUSD's first intermediate school, Clark, had opened a decade earlier and was already facing overcrowding. Kastner was needed to house seventh and eighth grade students residing north of Herndon Avenue plus students coming from coming Cole and Tarpey elementary schools.

To ease the high enrollment numbers at Clark as quickly as possible, Kastner opened for the 1979-80 school year in portable buildings at Clovis West High School, one mile away from where its permanent campus was being built by Harris Construction at a cost of $7,118,300. The new school was designed by Darden Architects.

Origins of a name

In 1979, a motion was entertained by then-governing board president Gerald G. Walker to name the new intermediate school after the recently retired George W. "Tink" Kastner. The board unanimously approved the name in honor of Kastner's impact on the local community.

The new school was dedicated on September 27, 1980, with Kastner's two grandchildren placing a time capsule in the cornerstone.

Kastner was a product of Clovis schools, attending Dry Creek Elementary, Garfield Elementary and graduating from Clovis Union High School in 1937. While a high school student,

Kastner participated in student government and activities, serving as freshman class president, student body president and assistant editor of the school's first edition of "The Cavalcade" yearbook (it had previously been called "The Argus"). He went on to receive bachelor of arts and master of arts degrees from Fresno State College. During his high school and college years, Kastner was a celebrated athlete.

After college, Kastner entered the U.S. Air Force in 1941, graduated from pilot training in 1942 and flew a P-51 Mustang fighter aircraft in 83 missions during World War II in the Mediterranean Theater. His 83 missions set a record at the time and his heroic service earned him a Certificate of Valor. Before his discharge from active duty in 1945, he served as base commander of the first helicopter unit in the United States.

When he returned to Clovis, Kastner began teaching at Dry Creek and Pollasky (in Friant) schools and then at Clovis Union High where he taught history. He would begin each day as a bus driver, crossing town nearly 30 miles to pick up children from the Friant community to the area around Belmont Country Club and

George W. "Tink" Kastner
Clovis Unified School District Archives

was reimbursed one dollar a day for bus driving duties. He also coached track and football at Clovis High, and would reminisce about first driving the student-athletes to their athletic event, then assuming the role of coach upon their arrival.

Kastner was recalled to active duty in 1951 during the Korean Conflict and, during this second term of service to his country, was graduated from the Command and General Staff Air University, Maxwell Air Force Base in Alabama, served at Strategic Air Command Headquarters in Omaha, Nebraska, in the Air Inspector's Office and served as Security Education Officer for Strategic Air Command.

After his discharge from active duty in 1953, he became Group Commander 93, 72nd Reserve Wing for Central California and Southern Nevada, 1958-63. He retired from U.S.A.F. as a full colonel in 1963.

Kastner returned to Clovis Union High School where he served as vice principal, and in 1956, principal. In 1961, Kastner became the first assistant superintendent in Clovis Unified, and in 1976, until his retirement in June 1979, he served as associate superintendent.

Kastner was innovative and devoted to the school district and its students. As former Superintendent Dr. Terry Bradley recalled: "One day, Tink was leading a group of visitors around the district and showing them various schools. When he got to the Clovis High School track he found the track coach on a tractor, attempting to drag the dirt track to smooth out the ruts. The old track coach in Tink immediately surfaced and he pointed out that the drag did not have enough weight on it to accomplish the task. The solution? Tink jumped on the drag and had the coach drive the tractor, with Tink and the drag in tow, around the track while the visitors tried to get clear of the dust cloud!"

Actively involved in the campus, Kastner could often be found helping run a track meet; bringing candy to staff at Christmas; sharing stories of World War II; donating to those students at the school in need; attending, along with his wife Thelma, CHARACTER COUNTS! awards banquets for Clovis West area students; and being present for every event he could attend.

According to former Principal Rick Gold, Kastner's namesake truly represented "Excellence in Education" and the spirit of the school named for him. "Like the school's namesake, the Kastner staff strives for excellence in serving the needs of its students," he said.

Origins of a mascot

While other schools across the nation have the "Thunderbirds" as their mascot, Kastner is the only school in the nation with the permission to have the "U.S. Air Force Thunderbirds" as its mascot, as well as the rights to its logo. This was due to George W. Kastner's years of dedicated service to the Air Force.

The Air Force's official air demonstration team based out of Luke Air Force Base, Arizona, adopted the "Thunderbirds" as its mascot in 1953. According to U.S.A.F., the mascot was "influenced in part by the strong Indian culture and folklore of the southwestern United States where Luke is located. Indian legend speaks of the Thunderbird with great fear and respect. To some it was a giant eagle… others envisioned a hawk. When it took to the skies, the earth trembled from the thunder of its great wings. From its eyes shot bolts of lightning. Nothing in nature could challenge the bird of thunder, the story said, and no man could stand against its might. The story of the Thunderbird was repeated, voice-by-voice, across the generations, until at last, it assumed the immortality of legend."

ESTABLISHED: 1979
GRADES: 7-8
MASCOT: U.S. Air Force Thunderbirds
COLORS: Cardinal and gold
MOTTO: "T-Birds… Transforming to Greater Heights!"
LOCATION: 7676 N. First Street, Fresno
ACREAGE: 45

At Kastner's 25th anniversary celebration September 22, 2005, two new Thunderbird mascots were introduced named "Tink" and "Thelma" in honor of Kastner and his wife, both of whom were present for the celebration and the unveiling of the mascots. Not long after the celebration, on April 1, 2006, Tink Kastner passed away at the age of 86.

To correlate with the Thunderbird fighter plane, the school's colors were going to be red, white and blue. However, before the official opening it was determined that the colors of cardinal and gold would be preferable in order to match Clovis West High's school colors.

Over time

In its more than 30-year history, Kastner has had eight principals at its helm: Fugman, Dr. Thomas Crow, Dr. Ginny Boris, Lyn Snauffer, Walt Byrd, Rick Gold, Rick Watson and Johnny Alvarado, who currently holds the position.

The school has been an innovator in developing character, with the physical education department first bringing the CHARACTER COUNTS! program to the district in the 1996-97 school year. All Clovis Unified schools now integrate the character building program that emphasizes six pillars of character: caring, citizenship, fairness, respect, responsibility and trustworthiness.

Kastner was first in the district to pilot the Where Everyone Belongs (WEB) program in 1998. A national curriculum for intermediate school students, WEB is designed to involve older students in the success of younger students, focusing on both their social and academic success in school as they transition into the intermediate school setting. Student leaders can call their younger charges at home, invite them to different school functions, coordinate monthly activities, or make presentations on subjects as diverse as good study habits, using time wisely and making honorable choices. WEB is now successfully operating in all five Clovis Unified intermediate schools.

In the 2009-10 school year, Kastner introduced the Time To Teach! classroom management model using practical and proven teaching strategies that maximize instructional minutes. Also in that school year, Kastner introduced an ambassadors program with representatives from all of its feeder elementary schools participating. The goal of the students involved is to go back to their home campuses and recognize good behavior and citizenship displayed by their peers.

In the 2010-11 school year, Kastner is the first intermediate school in the district to pilot an all-inclusive laptop program for all seventh-graders.

Awards

Kastner's success on state standardized testing was recognized by Standard & Poor's School Evaluation Services on September 12, 2006. Kastner was one of 103 California schools identified by S&P to have significantly narrowed the achievement gap between higher- and lower-performing student groups during the 2003-04 and 2004-05 school years. Specifically, the school was recognized for reducing the achievement gap between eighth grade students of diversity who attained a level of "proficient" or above in reading and math in their Standardized Testing and Reporting (STAR) results over the two-year timeframe.

In 2008, Kastner was named a School To Watch — Taking Center Stage Model School, a designation given on behalf of a collaborative endeavor of 10 organizations that form the California Middle Grades Alliance. Schools receive the award for implementing replicable practices focused on academic excellence, responsiveness to the developmental needs of young adolescents; fair and equitable education for all students; and organizational processes and procedures that foster and sustain academic growth. Kastner's award made history: for the first time in the history of California's Schools To Watch program, two of the honored schools were from the same district with both Alta Sierra and Kastner intermediate schools being selected for the very short list of honorees.

Recognized Excellence

Kastner Intermediate has received:
>> National Exemplary School (1985)
>> National Blue Ribbon School Award (1993)
>> California Blue Ribbon Nominee (1993)
>> State Distinguished School Award (2005)
>> School To Watch - Taking Center Stage Model School Award (2008)
>> CSU Fresno's Bonner Center Character for Education's Exemplary Middle Schools of Character Award (1999, 2001, 2003, 2005)

During the Schools To Watch judging committee's visitation, then-Superintendent Bradley poignantly described the spirit of Kastner, according to the school's principal at the time, Rick Watson. "The question 'What makes Kastner so special?' was asked by the committee," said Watson, "and Dr. Bradley said something to the effect of, 'Kastner has such a unique feel to it when you walk on this campus. It is a diverse microcosm of society and students who attend here have such a rich experience. Staff here buys into the tradition and history so strongly and they believe in each other and in their students. All who attend here or work here are so blessed by their experience!'"

Student awards

Unique to Kastner are the Thunderbird Award, George Kastner Award and James S. Fugman Award, all of which are presented to students at the annual Principal's Awards Reception at the end of the school year.

The Thunderbird Award is a tribute to those students at Kastner whose involvement reflects the spirit of the Sparthenian Concept of the total child — developed in mind, body and spirit. It is the most significant award a student can earn while at Kastner.

The James S. Fugman Award is given to students who exceed all expectations in both the curricular and co-curricular activities. It represents the finest Kastner has to offer and perpetuates the goals and standards set by Fugman, the school's founding principal.

The George Kastner Award is presented to eighth grade students with 4.0 grade point averages.

A school with heart

Every May, special needs athletes are given a chance to shine in an annual event hosted by Kastner Intermediate School that started in 2000. The Frisbee Golf Tournament includes special needs students from not only Clovis Unified schools, but from across the Central Valley, from Modesto to Bakersfield.

Scores from the Frisbee golf games are kept and at the end of the event, each student is awarded a medal to emphasize that they are all winners.

The tournament brings together students with special needs and general education students who help run the event. At the close of the 2007 tournament, Kastner resource specialist Erin Atchley noted, "All adults and general education peers came away with a better understanding of the needs of our population of students. Our leadership students were able to see the trials and tribulations that our students face on a daily basis."

GETTYSBURG ELEMENTARY SCHOOL

By Carol Lawson-Swezey

Gettysburg Elementary, located on Gettysburg Avenue between Fowler and Armstrong avenues, formally opened in September 1989 with Tony Petersen, Jr., as principal. The school was in good hands with Petersen having previous experience opening both Miramonte Elementary and Kastner Intermediate schools.

Petersen, who was involved in the designing of Gettysburg early on, helped develop a unique cross-ventilation classroom design for Gettysburg in which a door was placed at the front and back of each classroom to enhance student and teacher comfort. Gettysburg's 21 classrooms and two kindergarten rooms were built around three sides of a courtyard.

Students were transferred from Miramonte, Temperance-Kutner, Jefferson and Mickey Cox elementary schools to attend the new Gettysburg Elementary. Despite challenges of some families not wanting to change boundaries, it was, in the end, strong parental and staff support that led to the successful transition of students to their new school, said Petersen.

Adaptive climate

Even before the official Gettysburg site opened in the fall of 1989, the school's staff and students had to adapt to a variety of unusual circumstances. The school community rose to the early challenges with ease and has continued that same spirit of adaptability in the face of anything that has come their way.

In 1987, Gettysburg first began operating in portables at a temporary location behind Clovis High. While contractor Lewis C. Nelson and Sons completed Gettysburg's new $6.3 million school facility, students attended the portable school through June 1989.

Because the portable campus had no cafeteria, the students had to eat on the bleachers at Clovis High's Lamonica Stadium, which was situated just west of the campus.

"Some of the kids could barely see over the counter at the snack stands to order food," recalled Petersen.

Five current teachers began with Petersen at Gettysburg when it opened at the temporary school in 1987 including Dawn Couchman, Judy Harris, Stacy King, Richard Kopper and Dawn Rohm; Mike Murphy joined the team the following year and remains at Gettysburg today. They recalled that the early days required some creativity in order to make do and be resourceful as they awaited the opening of their permanent campus.

"The first time I visited my new portable," recalled King, "I actually had to climb in because the portable site had no sidewalks yet. We barely got electricity in time for school to start. At lunch time, while the students ate on the bleachers in the end zone of Lamonica Stadium, some of us teachers walked over to the Clovis High teachers' room. It was a huge day when we got to watch as our cafeteria was brought in by crane and placed in its spot."

"During the preliminary days before the students arrived, we were setting our classrooms up before the blacktop had been laid at the portable site," added Kopper. "We were walking over the blacktop as it was being laid for the walkways. After school started, we watched the grass seed being sprayed on to the grounds. The school was literally taking final shape before our eyes."

Challenges arose at Gettysburg's new, permanent facility as well. The lawn had to be torn out and replanted later due to the relocation of the kindergarten portables, and the opening date was pushed back because of transportation issues with building supplies. The sidewalks were yet to be completed when students began their first year on the Gettysburg campus.

Teachers recalled the multiple challenges they faced as well.

"We opened school in the fall of 1989 at our permanent campus with a half-finished school," said King. "We didn't have sinks or any cupboards in our classrooms. We had to move all of our furniture into the middle of the room before leaving each day, just in case they were going to install the cabinets that night. We had no cafeteria (again) and the kids ate lunch in the covered hallways. Our library was not finished, either. Our secretaries had a phone plugged in to the telephone pole out by the street for a day or two, because that was the only phone service we had."

"Sometimes it looked like the person was talking to the pole!" Kopper mused. "We had outside light poles and light tube boxes inside some of our rooms when we were trying to set up class. The office was set up in the primary grade hallway wing. From the beginning, all of these so-called adversities were really things that helped pull us together as a team."

ESTABLISHED: 1987 in portables; 1989 in its permanent facility
GRADES: K-6
MASCOT: Generals
COLORS: Purple and gold
MOTTO: "Reach for the Stars"
LOCATION: 2100 Gettysburg Avenue, Clovis
ACREAGE: 15

Another challenge that the Gettysburg community has faced is multiple boundary changes. When the school started, it was part of the Clovis Area which meant that sixth grade students went on to attend Clark Intermediate and then Clovis High schools. In the 1999-2000 school year, boundaries were changed to accommodate the opening of Clovis Elementary, which opened as part of the Clovis Area schools. These boundary area changes resulted in Gettysburg students now advancing to Reyburn Intermediate and Clovis East High schools. In the 2007-08 school year, Gettysburg changed back to a feeder school within the Clovis Area. This educational track remains in place today.

"The boundaries might change, but the expectations never change and our kids just rise to the expectations," said Couchman.

Gettysburg faced another challenge in the 1992-93 school year when it, along with Cole, Miramonte, Tarpey and Weldon elementary schools, was placed on a year-round, multi-track schedule. It was a difficult and trying time for parents, students and school personnel. The decision to try this change was due to growth; overcrowding; obtaining construction funds from the state that required 30 percent of a district's kindergarten through sixth grade students to be enrolled in year-round education; and a need for a bond measure to pass in order to build a new school.

The year-round experiment lasted two years. Under pressure from dissatisfied parents and the community, the school board voted to return to the traditional schedule. At that time, a school comprised solely of portables opened on the southeast grounds of Clovis High as a site that would temporarily accommodate overcrowding.

Core of school's success

At the core of Gettysburg is a dedicated and committed staff.

There is little turnover in the teaching staff. Some teachers were once dedicated parents, current Principal Scott Dille said. "The staff is really committed to the school. They bleed purple," he said, referring to school's colors of purple and gold.

When custodian Rick Smith was killed in a horseback riding accident a decade ago, the staff quickly came together to support his family, especially Smith's granddaughter, who attended the school.

Gettysburg staff and students have consistently worked well together. "I've never been at a place where the kids were so comfortable with the teaching staff," said Doris Brosi, who taught for the district at Cole Elementary and then at Gettysburg a total of 38 years before she retired in 2002. "They would come before and after school just to hang out. A group of the staff used to have dinner at a neighborhood Mexican restaurant when we had Parent Teacher Club meetings once a month since we didn't have time to go home to eat. One time, one of the fifth-graders just came over with his plate, plopped down between our principal, Tony Petersen, and vice-principal, Scott Steele, and asked to eat with us. I'll always remember that fondly."

Unique lessons evoke innovation, creativity

Although they might be veteran staff, creativity and innovation are the names of the game as teachers continue to try new ways to stimulate learning, both inside the classroom and out.

"We are always searching for ways to make the education real, to bring history and science to life," said Kopper. "We have tried to keep our students at the center of our curriculum and not the other way around."

For example, fifth grade teacher Mike Murphy created a tradition of teaching students firsthand what life was like for American Plains Indians and pioneer settlers in the 1840s. One day a year, students wear period clothing, build teepees, use tools and weapons from that time, and cook a lunch of stew in cast-iron pots. Outside the classroom, Murphy has led students and their families on educational summer backpacking trips over Mount Whitney. In the winter, Murphy spearheads an annual fifth grade ski fieldtrip to Badger Pass Ski Resort to teach students lessons in science and physical education. Other Gettysburg fieldtrips have included tours of Selma's Pioneer Village, Kearney Mansion, Monterey, Sacramento, Challenger Learning Center and La Purisima Mission.

History in a name, mascot

Gettysburg was named for the street on which it is located, Gettysburg Avenue. The school colors of purple and gold were selected by students who would be attending Gettysburg when it opened and were approved by the governing board. The mascot, the Generals, was a nod to the Civil War/Gettysburg influence. "This was an opportunity to look toward the future with hope and with respect for the past," said teacher Judy Harris.

The school's motto, "Reach for the Stars," has been in place from day one. "We believed and continue to believe that every child possesses 'star' qualities," said Harris.

> **Recognized Excellence**
> Gettysburg Elementary has received:
> - National Blue Ribbon School Award (1999, 2007)
> - National Drug-Free Schools Program Award (1995)
> - State Distinguished School Award (1998, 2006)

New generals take charge

After Petersen left, Rick Talley, Todd Bennett and Carl Tomlinson each took turns as principals at Gettysburg. The newest principal on campus as of the fall of 2009 is Scott Dille who has a laundry list of goals and aspirations for his new school, which isn't so new. "I want us to reach an Academic Performance Index of 900," he said. "It's currently at 898 as of 2010 — a challenge very much within reach."

Added Dille: "This is a school with great character. It really shines."

HAROLD L. WOODS
ELEMENTARY SCHOOL

By Carole Grosch

Harold Lloyd Woods

Clovis Unified's twenty-ninth elementary school, Harold L. Woods Elementary, was so named in honor of the longest serving teacher in the district. In 2004, the CUSD Governing Board determined that the new school would be named for Woods to recognize his service and dedication to students for 46 years, all of which were spent at Jefferson Elementary School where he taught grades five, six and seven before retiring in 2001. Today, Woods still serves Clovis Unified by mentoring future teachers.

Woods is a lifelong resident of the Fresno-Clovis area. He attended Clovis Grammar School, located at the site where Weldon Elementary now sits in Old Town Clovis, and graduated from Clovis High School. Immediately after graduating from Fresno State College in 1955, Woods was hired at Jefferson. During his career with Clovis Unified, he has received numerous awards and honors for his dedication and commitment to children including winning the Crystal Award, Clovis Unified's employee recognition program, three times, and being named a Gamma Psi Master Teacher by California State University, Fresno.

Balloon day

As the student populations grew at Garfield and Century elementary schools, Clovis Unified School District made plans for building a school at the intersection of Clovis and Teague avenues in northeast Clovis.

After three years in the planning stage, the school, which was designed by S.I.M. Architects and constructed by Harris Construction, was ready for students in August 2005. The school's Parent Teacher Club was already organized and enthusiastic. Prior to opening day, students from Garfield and Century who were going to be attending Woods chose the school colors and mascot by voting in official voting booths. Selected as school colors were silver, navy blue and Columbia blue. "Wolverines" was chosen as the mascot.

The new school opened with a total of 490 students and 40 staff. Twenty-eight classrooms and three portables were in place. Celebrations kicked off with a rally, which was attended by the school's namesake. The pep and cheer squads performed for the first time. As a finishing touch, the students had a balloon launch, releasing a flood of hundreds of light blue balloons over the campus.

> **ESTABLISHED:** 2005
> **GRADES:** K-6
> **MASCOT:** Wolverines
> **COLORS:** Silver, navy blue and Columbia blue
> **MOTTO:** "Respect Yourself, Each Other and the Place in Which We Learn"
> **LOCATION:** 700 Teague, Clovis
> **ACREAGE:** 16.33

Vision for a school

Two different school communities merged together to form a cohesive unit. Since Woods opened, the community has been supportive of the school, staff and students, not only financially, but also in the desire to create a fun and successful learning environment.

The school is also known for its innovation. According to Tracy Smith, Woods' principal since opening day, "We were the first elementary school to have an electronic marquee in front of the school to display announcements, and we were able to put in a computer lab by the second year. We have a young staff that chose to come to our site when it first opened and is willing to try new ideas and strategies if it is going to help our students academically."

Professional Learning Communities are utilized in meeting the needs of all students by increasing staff collaboration with special attention to academics and student achievement. Through teacher collaboration, data analysis and deployment of students to various classrooms students are taught at their level on specific state standards in the area of language arts.

Harold L. Woods, 1951
Clovis Unified School District Archives

Virtues and character

Emphasis is placed on curriculum in character as well as curriculum in knowledge. The staff promotes the CHAR-

ACTER COUNTS! program with the belief that instilling ethics and morals will assist with lifetime learning.

The school's strong peer mediation program implements restorative justice so both the victim and perpetrator have the opportunity to talk through a conflict at hand.

Recognized Excellence

Woods Elementary has received:

>> CSU Fresno's Bonner Center Character for Education's Virtues and Character Education Award (2008)

As another way of instilling values, students can earn a "Random Acts of Kindness" reward for doing a good deed. Once spotted doing a good deed, they are given an entry into a weekly drawing for a prize of their choice from the prize bin.

The culture at Woods Elementary is one of support and caring: for each other as well as for academic achievement.

JAMES S. FUGMAN ELEMENTARY SCHOOL

By Janice Stevens

In 2004, a new school was opened to accommodate the rapid growth taking place in the northeast area of Fresno. Students from nearby Riverview and Copper Hills elementary schools comprised the original population.

When it opened to students for the 2004-05 school year, the brand new Fugman Elementary School included five buildings and 28 classrooms covering nearly 52,000 square feet on 16.5 acres of land. The school is located at North Cedar Avenue and East Olympic Drive in northeast Fresno and today serves more than 600 students in grades kindergarten through sixth.

A fish tale

When choosing its mascot, the Mighty Marlins, James S. Fugman Elementary set its sights on the "big one," big fish, that is. Indeed, today, the Mighty Marlins are swimming with the big ones, achieving awards and recognitions that are elusive to many long established schools, but which came early to this northeast Fresno school. Fugman Elementary received a Bonner Award for Virtues and Character Recognition, was named a California Business for Education Excellence Honor Roll School, was given a Just for the Kids Award by the National Center for Educational Achievement, and earned the prestigious California State Distinguished School Award in 2008, all in its first four years.

From the beginning, only one name was considered for the new school. Fugman Elementary is named in honor of James S. Fugman, Ed.D., retired CUSD administrator who served Clovis Unified for 28 years. He began his CUSD career in 1974 as a physical education teacher

James S. Fugman *Clovis Unified School District Archives*

and head football coach at Clovis High School. He soon decided to enter administration serving as a Clovis High learning director, deputy principal and, later, principal. He also opened Kastner Intermediate School in 1979 as its first principal, and was later appointed assistant superintendent over the Clovis Area schools. In 1993, Fugman was named deputy superintendent for curriculum and instruction, a position he held until his retirement in 2002.

Fugman took an active interest in the school from its start. Upon learning the school to be named after him would also sport the mascot of the Marlins, Fugman, an avid fisherman, began dreaming of catching a marlin himself. With his sense of humor intact, Fugman longed to catch a marlin in the school's colors of blue, black, silver and white. His wish soon came true: Fugman caught a perfectly colored marlin off the coast of Mexico in June, just prior to the fall 2004 opening of Fugman Elementary. The fish was mounted in the school's library and presented at a special dedication ceremony celebration.

Fugman continued to be active in the school after its opening. He launched the school's first ever first Fitness Frenzy school fundraising event, which has since become a school tradition, and has also served as a guest reader for which he selected a book about marlin fishing and brought equipment for students to see.

"Dr. Fugman was a renowned educator who truly made a difference for all kids," said Principal Sharon Uyeno, who opened the school and still serves there today. "His dedication to academic excellence through high standards provided a blueprint for our rigorous and effective instructional standards-based system at Fugman. His love for the ocean and fishing inspired the naming of our school mascot, the Mighty, Mighty Marlin."

ESTABLISHED: 2004
GRADES: K-6
MASCOT: Marlins
COLORS: Blue, black, silver and white
MOTTO: "Marlins Swim with the Best!"
LOCATION: 10825 N. Cedar Avenue, Fresno
ACREAGE: 16.5

Educational priorities

The school was proud to serve as a charter member of the Clovis North Area when the area was first established in the 2006-07 school year. Once Fugman students complete the sixth grade, they attend the Clovis North Area secondary schools, Granite Ridge Intermediate followed by Clovis North High School.

With the dedication of teachers, parents and students working together to open the school, Principal Uyeno, who transferred from serving as principal of nearby Valley Oak Elementary, had marlin-sized dreams for her new school. "Since opening our doors in 2004, the Fugman Marlins have already established a tradition of exemplary education for all students," she said.

In its first year, Fugman Elementary earned a California Academic Performance Index score of 930, the second highest score earned by a CUSD school that year. Students, parents and staff continue to take pride in their high performance, and each year aim to improve upon their already excellent standards.

Cultural diversity

Involving staff, community and parents in the activities of the school has been a priority for everyone at Fugman Elementary. Programs such as Diversity Day Celebrations, which are organized together by parents, community members and staff, offer an annual cultural fashion show, diversity art lessons and exhibits, music and dance presentations, cultural games, and a food fair representing cuisine from around the world. The programs and events are designed to enhance students' educational experience and offer understanding and unity in diversity.

Fugman Elementary's Mighty, Mighty Marlins continue to be a force to reckon with as they strive to be America's benchmark for excellence in education, through the strength of a cohesive and united community.

> ### Recognized Excellence
> Fugman Elementary has received:
> >> State Distinguished School Award (2008)
> >> California Business for Education Excellence Foundation's Honor Roll School Award (2009)
> >> National Center for Educational Achievement's Just for the Kids Award

JEFFERSON ELEMENTARY SCHOOL

By Charlotte Hutchison

Jefferson School District

Several years before the town of Clovis came into existence, a one-room country school was built on the corner of a wheat field. After a petition was circulated and filed by Joe P. Vincent, the Jefferson School District was established May 6, 1884, by the Fresno County Board of Supervisors. At that time, the Clovis Cole family donated one acre of land on the corner of Shaw and Fowler avenues for the new school site where the school remains today.

In 1884, the new Jefferson School District consisted of 20 sections of land bounded on the north by the present-day Bullard Avenue, and the south by Shields Avenue. The western and eastern boundaries were Peach and Highland avenues respectively.

In an article written by G. M. Reyburn, one of Jefferson's first students, in the June 12, 1952, issue of the *Clovis Independent*, Reyburn recalled how before the Jefferson District was established, "the children in the area had to ride between five and six miles on horseback to attend classes at Garfield, Red Banks, Temperance or Scandinavian schools. The dirt roads were dusty in the summer and muddy in the winter."

A new school is built

Lumber was hauled down from a Tollhouse-area sawmill to build the new one-room, frame building. By the fall of 1884, the new school was still under construction. During the first four months of the term, Jefferson's first teacher, Alice Pratt, conducted classes for 18 students in a dirt-floored washhouse at the home of Charles H. Boucher. Pratt's salary was $560 per year.

The one-room school was completed later that fall. The rustic pine building was 24 feet wide by 36 feet long with a 16-foot ceiling. It had a tongue and groove finished lumber interior, and a cedar shingle roof. In his article, G. M. Reyburn further described the building:

> "There were two entrances; one at each end of the south front; one front window and three windows on each side. Inside the center front was a small library and storeroom. On each side of that, just inside the entrance, small recesses provided cloak and lunchbox space. The blackboards were built-in on the north and east walls.
>
> "A large cast-iron stove in the center of the room, with stove-pipe extending to the terra cotta chimney through the ceiling and roof, was used for heating.
>
> "Old Sol provided lighting, but was supplemented by four kerosene lamps supported on wall brackets. These provided at least some illumination for night meetings.
>
> "The water supply was from a deep well hand pump in a 6-inch well about 50-feet east of the building. Inside, a bucket and dipper provided drinking water during school hours. Not sanitary, but what we didn't know didn't hurt us.
>
> "Lavatories consisted of two earthen pit toilets at the north end of the schoolhouse."

Jefferson's second schoolhouse, built in 1907 in the same location as the original 1884 school house at Shaw and Fowler avenues.

Community hub

The new building faced Shaw Avenue and was the pride of the community. Jefferson was more than just an educational center; it also served some of the recreational and religious needs of the community. Before Clovis was a town, Jefferson was a common meeting place for social events, religious meetings and political events. According to an excerpt from "History Memories — Jefferson Elementary School 1884-1984," "Here, people of the surrounding community gathered for their May Day Festival, the frequent dance, and the Friday night 'Literary Society' meetings. The earliest religious services were conducted by a Methodist circuit preacher."

One of Jefferson's first students, Charlie Reyburn, wrote in his diary about everybody in the community going to Christmas programs at the school. He further described how the whole community came to Jefferson to celebrate Thanksgiving Day where a potluck-style dinner was served on tables created out of sweat boxes and boards.

Alma (Dawson) Lemmon recalled, as documented in "History Memories — Jefferson Elementary School 1884-1984" compiled by Jake Smith, principal of Jefferson Elementary School from 1958 to 1986, "The first movie that we ever saw came to Jefferson. It was done with a Magic Lantern. A very fat man was asleep on a bed and there was a mouse that kept running in and out of his mouth. How we all laughed! And, it only cost 10 cents to see it."

ESTABLISHED: 1884
GRADES: K-6
MASCOT: Blue Jays
COLORS: Blue, white and red
MOTTO: "Try Hard and Never Quit"
LOCATION: 1880 Fowler Avenue, Clovis
ACREAGE: 17

Early enrollment

Historically, Jefferson Elementary served grades one through nine, and early statistics indicated that Jefferson's average daily attendance was 15 students. By 1887, enrollment dropped to 11, and in 1888, the student enrollment was down to 10; which was small enough to put the school in danger of closing. In order to save the school, Alvin R. Cole's two sisters and brother (cousins to Clovis' namesake Clovis M. Cole) moved in with him and attended Jefferson until after the census was taken, thereby raising the enrollment to 17 students. Afterward, the community began to grow, and the number of students increased.

The Clovis Union High School District was established June 27, 1899. The seven participating elementary school districts in the Clovis area — Jefferson, Clovis, Garfield, Red Banks, Mississippi, Temperance and Wolters — were united to the new high school, but they retained their status as separate districts.

When the Enterprise Canal was completed in the late 1890s and agricultural water became available, the Muscat Boom Era was ushered in. During this time, agriculture land was subdivided to grow cultivated crops. New settlers moved into the district, but Jefferson continued to be a one-teacher school until 1902. The following year, a lean-to was added to Jefferson's building to accommodate the influx of students and a second teacher was hired. The school remained a two-teacher school until 1907.

Jefferson's original one-room building and its lean-to annex were too small by 1907. The building was sold and moved off the site to make room for a more up-to-date four-room school with a bell tower complete with a large bell. That same year, the Cole family donated a second acre to be added to the playground, and a third teacher was hired.

The Green Grasshopper

In 1925, a bungalow was built, and a fourth teacher was added to the staff. This was also the year the district initiated bus service to transport the students. A green Model T Ford bus nicknamed "The Green Grasshopper" served the district well into the next decade. During the first year of service, Principal Louise Asplund drove the school bus. The following year, Robert Dalton became the bus driver. Dalton also succeeded Luther Rogers as the school's custodian, caretaker and furnace tender.

By 1944, enrollment at Jefferson had increased to 113 students; that year Hazel Reyburn was principal, and that year was the last for Jefferson to exist as a separate district.

Jefferson Union School District

On May 8, 1945, voters approved the merger of Red Banks School District into the Jefferson School District. On July 1, 1946, the two districts joined to form the Jefferson Union School District. The new district's first year average daily attendance was 134 students and Hazel Reyburn remained as principal.

By 1949, the Jefferson school building was more than 40 years old, and the number of students in the new district continued to grow. A larger building was necessary to accommodate the constant influx of students. The old structure was sold and moved to another location, and a new school was constructed on Jefferson's original site at Shaw and Fowler avenues.

The population around the Clovis area continued to increase rapidly. A third wing of classrooms was added in 1955. During the following five years, more classrooms were added to accommodate the ever-increasing number of students moving into the district.

In 1957, a newcomer by the name of Dr. Floyd B. Buchanan came to town from Walnut Creek to accept the job of superintendent of the Jefferson Union School District. A few months later, he promoted Jefferson's vice-principal, Albert "Jake" Smith, to principal. Smith served as Jefferson's principal for 28 years. When he retired in 1986, he was honored as the district's longest-serving principal.

Student enrollment continued to increase in the Jefferson area, and the district found it necessary to approve an additional school to be built on a second site. The new Tarpey Elementary School, located at 4655 Minnewawa Avenue, was dedicated on October 23, 1958. The Jefferson Union School District office was moved from Jefferson to the new library at Tarpey.

The 1959-60 school year was Jefferson Union School's last year of separate operation; average daily attendance at that time was 830 students. That year, a unification initiative was passed by the voters December 22, 1959, with seven individual school districts in the Clovis Union High School District consolidated to form Clovis Unified School District.

One hundred years

By 1984, the area of the Jefferson District had been reduced to about 7 percent of its original size. Tarpey, Miramonte and Mickey Cox elementary schools, and portions of Dry Creek, Temperance-Kutner, Weldon and Sierra Vista elementary schools were chiseled out of the original Jefferson Union District.

When Jefferson celebrated its centennial year in 1984, enrollment exceeded 780 students. The school had a staff of 25 teachers, a resource specialist, speech therapist, psychologist, a nurse and Smith was in the 25th of his 28 years as principal.

Try Hard and Never Quit – The origin of a motto

In February 1993, Jefferson's new custodian, Sing Houngviengkham, told then-Principal Mike Young about his escape from Laos after the communists gained power. After the fall of Saigon, the Vietnam War ended in April and Laos officially became a communist country in December 1975.

Houngviengkham's first attempt to escape in November of 1980 failed. He and two of his young children were captured. After his family paid a bribe to the guards for his release, Houngviengkham was afraid for his life. His second attempt to leave Laos succeeded, and he crossed the Mekong River into Thailand. His wife and four children followed three weeks later. He brought his family to America in 1981, and settled in the Fresno area in 1984.

When Houngviengkham first inquired about a custodial job at CUSD, he was told he did not qualify because he did not have the proper work permits needed for employment in the United States. In March of 1991, Sing Houngviengkham was sworn in as an American citizen and was later hired by CUSD as a custodian at Jefferson Elementary.

Young was inspired by Houngviengkham's constant pursuit to achieve each of his goals. Three weeks after hearing the story, a banner displaying Jefferson's new motto, "Try hard and never quit," printed in English, Spanish and Hmong, was hung in the cafeteria.

The Jefferson Bell

The epic of Jefferson Elementary would not be complete without telling the story of the Jefferson Bell. It had no identifying marks, and not much information was known about its origin. However, it can be seen hanging in the bell tower in a 1907 picture of the Jefferson School building.

During the construction of the new classrooms in the mid 1950s, it was necessary to take down the Jefferson Bell to accommodate the building process. Buchanan recalled, "There was a house across the street [on the northeast corner of Fowler and Shaw] down the way from here, about a quarter of a mile. The guy that owned it was an insurance agent. And somehow, when Jefferson remodeled, he ended up with the bell. We had to pay him three hundred bucks to get the bell back from him."

In his poem, "An Old Bell Speaks," Principal Smith recounted how the Class of 1963 restored the Jefferson Bell and mounted it on a brick pedestal placed on the front lawn of the school campus.

Twenty-one years later, in 1984, when Jefferson celebrated its centennial year, the bell was dedicated to Smith for his many years of leadership. A bronze plaque was placed on the bell's pedestal to commemorate the event.

The week before the 2007-08 school term began, all of the bronze plaques on Jefferson's buildings were stolen, including the one on the bell. The following year, they were replaced with stone plaques, since stone has no recycling value to thieves.

A significant and symbolic annual event at Jefferson is the long-standing tradition of ringing the Jefferson Bell. On the first day of each new school year, the principal, students, staff, employees, district superintendent and other notables gather on the lawn. The 10-minute ceremony includes singing the national anthem, recitation of the flag salute and ringing the bell. On the last day of each school term the regular bell rings to dismiss classes; afterward the old

Jefferson Bell can be heard ringing across the campus as students head home for summer vacation.

Jefferson News Network

Jefferson is one of the first schools in CUSD to initiate a videotaped student news network, which premiered in September 1991. The Jefferson News Network (JNN) covered a visit by then-President George Bush to Fresno. Additionally, the many prominent citizens interviewed by JNN include: Vice-president Dan Quayle; New Mexico Senator Harrison Schmidt, who was the Apollo 17 Lunar Module Pilot in 1972 and the last astronaut to land on the moon; California Secretary of Education Bill Honig; Olympic Gold Medal Winner John Neighbor; Fresno Mayor Alan Autry; and Fresno State football Coach Jim Sweeney.

Inspiration for naming a new school

Jefferson's most notable teacher, Harold L. Woods, retired in 2001 after teaching at Jefferson for 46 years, all in the same classroom. The school's new library media center was named in his honor. He was also the first teacher in the district to have a school named for him. Harold L. Woods Elementary School located at 700 Teague Avenue opened in the fall of 2005.

Recognized Excellence

Jefferson Elementary has received:

>> National Blue Ribbon Award (1997, 2010)

>> State Distinguished School Award (1987, 1995)

>> California Blue Ribbon Nominee (1992, 1997)

>> California Business for Education Excellence Foundation's Star Schools Award (2009)

>> Title I Academic Achievement Award (2009, 2010)

JOSEPH D. REYBURN
INTERMEDIATE SCHOOL

By Carole Grosch

Three for one

In the late 1990s, a huge crop of subdivisions were sprouting out of the fertile agriculture fields of southeast Clovis. According to CUSD's housing projections, the area was showing great potential for continued growth and schools, including a high school and intermediate school, were going to be needed to house the influx of students.

A successful educational complex had been constructed for the first time in the district in 1991 comprised of Buchanan High, Alta Sierra Intermediate and Garfield Elementary schools all sharing one plot of land. A primary advantage to housing the three schools in close proximity was the ability to provide students a seamless transition through grades kindergarten through 12. Additionally, the three schools would have the advantage of being able to share facilities and grounds.

Clovis Unified opted to replicate the effective educational complex concept with its new school construction in southeast Clovis. A 160-acre parcel of land bordered by DeWolf, Gettysburg, Leonard and Ashlan avenues was selected to serve as the site of the new complex which would become the Reagan Educational Center, or REC.

The Clark and Alta Sierra intermediate students slated to attend the new schools chose the school colors of hunter green, navy blue and silver, and the Timberwolves as their new school's mascot. It was decided that all three Reagan Educational Center schools would share the same colors and mascot in order to ensure an all-inclusive feel.

Of REC's 160 total acres, 55 acres were purchased from the Reyburn family who had farmed the land since the 1870s. The intermediate school would later be named after the family's patriarch, Joseph D. Reyburn.

Origins of a name

Joseph Davidson Reyburn was an adventurer. Born in Des Moines County, Iowa, on December 25, 1840, Reyburn attended log cabin schools and worked a variety of farm jobs before traveling to Oregon with mule teams in 1862.

For the next several years, Reyburn worked as a teamster, homesteader and farmer, and ran a lumber company.

He traveled throughout Nevada and California, arriving in Fresno County in 1881 where he built a house and barn on property near present-day DeWolf and Gettysburg avenues. He became a specialist at dry-farming wheat and barley.

Reyburn was married twice and was the father of 15 children. His first wife, Mary Ella Lester, was the mother of nine children when she died October 7, 1893, just 10 days shy of her 42nd birthday. Her death left Joe with children ranging in ages from one-and-a-half to 19 years old. Four years later, he married Annie Predmore Buckley; they became the parents of six additional offspring. All but two of his 15 children lived to adulthood.

Joe Reyburn was a well-liked and respected member

Joseph D. Reyburn, 1888
Photo Courtesy of Clovis-Big Dry Creek Historical Society

of the community. He served on the first board of trustees for Jefferson School District; was an elder and Sunday school superintendent at his church; director of Red Bank Cemetery Association; built the Enterprise Canal in 1893 with the help of five people; and built a canal in the Garfield District. He died in Pacific Grove, California, in 1914 from pleural pneumonia at the age of 74.

Cornerstone for Reyburn

By September 1999, Reyburn Intermediate was the first REC school to be completed on the 160 acre site. At the time Reyburn opened, Clovis East High School was yet to be finished and adjoining Reagan Elementary School yet to be built. All three sites of entire REC complex represented an investment of $90 million. In the first year the intermediate school was open, Clovis East ninth-graders shared the new campus with Reyburn's seventh and eighth grade students.

A local chapter of the Masonic Lodge conducted the cornerstone ceremony to officially open the school for the 1999-2000 school year. District and elected officials attended the ceremony as well as members of the Reyburn family. A time capsule, to be opened 100 years later, was placed in the cornerstone.

The administration, support staff and teachers were eager to create their own culture at the brand new school. According to Stacy Dunnicliff, Reyburn's first principal, "Teachers who transferred from other schools brought with them the best practices from other sites. By blending and discussing a variety of practices, the teachers at Reagan Educational Center developed a new culture and norms specific to the Reagan Area."

Title I

Reyburn was the first intermediate school in CUSD to be classified as a Title I school, a declaration based on at least 40 percent of the children in the school attendance area or student enrollment being from low-income families. These schools receive Title I funding to be used for programs designed to improve the academic achievement of children from low-income homes.

> **ESTABLISHED:** 1999
> **GRADES:** 7-8
> **MASCOT:** Timberwolves
> **COLORS:** Navy blue, hunter green, silver
> **MOTTO:** "P.A.C.K. Pride – Perseverance, Academic Achievement, Community and Kids First"
> **LOCATION:** 2901 DeWolf Ave., Clovis
> **ACREAGE:** Part of the 160-acre Reagan Educational Center

The funding allowed for innovative programs on the Reyburn campus including the Anywhere Anytime Learning Program, in which every seventh-grader was issued a personalized laptop, enabling teachers to use computers and the Internet as a teaching tool. Due to a change in student demographics, Reyburn is no longer considered a Title I school, but laptop labs and the traditional Laptop Academic Block classes remain.

Best practices

In January 2006, the California Department of Education's School Improvement Office (SIO) visited Reyburn Intermediate to film some of the school's best practices. "We were recommended as being a place rich in best practices by several principals who had visited Reyburn," said Dunnicliff. "Two principals actually cited Reyburn as one of the most valuable resources they had found."

Over a three-day period, the department of education representatives and film crew took footage in six Reyburn classrooms, one department meeting and one team meeting, met with the faculty as a whole for input, and filmed and interviewed six students and 14 individual teachers.

Reyburn, along with 15 other schools in California, was cited in the state document, "Taking Center Stage, Act II," which was released in spring 2007. A link in "Taking Center Stage, Act II," took readers to an online toolkit with videos and voiceovers of the best practices from Reyburn and the other schools.

One of the best practices that interested the SIO was Reyburn's Interdisciplinary Teaming in which teachers are assigned to one of four teams with approximately 370 students, 16 teachers and an administrator in each. These teams, or small learning communities, make it difficult for Reyburn students to "slip through the cracks." Teachers share their best practices, develop common academic vocabulary and use similar methodologies classroom to classroom. To promote collegiality further, teachers are housed in wings based on team assignment.

A second best practice highlighted by the film crew was Strategy Electives, which offer academic support during the regular school day for students who want to gain proficiency in a core subject. The electives include a Math Strategies class and Academic Seminar/Reading Strategies.

The third best practice featured was Reyburn's After-school Intervention Lab, a state-standards specific program focusing on students who are below grade level. The goal of the lab is to teach test-taking strategies as well as break down each standard to catapult students toward achieving proficiency in language, reading and math.

Reyburn Intermediate's unique English Learner program was also explored by the SIO. Specially designed academic instruction in English classes has been developed at the school to target instructional learning and standards based on California English Learner Development Test placement levels. Classes are designed for beginning, early intermediate and intermediate level English learner students, and have had a successful track record for reclassifying English learner students as "Fluent English Proficient."

> ### Recognized Excellence
>
> Reyburn Intermediate has received:
>
> >> School to Watch - Taking Center Stage Model School Award (2010)
> >> CSU Fresno's Bonner Center Character for Education's Exemplary Middle Schools of Character Award (2001, 2005)

Agriculture program

Unique to Reyburn is the McFarlane-Coffman Ag Center. The Ag Center serves both Clovis East High School and Reyburn, giving students the opportunity to be part of a rigorous elective program in agricultural science for grades seven through 12.

The McFarlane-Coffman Ag Center is a comprehensive, state-of-the-art facility offering students real-world hands-on experiences in animal science, plant science, agricultural engineering and environmental/natural resources.

The seventh/eighth grade agriculture elective class is ideal for the hands-on learner. The connection to the agriculture industry gives students the opportunity to be part of the San Joaquin Valley agriculture global powerhouse. Reyburn's interactive ag elective class allows seventh and eighth grade students to build a foundation where the primary focus is premiere leadership, personal growth and career success.

P.A.C.K. Pride

The school motto of "P.A.C.K. Pride" stands for Perseverance, Academic Achievement, Community and Kids first. According to current Principal Barry Jager, who assumed the job upon the departure of Dunnicliff in July 2006, "Character continues to count on our campus. Respecting one another is a priority."

LIBERTY ELEMENTARY SCHOOL

By Carole Grosch

In the late 1980s, it became evident student enrollment was rapidly increasing in the northeast parts of the City of Fresno. Plans were made to build an elementary school on 15 acres at the corner of Liberty Hill Road and Perrin Avenue to house these new students. In recognition of its 1250 East Liberty Hill Road location, the school would be named Liberty Elementary.

The 1986 Clovis School Bond Measure and State Building Program covered the $6.98 million cost of construction of the school. Temple Andersen Moore Architects designed the school and Schaal Lechner Corporation served as the contractor.

Ground breaking

When the school was 70 percent finished, a ground breaking ceremony was held on April 23, 1991. It was the last school ground breaking ceremony in which Dr. Floyd B. Buchanan would participate as superintendent of the Clovis Unified School District before his departure in June 1991.

Construction of the school continued during spring and summer to prepare to open for the 1991-92 school year. The buildings were wood frame with stucco and concrete blocks. The campus consisted of 20 first through sixth grade classrooms, two kindergarten rooms, two special education rooms and a multipurpose room. The administration building held a nurse's office, a library media center, a teachers' workroom and various offices.

The stark new school needed shade trees and a playground. Robert Sanchez, who served as plant manager when Liberty opened, created planters with benches, both scaled to students' height, so they could enjoy sitting in the shade. Arbors had been designed by using steel tubes for columns. He cleaned up the playground, helped to get rooms ready and even organized a place for serving lunch in the hallways, as the multipurpose room was not yet available.

"Teachers were busy preparing their classrooms," he remembered. "My classroom was the whole school."

In the spring of 1991, suggestions were taken for a mascot and school colors from staff, parent club members and students preparing to attend Liberty in the fall. The students voted on the most popular choices collected from the various groups.

"The colors of royal blue and white with Kelly green and silver accents were chosen because of their uniqueness," recalled Liberty's first principal, Carol Putnam. "No other school had them at the time. As far as the mascot, we came close to being Longhorns — but the Skyhawk won out in the end. It was felt that the Skyhawk was a fitting symbol for our school representing the 'freedom' of soaring hawks, native to this part of the valley and would provide a transition to the 'Thunderbirds' of Kastner Intermediate and the 'Golden Eagles' of Clovis West High School."

Principals at the school have included Putnam (1991-2001), Sylvia Borges (2001-2007) and George Petersen (2007-present).

Overflow school

The enrollment at Liberty surged from 495 to more than 700 students during its first four years of operation. During the 1995-96 school year, when nearby Friant Elementary closed and those students transferred to Liberty, it was nearly at full capacity with 710 students. The following year, enrollment dropped to 580 with the opening of Copper Hills Elementary less than a mile away.

The sudden growth early in the school's history presented many challenges. Dedicated teachers were hired and staff members took on extra co-curricular responsibilities. The school was supported by parents who became involved by volunteering as classroom tutors, and serving as activity co-coordinators, library assistants, crossing guards and coaches. A partnership was born, grew and flourished.

"Liberty staff, parents and students worked hard to develop a sense of community and belonging, and were able to form a partnership which supported quality education, held high expectations and were willing to work together in the development of a highly functioning school," said Putnam. "Liberty was strengthened by being an 'overflow' school. Because so many students came from other schools in the area there was never any 'them' and 'us.' Every student belonged and every parent was considered a partner."

ESTABLISHED: 1991
GRADES: K-6
MASCOT: Skyhawks
COLORS: Royal blue, Kelly green, white and silver
MOTTO: "T.E.A.M. Liberty" (Together Everyone Achieves Mastery); "Let Skyhawk Spirit SOAR"
LOCATION: 1250 E. Liberty Hill Road, Fresno
ACREAGE: 15

Supporting students

Principal Petersen reflected on Liberty's future. "For a small school, we have a diverse student body from a unique blend of cultures and socio-economic groups," he said. "Because of the apartments within our boundaries, some children are only here for a year or two, and we want to get them to grow while we can. Our goal is to serve all kids and have 90 percent of the students on grade level in reading and math."

Faculty and staff are fully committed to Liberty's students. To increase instructional opportunities for students, many teachers hold academic interventions before and after school with small groups of students needing extra assistance in various subjects.

Teachers and staff have a family mentality and enjoy working together and also connecting with students through fun educational activities.

The surrounding community takes pride in this neighborhood school, working together with staff and students to prepare for the future. Parents play an integral part in the success of the school, too, noted Petersen. Through parental support, a new computer lab with 25 computers became a reality, as did a document camera, media cart, and LCD projector in every classroom.

"Liberty parents are active in their children's education as evidenced by the personal involvement and participation at school," said Borges. "Parents believe in high standards for their children and the school, and support a challenging academic curriculum, a broad-based co-curricular program, and innovative instructional strategies."

Recognized Excellence

Liberty Elementary has received:
>> National Blue Ribbon School Award (1997)
>> State Distinguished School Award (1995, 2000, 2004, 2009)
>> California Blue Ribbon Nominee (1997)
>> California Business for Education Excellence Foundation's Scholar Schools Award (2009)

LINCOLN ELEMENTARY SCHOOL

By Naoma Hayes and Susan Sawyer Wise

On January 21, 1909, Lincoln District was organized, and a one-room wood school was soon built on present-day Alluvial Avenue between First Street and Millbrook Avenue in Fresno.

The new Lincoln Grammar School, named after President Abraham Lincoln, consisted of one room and one teacher who taught all eight grades. Gertrude Drew gave class lessons to each grade in turn. Eighteen students were enrolled in the school's first year of operation, 1909-10.

There were shelves to store articles of clothing as well as supplies for the students and Mrs. Drew. Mr. Cheney, a music teacher, visited the students once a week with his guitar. Sometime later, the school acquired a piano.

Grapes were the foremost crop grown in the area where Lincoln School was built. Plants had to be replaced as they ceased to produce the required amount of grapes. The discarded grape stumps were efficiently used as burning material in the school's huge cast iron stove.

The school took pride in the hand pump installed for drinking water and washing hands. The outhouse was just that, located outside and at the end of a well-worn path.

One student graduated from Lincoln Grammar School in 1916. By 1921, the graduating class was up to 10.

The Woodpecker School

The 1909 school was called Lincoln Grammar School, but it wasn't long before it had a second name: "The Woodpecker School."

The world was tranquil in the early 1900s; no airplanes, phones or traffic other than an occasional horse-drawn wagon disturbed the peace. So when noisy woodpeckers began their merciless tapping outside the Lincoln students' classroom, the little birds became a significant distraction for the children trying to learn.

> **ORIGINALLY**
> **ESTABLISHED:** 1909
> **RE-ESTABLISHED:** 1979
> **GRADES:** K-6
> **MASCOT:** Lion
> **COLORS:** Cardinal and gold
> **LOCATION:** 774 E. Alluvial, Fresno
> **ACREAGE:** 15

The woodpeckers made holes under the eaves, and stuffed them full of food, until the building was ringed with penetrations. When the noise became unbearable, teachers sent the children out to throw rocks at the birds. Reaction was swift. The birds flew off for a short time, and returned with annoying regularity.

The food the birds stored regularly vanished from their holes. This occurred because often the birds would drill completely through the wood before pushing food into the hole. The food would then naturally fall to the interior floor of the school and be lost to them, swept up and discarded by the janitor.

A fire and a union

The course of Lincoln's history was forever changed Sunday afternoon, October 29, 1944, when the school was destroyed by fire. It was soon discovered in the meter box that one-cent pieces had been substituted for burned fuses, the likely cause of the fire. Damages were estimated at $2,500 ($2,000 for the building, $500 for furnishings).

The loss of Lincoln Grammar School resulted in the school's 34 students relocating to Fort Washington School at Friant Road and Copper Avenue. On March 23, 1945, the two schools officially merged to become the Fort Washington-Lincoln Union District.

All 45 students in the new district attended school at the 1906 Fort Washington School facility. Additional space was needed, so the old Pollasky District schoolhouse in Friant, which had closed in 1944, and barracks from a World War II Pinedale army camp were added on the site of the Fort Washington School.

Years later, on September 3, 1966, the long-gone Woodpecker School was celebrated by its past and present students and teachers who spent an afternoon at the Mesple Ranch in Fresno County. The potluck lunch reunion was all about camaraderie and the opportunity to renew old friendships. Partygoers visited the grounds where their Lincoln School once stood.

Charles B. Garrigus, poet laureate of California from 1966 to 2000, read a poem he penned especially for the occasion:

Salute to the Old Woodpecker School

For Honest Abe our schoolhouse bore
His proper and appropriate name:
For there the children of the poor
With faith in learning hopefully came.
Italians, Slavs, Armenians, too,
At lunchtime showed what each had brought.
The food we freely swapped to chew

Made each of us a melting pot!
The little boys, the big would beg
To let them share their fun and chat:
To flip the knife at mumbley-peg
And sock the ball at one-y-cat!

School on Teague Avenue

In 1956, Fort Washington-Lincoln district voters approved development of a new school at Teague and Millbrook avenues, four miles from the Copper Avenue and Friant Road facility, and just over one mile from where the original Lincoln School once sat.

For a cost of $193,000, William Hastrup designed, and Walker and Walker built the new Fort Washington-Lincoln School at 960 East Teague Avenue. Daniel Langpaap was the principal of the school, a position he held from 1957 until 1977.

Students started at the new Fort Washington-Lincoln School in the 1958-59 school year.

Sometime during the weekend of January 9-11, 1959, the bell that was transferred from the old Fort Washington-Lincoln School was stolen from its place in the new bell tower. The bell was of sentimental value to the people of the district, who had planned to mount it on the new school. In addition, the bell that had once rung at the original Lincoln School had been stored away since the school fire in 1944 and forgotten, leaving the new Fort Washington-Lincoln campus without a bell.

Unification

On December 22, 1959, Fort Washington-Lincoln was one of seven districts to unify to become the Clovis Unified School District. At that time Fort Washington-Lincoln had about 100 students enrolled in grades one through eight.

The decision to unify was not a popular one with voters of the Fort Washington-Lincoln District with 23 voters in the district voting for unification, and 85 against. However, with unification approved by the majority of voters in the other voting areas, Fort Washington-Lincoln became part of the new Clovis Unified School District. Those opposed to unification were concerned that they would incur costs with their area's children going to a big school district. Their concerns proved unnecessary as the community did not have to pay any additional expenses associated with being part of Clovis Unified School District, said Everett G. "Bud" Rank, Jr., who served as trustee of the newly unified district.

With the opening of Clark Intermediate in 1969, Fort Washington-Lincoln's seventh- and eighth-graders attended the new school, leaving the elementary school to serve grades kindergarten through sixth only.

During the 1976-77 school year, additions were made to the school, just after five acres had been added to the site, bringing the grounds to 15 acres. Thirteen new classrooms and a new kindergarten room were added as well as a multipurpose room, library media center, teachers' lunchroom, administrative offices, an outdoor amphitheater and tennis court.

Lincoln Elementary reborn

Despite the additions to Fort Washington-Lincoln, the school was still reaching capacity so planning and work began in 1977 to build a new Lincoln Elementary School, named in honor of and located near the original 1909 school on the northeast corner of Alluvial Avenue and First Street.

As plans for the new school continued, its future student body from Fort Washington-Lincoln was organized in 1979 with Dr. Tom Lutton serving as principal. Until the new school was completed, the more than 400 Lincoln students were temporarily housed one and a half miles away at Pinedale School, which was renamed "Lincoln" during this time, from September 1979 until June 1983.

Lincoln officially re-opened in 1983, thirty-nine years after the fire destroyed the original building, at its permanent site at 774 East Alluvial in Fresno. Unique elements of the facility include a triangular plaza, referred to as "The Lincoln Courtyard," which consists of a grassy area and a raised, concrete stage with a vertical panel containing a depiction of President Lincoln's head, backing the staging area. The courtyard is used for assemblies, presentations, rallies and carnivals.

When students first began at the school, only the kindergarten and administrative offices were completed while the cafeteria and library were under construction. The cafeteria was soon finished, none too soon. "The day the cafeteria was finally done and students could eat their lunch in there was the first time it rained that school year," said Lutton.

> ## Recognized Excellence
>
> Lincoln Elementary has received:
> - National Exemplary School Award (1990)
> - State Distinguished School Award (1997, 2004, 2008)
> - California Blue Ribbon Nominee (1997)
> - CSU Fresno's Bonner Center Character for Education's Virtues and Character Education Award (1996, 1998)

Classroom instruction was held in portables until permanent classrooms were completed for the 1987-88 school year.

Lincoln Elementary and the adjoining Kastner Intermediate School share an athletic field, on which students can play and practice sports.

The school's mascot is the lion for the alliteration of the Lincoln Lions and the colors are cardinal and gold to blend with Kastner's school colors.

PRIDE Academy

Lincoln Elementary sixth grade teachers began a new approach to educating their students in 2006. The teachers developed "PRIDE Academy," a small school within the Lincoln community.

PRIDE Academy, which stands for "Personal Responsibility and Integrity, Devoted to Excellence," is designed to more resemble the intermediate school setting. Sixth grade students have a homeroom, but rotate through the other teachers' classrooms for individualized instruction in the subjects of writing, history and science.

In the spring, students visit Kastner Intermediate, the school the students will attend after graduation from Lincoln Elementary. The innovative approach to teaching and class structure reduces many of the Lincoln sixth-graders' fears about attending intermediate school in the fall.

100 years celebrated

On December 16, 2009, in conjunction with its centennial celebration, the Lincoln community celebrated a little piece of its 100-year history when the original bell used to call kids to school each day from 1909 until 1944 was returned to the school. Current Principal Roann Carpenter presided over the unveiling.

Earlier in the year, the bell was returned to Clovis Unified by the Mesple family who had originally rescued it from the ashes of the school and stored it until a new schoolhouse could be built. Unfortunately, that would not happen until Clovis Unified opened today's Lincoln Elementary School in 1983, by which time those who had rescued the bell were no longer living. The bell was discovered in 2009 by members of the Mesple family, who coordinated its return to Clovis Unified.

A new pedestal was created for the restored bell that could once again be part of Lincoln's history. The bell is now displayed prominently in front of the campus as a reminder of the rich traditions and history of the school.

LUTHER E. WELDON ELEMENTARY SCHOOL

By Linda Robertson

In the late 1940s it became clear that the downtown Clovis building that housed Clovis Grammar School would not be able to withstand many more years of use. At that time, 10 acres of land, located two blocks west of Clovis Grammar, was purchased by the Clovis Elementary District from Lillian Underwood with the intention of building a new school on this property. Until then, the Underwood family had used the land to pasture cattle and grow wild grain.

When the new school was complete, Clovis Grammar's kindergarten through eighth grade students were rerouted to the campus at Dewitt Avenue between First and Second streets in Old Town Clovis. When Sierra Vista Elementary opened nearby in 1953, it was attended by former Clovis Grammar students as well.

Some of the bricks from Clovis Grammar School, which was demolished in 1952, are placed at the front of the current Weldon Elementary School, along with the Clovis Grammar School bell, which serves as an everlasting reminder of the original school.

When Weldon opened in 1949, it had eight classrooms. Permanent additions were made in 1957, and then again in 1999; and today the school houses 31 permanent and temporary classrooms.

Luther E. Weldon

Weldon Elementary School was named for Luther E. Weldon who was born September 7, 1869, in Denton County, Texas, and died on October 24, 1948, in Clovis.

After moving with his family from Texas to Fresno in 1887, and later Clovis, Weldon was employed as an engineer for a flour mill established by the Cates family, and later, as a night engineer working 13-hour days for the Fresno Flume and Lumber Company. He then moved to the Copper King Mining Company for nine years as a construction and shipping superintendent. When the mine closed, he returned to Clovis and went into the building business, buying the Clovis Drayage Company in 1914 from the widow of James Turner, and renaming it the Clovis Dray and Ice Company.

Luther E. Weldon, 1940s
Photo courtesy of Clovis-Big Dry Creek Historical Society

Weldon was a respected business and civic leader. He was highly thought of as a member of the board of trustees for the Clovis Elementary District (from 1912 to 1933) and Clovis Union High School District (from 1924 to 1945), of which Clovis Elementary District was a part. He served as president of the Clovis Union board for several years, as well as clerk for the Clovis Elementary District, which, during his time on the board, was comprised solely of Clovis Grammar School, though Weldon and Sierra Vista elementary schools were later opened by the Clovis Elementary District.

He also served as president of the County Association of School Trustees, and served as city clerk from 1912 to 1920. He was a member of the City Council and performed the duties of mayor from 1939 until his death in 1948.

As a trustee of both the Clovis Grammar School and the high school, Weldon wanted nothing less than the best education possible for the children of his community, and he worked to improve and raise the standards in all Clovis schools.

Transitions

Glenn Reavis was the first principal of Weldon when it opened in 1949. Other principals have included Ralph Lockwood, Tom Lutton, Ed.D., Sue Van Doren, Ed.D., Carl Tomlinson, George Thornburg, Scott Steele and the current principal, Ray Lozano.

Weldon, and the Clovis Elementary District to which it belonged, joined with six other districts to form Clovis Unified School District in 1960.

Kindergartners through eighth-graders were taught at the school from its inception until 1969 when Clark Intermediate School opened less than one mile east of Weldon. Clark was created to teach all Clovis Unified students in grades seven and eight. When Clark opened, Weldon became a kindergarten through sixth grade school. Weldon now teaches approximately

650 to 700 students and offers a preschool program on campus that is operated through Clovis Unified's Child Development Department.

The school's appearance has changed over time as well. "This school has grown over the years," said Lozano. "There was an area originally called the Conservation Acre that had a pond, with plants and birds and trees. It was a large park area, and there are still remnants of it [on campus]. We have a nice amphitheater that's very unique, and a stage that was renovated in 2004." The renovations included a new stage complete with electricity. The original wooden Weldon sign was kept as a backdrop for the amphitheater and a baseball field and more classrooms were added.

> **ESTABLISHED:** 1949
> **GRADES:** K-6
> **MASCOT:** Warriors
> **COLORS:** Black and red
> **MOTTO:** "Once a Warrior, ALWAYS a Warrior!"
> **LOCATION:** 150 Dewitt, Clovis
> **ACREAGE:** 15

Starting with the 1992-93 school year, Weldon, along with Cole, Gettysburg, Miramonte and Tarpey elementary schools, was placed on a year-round, multi-track schedule. It was a difficult and trying time for parents, students and school personnel. The decision to try this change was due to growth; overcrowding; obtaining construction funds from the state that required 30 percent of a district's kindergarten through sixth grade students to be enrolled in year-round education; and a need for a bond measure to pass in order to build a new school.

The year-round experiment lasted two years. Under pressure from dissatisfied parents and the community, the school board voted to return to the traditional schedule. At that time, a school comprised solely of portables opened on the southeast grounds of Clovis High as a site that would temporarily accommodate overcrowding.

Ensign Library Media Center

In April 1994, the library media center moved into a larger building and was dedicated to Gaylord Ensign in honor of his 27 years of teaching at Weldon. He not only oversaw the library, but the Gifted and Talented Education, or GATE, program as well. Even after he retired, Ensign remained in charge of the GATE program for several years. He also was very involved with the Conservation Acre. "He always reminded us that we were trying to show the children how an area would look in its natural state through conservation," said Van Doren.

Traditions

For more than 60 years, Weldon students have proudly worn their school colors of black and red and have boasted the "Warrior" as their mascot.

The close-knit community consists of many second and third generation Weldon students.

A tradition since 1990, Weldon students take to the streets of Old Town Clovis one morning during Red Ribbon Week each October declaring their choice to be drug-free. Weldon's entire campus, joined by the color guard and bands from Clark and Kastner intermediate schools along with guest school and government dignitaries, march through the streets carrying anti-drug signs and then reconvene back at Weldon for an energizing Red Ribbon assembly. Long known as an advocate for saying no to drugs, Weldon was named a National Drug Free School in 1991.

Programs

There are many programs at Weldon that not only provide education and build the character of the students, but add enrichment and enjoyment to their everyday lives. One of these innovative programs is ExCEL, or Excellence: A Commitment to Every Learner. The program, which began in the 2003-04 school year, places students into groups based on their instructional level and academic needs. ExCEL teachers spend a full 60 minutes per day with either one child or a group of students at their determined level of instruction.

In addition to Weldon's teachers participating in the small group instruction, resource specialist program, speech and bilingual instructional assistants as well as student teachers from Fresno State are also involved.

The results have been effective. "ExCEL is the reason we've shown academic gains as never before," said Lozano. "Weldon is performing at higher levels than ever before. Our standardized testing scores are up, and we believe that it is because of our differentiated instruction, giving all children what they need to be successful. We've really personalized it."

An incentive program currently in place at Weldon is the Star program. Focusing on the positive, each time a student excels in class, he or she is rewarded with a Star Ticket. If a student qualifies with exceptional learning and behavior, he or she can earn several Star Tickets and trade them in for prizes.

Another program found on the Weldon campus is ACES (After-school Co-curricular Education and Safety), which meets every afternoon until 6 P.M., and is open to second-through sixth-graders who would benefit from additional academic support, providing them with a nutritious snack, help with homework, organized recreation and academic enrichment. Fresno State teaching fellows teach each grade level to help the children succeed.

Recognized Excellence

Weldon Elementary has received:

>> National Drug-Free Schools Program Award (1991)
>> Title I Academic Achievement Award (2006, 2008)
>> CSU Fresno's Bonner Center Character for Education's Virtues and Character Education Award (1998)

A Title I school: Categorical funds

Because a significant percentage of Weldon Elementary School's population is socioeconomically disadvantaged, the school is designated a Title I school. Weldon Elementary was awarded the California Title I Academic Achievement Award in both 2005-06 and 2007-08 for effectively using its federally issued Title I funding to help all students make significant progress toward proficiency on California's academic content standards. "This demonstrates our commitment to every learner!" said Lozano.

Through its Title I categorical funds, Weldon is able to offer its newsletter, Make-A-Difference, free to all families in English, Spanish and Hmong languages. The effective communication piece provides parents with tips on health topics, advice on how to talk to their child, suggested study habits and information on how to help their children succeed at school.

Weldon is also able to host an annual Reading Night during which students are given free books, and parents are given information on ways to help improve their child's learning and how to use language as an instructional tool at home.

MAPLE CREEK ELEMENTARY SCHOOL

By Carole Grosch

Let the public vote. This was the plan of the governing board when deciding on a name for a new school to be built on the southeast corner of Maple and Teague avenues.

Approximately 180 homes within one-half mile of the school site were sent ballots with name suggestions such as "Discovery" and "Sentinel," as well as a "write-in" alternative. "Maple Creek" won. The name was in recognition of the creeks and streams that once flowed northeast of Fresno in the area around modern-day Maple Avenue, prior to the 1948 completion of the Big Dry Creek Dam and Reservoir, located north of Shepherd Avenue and west of present-day State Route 168.

The Schoenwald-Oba-Mogensen-Ashida-Miller architectural firm designed the school with Schaal Lechner Corporation serving as the general contractor.

Land at the corner of Maple and Teague avenues, which formerly served as a fig grove, was purchased from the California Baptist Foundation and the Janzen family in 1990 to be used for the school. A ground breaking ceremony was held at 10 A.M. on April 21, 1995.

Construction was completed on the Fourth of July 1995. On September 28 of that year, a cornerstone ceremony was conducted by Masonic Lodge #417 in Clovis. A time capsule bearing information on the school, how it was built and how people lived at the time, was placed in the cornerstone, to be revealed 50 years later.

Opening day

Maple Creek consisted of an administration office, library, kitchen, multipurpose room, special education room, two kindergarten rooms and 20 classrooms. As the need arose, two portable units were added.

Ann Lindsey was the school's first principal. She supervised 21 teachers and 10 staff members. "I had a fabulous staff," she recalled. "Every day was a pleasure."

Students who had previously been part of the Liberty, Mountain View and Garfield elementary school boundary areas now comprised the Maple Creek enrollment. When the new school opened on September 5, 1995, more than 480 students were enrolled in kindergarten through sixth grades. Huskies were chosen to be the school mascot; silver, burgundy and hunter green were selected as the school's colors.

Better and better and better

Maple Creek's mission is "to establish an effective educational team of students, parents, educators and community members to direct and facilitate the delivery of exemplary curricular and co-curricular services that prepare individuals to deal successfully with a changing world and become contributing members of society." In its 15 years, the school has consistently honored its mission.

"Maple Creek is truly a treasure!" said current Principal Gina Kismet. "We have a great team of dedicated professionals from the teachers to office staff and all of the support staff. We also have a very supportive parent community and it is that support that undoubtedly contributes to our student success. Partnerships with our parents and students are at the forefront of all decisions, as well as doing what is right for students."

Shannon Lawrence, who served as principal from 2006 to 2009, referred to the concept of the staff, parent community and students working closely together as a model called Maple Creek's "Triangle of Success," which was developed by Rick Watson during his service as the school's second principal. "Together, the 'Triangle of Success' provides a supportive environment in which each student is provided an opportunity to become proficient or advanced in their performance on grade level standards in an engaging, stimulating, safe and respectful environment," she said.

The school also faithfully follows its motto: "Every day, in every way, Huskies get better and better and better."

The staff's approach to teaching has been traditional, open and friendly, with an emphasis on academics and excellence. "Maple Creek strongly believes that academics are why we attend school," recalled Lindsey. "Our goal during those years was to have 100 percent of our students on grade level in reading, math and language. Teachers individualized their instruction to meet the needs of their students, who then set goals and tracked their progress." These standards have continued through all of the school's principals — Rick Watson, who served July 2003 to March 2006, Shannon Lawrence, March 2006 to June 2009 and Gina Kismet, July 2009 to present.

ESTABLISHED: 1995
GRADES: K-6
MASCOT: Huskies
COLORS: Silver, burgundy and hunter green
MOTTO: "Every Day, in Every Way, Huskies Get Better and Better and Better"
LOCATION: 2025 E. Teague, Fresno
ACREAGE: 15

On the forefront of technology

Maple Creek parents have faithfully supported the school financially, a portion of which has been used to purchase needed technology.

It was Lindsey's goal to make Maple Creek a frontrunner in technology. The elementary school was the first in Clovis Unified to have video announcements every morning, the first to connect to the Internet through a wireless system and the first elementary school to have a computer lab with an instructor.

According to teacher Christen Otta who currently oversees the school's computer lab, "Maple Creek's computer program was started in 1999 to give students a good foundation for technology. There is also a comprehensive laptop program for sixth grade students."

Students in grades two through six make weekly visits to the computer lab for technology instruction. Each week, students are recognized for enthusiastic participation, exceptional character, eagerness for learning and outstanding work. These students are then invited to the monthly Computer Lab Hall of Fame gathering which takes place before school in the lab. Here students have free computer time to explore the Internet, take advantage of the Type to Learn program, use the scanner, take digital pictures, play a game or learn something new.

MAC & KIDS

The MAC & KIDS (Multicultural Advisory Committee and Kids Interested in Diversity in School) club was started at Maple Creek by Lindsey and teachers Carol Hensley and Rhoda Woo in an effort to promote awareness and understanding of cultures, ethnicities and disabilities. The club includes parents, staff and students. With the encouragement of Maple Creek staff, the parents have taken ownership of MAC & KIDS by running meetings and organizing events on campus that celebrate diversity. In fact, since the beginning, parents have been the key component of the club, bringing to meetings various clothing, food, traditions and artifacts representative of their own heritage.

Recognized Excellence

Maple Creek Elementary has received:

>> State Distinguished School Award (1998, 2006, 2010)

>> California Business for Education Excellence Foundation's Scholar Schools Award (2009)

>> Cesar Chavez Peace Maker Award (2009)

Over time, the popularity of the very active MAC & KIDS program has grown requiring a change of meeting venue from the library to the multipurpose room in order to accommodate all of the club's participants.

Not only has MAC & KIDS been successful on the Maple Creek campus, it has served as a multicultural educational model for other schools within the district. Elementary schools including Fort Washington, Freedom and Liberty now have their own versions of the MAC & KIDS club.

Peer Mediators

In 2007, more than 70 Maple Creek third through sixth grade students received a two-day training course at California State University, Fresno in peer mediation that assisted them in becoming skillful problem-solvers. The school's first-ever Peer Mediators returned to Maple

Creek to help their classmates solve conflict peacefully. The students worked during recesses in pairs to assist students with communication and strategies for effective interpersonal problem solving. Maple Creek's successful program, still active on campus today, was honored by Fresno State as the recipient of the 2009 Cesar Chavez Peace Maker Award.

MICKEY C. COX ELEMENTARY SCHOOL

By Marjorie M. Allen

School odyssey

Four hundred and twenty students in classrooms at Temperance-Kutner, Fort Washington and Dry Creek elementary schools had to wait patiently for their move to the new suburban Mickey Cox Elementary School. The students were originally intended to start the 1980-81 school year at Cox Elementary, but that plan was thwarted by building glitches.

Five months after the school was set to open, 285 kindergarten through fourth grade students started classes at their new school on February 2, 1981. Four weeks later, they would be joined by 135 fifth- and sixth-graders who were transferred to Cox after the winter sports and musical competition seasons were completed.

When the school opened, students came from a 12-square-mile attendance area bordered by Ashlan, Herndon, Fowler and McCall avenues. Just 10 years later, due to the rapid growth of Clovis combined with the opening of five additional CUSD elementary schools, Cox' original geographic boundaries were decreased by one-third.

The 23-classroom school, including a library, an office and a multipurpose room was designed by Gene Zellmer Associates for a cost of $2,458,000.

Origins of a name

Mickey Cox Elementary School was dedicated on September 27, 1979, at which time appointed Principal Lloyd Harline said, "Our school was named after Mickey C. Cox, a highly respected former long-time administrator in the Clovis Unified School District. He was principal of the Clark Intermediate School at the time of his death on June 3, 1979."

Born in 1934, Mickey Cochran Cox was named by his father, Howard, after Major League Baseball catcher and manager for the Philadelphia Athletics and Detroit Tigers, Mickey Cochran. This is the name on his birth certificate. However, his family called him "C.H." — Charles for his grandfather, and Howard for his father. He was known as Charles Howard and C.H. all through school until he registered for the U.S. Army draft in 1952 when he began going by his birth name of Mickey Cochran.

Mickey Cox was born in Okemah, Oklahoma, on December 15, 1934. He traveled with his parents and siblings to California at the age of 5, settling in the Kerman area west of Fresno where young Mickey Cox started school. Later, the family moved to San Francisco, where most of the relatives worked in the Kaiser shipyards during World War II. After briefly farming in the Clovis area, the family returned to the shipyards before permanently settling in Clovis after the war.

While Mickey was still in elementary school, the Cox family moved to the Clovis area in the late 1940s where his father farmed. He went to Jefferson, Garfield and Clovis elementary schools, and graduated from Clovis Union High School in 1953.

After a two-year stint in the Army, his wife, Ellen, persuaded him to go to college on the G.I. bill. They moved back to Clovis, and Cox enrolled at Fresno City College and never looked back.

He graduated from Fresno State in 1960, where he obtained his teaching credential. Cox began his teaching career at Nelson and Fort Washington-Lincoln elementary schools. He obtained his master's degree in 1970 before becoming an administrator at Clark Intermediate School in 1971. He served as the school's learning director prior to becoming the principal of Clark in 1976. During his academic career at Clovis Unified, he served as teacher, coach, resource specialist, learning director and principal.

Cox was the principal of Clark at the time of his death on June 3, 1979, after undergoing surgery for stomach cancer at a Fresno hospital. His sudden passing saddened his colleagues, the many friends he had in the community, and his family — his daughter, Leslie, was due to graduate from Clovis High School the day after his funeral. As a display of their loss, school officials directed the district's flags to fly at half-staff in memory of Mickey C. Cox.

At the dedication of the school bearing Mickey's name, his brother, Sid, said, "If Mickey Cox could give this school a motto, it would be: 'Work hard, play hard and succeed.'"

Builders' mistake is students' gain

Cox Elementary School's spacious new library was the dream of any school librarian. The library was designed to be half as large as it actually turned out to be. The builders misread the plans and, to Cox's benefit, the library turned out to be the largest in any of the elementary schools. On one side of the library were 5,000 new books, newspapers, magazines and study aids waiting to be opened.

Mickey C. Cox
Photo Courtesy of Clovis-Big Dry Creek Historical Society

On the other side was an array of electronic learning devices for modern media usage. CUSD Superintendent Dr. Floyd B. Buchanan said in a *Clovis Independent* article, "This equipment is absolutely necessary if children are to be given a complete education, preparing them for the world of the future. Cox' library, with its $50,000 worth of books, records, tapes, film strips and other assorted media, is a shining example of the integral part libraries play in Clovis' 'good solid program with no frills.'"

"Damper Song" on a rainy day

Lloyd Harline served as Cox's principal from 1981 to 1989. Tom Schultz, who taught third grade at Cox since it opened until he retired in 2010, reminisced how Harline, when the school was new, would not allow any students off the blacktop when the grass was first planted. As the hybrid Bermuda came up, so did the weeds. He called all the kids into the cafeteria and taught them what a blade of grass looked like and what a weed looked like. Then, for a short time each day, Harline would have the whole school out on the new turf pulling weeds.

On rainy days, Harline would let the teachers take a longer lunch break while he would entertain the students in the cafeteria. He would get up on the stage and lead the entire group in singing and acting out the campfire song, "Damper Song." The kids loved it, Schultz said.

Harline set a precedent that the school still follows in which staff takes a genuine interest in students. He would review all the students' report cards three days before they were given out. He knew every student by name, and would call them over if he saw them on campus to either compliment them or encourage them to do better, based on their report cards.

ESTABLISHED: 1980
GRADES: K-6
MASCOT: Cowboys
COLORS: Blue and grey
MOTTO: "Carpe Diem"
LOCATION: 2191 Sierra Avenue, Clovis
ACREAGE: 15

Upon Harline's retirement in 1989, Superintendent Buchanan described him as "one of the best kid men in the district." The school's library media center was named after him in recognition of his pursuit of excellence in education and dedicated service to Clovis school children.

With Harline's retirement, Colin Hintergardt became principal, serving from 1989 until 1996 when he became principal of the brand-new Cedarwood Elementary, located just one mile east of Mickey Cox. Ken Wulf was Cox Elementary's next principal from 1996 to 2006. Today, Cheryl Floth continues to serve as Cox's principal since assuming the position in 2006.

Renovation

With the passage of Measure A, the 2004 bond measure, monies and matching state dollars in 2005, Cox underwent extensive renovation that included a more spacious front office, teacher work room, library and technology classroom. Also modernized were the office, classrooms, bathrooms and cafeteria. Additionally, the school grounds received some attention with the installation of new sprinkler systems and new landscaping.

During the summer of 2007, the amphitheater area was completely remodeled. Included in the renovation were benches for seating, shade trees, improved landscaping and lighting.

Cox's community

One of the special attributes of the Mickey Cox community is the concept of family. For example, two of Cox's teachers announced their engagement the last morning before one winter break. "They invited the whole community to attend the wedding ceremony in the cafeteria, and the community came," said Schultz.

Overall, Schultz commented, Cox Cowboys and Cowgirls have always been strong in heart. "They stick together all the way through high school. Most of the Cox teachers made it a point to work together and play together, even during off times," he said.

The school's students are also known for serving together. Over the years they have reached out to the community in a variety of ways. For example, during Hintergardt's time at the school he helped develop the school's Adopt a Grandparent program in which kindergartners befriend residents of a local retirement home. During Wulf's period at the school he encouraged students to reach out to others as well by setting an example himself. Whenever there was a need — death, sickness, kids without food or clothing — Wulf was the first to offer help, generously giving everything he could. He served the Mickey Cox community as if he were their father. "A more giving man you'll never meet," said Schultz. Upon Wulf's retirement, the school's baseball field was named after him.

> **Recognized Excellence**
>
> Mickey Cox Elementary has received:
> >> State Distinguished School Award (1998, 2004, 2010)
> >> National Blue Ribbon School Award (1999)
> >> California Business for Education Excellence Foundation's Star Schools Award (2009)

Creating a connection

To keep students and families informed of happenings on campus, the school newspaper, the Pony Express, is sent home to every family.

A long-standing tradition includes the school's administrators sending kids home on Friday to the sound of "Happy Trails to You" playing over the Cox loudspeaker, setting the mood for a great weekend.

MIRAMONTE ELEMENTARY SCHOOL

By Earlene Holguin

The school around which a community grew

When Miramonte Elementary School opened in 1979, the area surrounding the school site was primarily rural. At its start, the largest population of students and parents were comprised of predominantly farm working families.

Growth in the Tarpey area around Fowler and Ashlan avenues spurred the need for Miramonte, the first Clovis Unified elementary school to open since unification in 1960.

While the school was being built, Miramonte's prospective population of approximately 400 students was bused to Pinedale Elementary School, 6.7 miles northwest of Miramonte, during the 1978-79 school year through Miramonte's January 1979 opening.

The school mission has continued to be "a quality educational system providing the opportunity for all students to reach their potential in mind, body and spirit." This ideal has been in place since the first principal, Carl Drow, dedicated the school in 1979 and has continued through principals Ginger Thomas, then Jeanne Hatfield, to current principal since 1995, David Bower, and all their staff.

Pod concept

The campus was designed by Allen Y. Yew and William E. Patnaude, Inc., and constructed by Robert G. Fisher Company for $2.7 million.

One of Miramonte Elementary's most unique attributes is that it was the first Clovis school to be built in the innovative pod concept, which resulted in each grade being taught in its own individual pod. This enabled teachers to build and develop grade levels as a team in close proximity.

Cited as a positive force in the school's continued success is parental support, which the school considers paramount in providing a strong base in student achievement. Each year, a Family Appreciation Day is held in which the school's activities team creates decorations and displays showing parents and families how much they are appreciated at Miramonte.

The Miramonte community is close-knit. "Miramonte truly is a neighborhood school," said Thomas. "Everyone walks to school. It's got such a diverse population and everyone supports one another."

Tiggertown Tigers

Serving kindergarten through sixth grades, Miramonte Elementary School sports colors of orange and royal blue, and boasts two mascots. The Miramonte Mustangs, the mascot adopted at the school's inception by parents, teachers and incoming students is the primary mascot. Its companion motto continues to be "Once a Mustang, always a Mustang."

The second, more informal mascot is the "Tiggertown Tigers" created by Principal Bower, who was inspired by the orange color and energy of the Disney character, Tigger, friend to Winnie the Pooh. Tigger's personality and positive qualities, Bower believed, best represented the theme and the principles espoused by the school's CHARACTER COUNTS! standards.

The school takes pride in the fact that their principal carries a Tigger backpack around the school from which he randomly dispenses "Tigger Treats" to the students. He also sings "Happy Birthday" — in off-key Tigger fashion — to each student on his or her special day.

ESTABLISHED: 1979
GRADES: K-6
MASCOT: Mustangs
COLORS: Orange and royal blue
MOTTO: "Once a Mustang, Always a Mustang"
LOCATION: 1590 Bellaire, Clovis
ACREAGE: 15

The bold orange color has more than defined the school's secondary mascot, it has shaped a school-wide attitude. The orange and blue school colors have come to equate "loud and proud," "continuous improvement" and "personal best." Fridays, or "Big O" (Big Orange) Day, turn the school into a sea of orange when students, staff and visitors proudly sport the school colors.

Year-round

Starting the 1992-93 school year, Miramonte, along with Cole, Gettysburg, Tarpey and Weldon elementary schools, was placed on a year-round, multi-track schedule. It was a difficult and trying time for parents, students and school personnel. The decision to try this change was due to growth; overcrowding; obtaining construction funds from the state that required 30 percent of a district's kindergarten through sixth grade students to be enrolled in year-round education; and a need for a bond measure to pass in order to build a new school.

Ginger Thomas was principal at the time year-round was implemented at the school. "A lot went into it preparing for the change. We needed to educate parents and the community on what year-round was all about. Teachers visited different year-round schools in Fresno Unified to get ideas. It was a challenge getting our brains around the concept," she said. "The community was really good about the change, really embraced it."

The year-round experiment lasted two years. Under pressure from dissatisfied parents and the community, the school board voted to return to the traditional schedule. At that time, a school comprised solely of portables opened on the southeast grounds of Clovis High as a site that would temporarily accommodate overcrowding.

When the program ended, then-Principal Jeanne Hatfield was faced with severe overcrowding. "Miramonte had over 900 students until a portable school of east of Lamonica Stadium at Clovis High was opened," Hatfield said. "The portable school accommodated schools with huge enrollments. Our third-graders were sent there for a period of time to relieve overcrowding at Miramonte. Our teachers went with the students to teach at the portable school, and everyone was bused back for rallies, assemblies, events. I would go to that site to give awards or do teacher observations. The students were still very much a part of the Miramonte campus."

Initiating character

Miramonte was the first CUSD elementary school to develop and implement a full character education program. In 1996, the Miramonte team established a program called "Values in Education" in which a different character trait was emphasized each month. The program was effectively utilized until the district adopted the CHARACTER COUNTS! program in 1996, a national non-partisan character education program that has been included in the district's curriculum. Basic values that are integrated into the program are trustworthiness, respect, responsibility, fairness, caring and citizenship, also referred to as the "Six Pillars of Character."

Today, across the Miramonte campus it isn't uncommon to hear students say that they "MRD" — make right decisions.

Recognized Excellence

Miramonte Elementary has received:

>> State Distinguished School Award (2000, 2006)

>> Title I Academic Achievement Award (2005, 2006, 2009 and 2010)

>> CSU Fresno's Bonner Center Character for Education's Virtues and Character Education Award (1998, 2004)

The Freedom Flag Project

Miramonte Elementary School also connected with world events following the tragic terrorist attacks on the World Trade Center and Pentagon on September 11, 2001. The school participated in the Freedom Flag Project, a competition developed and sponsored by AT&T Broadband to allow children across the United States an outlet and avenue by which to communicate their emotions in the aftermath of the events of 9/11.

For the project, more than 1,000 students representing 17 cities each created artwork on 10-by-10-inch squares expressing what freedom means to them. Once the 42- by 22-foot Freedom Flag, made up of a total of 1,034 decorated squares, was complete in mid-October 2001, it toured the country, stopping at each participating school including Miramonte.

"The project was the driving force in the enhancement of the school's patriotism and solidified their national bond," said Bower. "As a result, the entire school, including faculty and administrative staff, join in the daily morning recitation of the pledge of allegiance."

MOUNTAIN VIEW ELEMENTARY SCHOOL

By Carole Grosch

Beginning the journey up the mountain

Mountain View Elementary's beginnings can actually be traced 2.7 miles southeast from its permanent home at Maple and Alluvial avenues to Clovis Unified's Pinedale Elementary School. During the 1989-90 school year, this temporary location was home to more than 650 Mountain View students while they waited on the completion of their new school.

The Fresno architectural firm of Temple Andersen Moore designed the buildings and construction was completed in September 1990 in time for the 1990-91 school year. Enrollment had grown the summer leading up to that school year, and when the new school facility officially began operation, 843 students filled its classrooms.

Mountain View opened the same year as Fancher Creek Elementary, located about 18 miles to the southeast. "This was part of a series of schools to be built in response to increasing enrollment at both ends of the district," said Mountain View's first principal, Dave Derby.

Enrollment for Mountain View was formed by combining students from Cole, Lincoln and Fort Washington elementary schools. "There was a little bit of a struggle bringing those parents on board at the very beginning," said Derby. "But once the decision was made final, I received a great deal of support from even those who did not want to move. They quickly became a part of something very exciting in opening a new school."

Prior to the official opening, the school's mascot, Golden Bears, was chosen by popular vote of the school community. A contest was held to name the mascot; "Rocky" was the winning name. School colors of royal blue, Kelly green, gold and white were also chosen by vote.

Students, parents and teachers submitted suggestions for the school name, including Golden View, but according to Derby, that name was out of the running quickly as many members of the school community noted that it conjured up images of a rest home. "Mountain View was eventually chosen as our recommendation to give the CUSD Governing Board after a great deal of input from parents and students alike," said Derby. "We were captured by the view of the mountains from the location on Maple and Alluvial and so the name was adopted. At that time there was not much else between us, the foothills, and the Sierra Nevada Mountains."

ESTABLISHED: 1989
GRADES: K-6
MASCOT: Golden Bears
COLORS: Blue, green, gold and white
MOTTO: "Golden Bears Lead with Heart, Spirit and Pride"
LOCATION: 2002 E. Alluvial, Fresno
ACREAGE: 15

The name of Mountain View was adopted "with a challenge that I later gave to the students," said Derby. "That challenge was that when our students left Mountain View, how would they ensure that we would actually be able to see the mountains (from the school campus) twenty years from then? The challenge was perhaps the first 'green' message of their lives. It was a dream and vision of the future."

Derby's vision was to create a place for children where they could be the best they could be, where they could be loved, cared for and challenged. This was to be achieved by staff, parents and students, coming and working together as a community for teaching and learning. A strong emphasis was put on college as a future goal.

A casual get-acquainted meeting, sponsored by the Parent Teacher Club (PTC), was held at Woodward Park in the summer of 1989. Staff and PTC introductions were made, and Derby presented the school theme, "Begin the Journey up the Mountain," highlighting his goals and vision for the school community.

Kid Country

With the completion of the new school buildings, a ribbon-cutting ceremony was held in September 1990 for the grand opening. It was important that students feel Mountain View was a place that was made and built especially for them — Kid Country, as it was to be known. Students were to "climb their own mountain, overcome their own obstacles…and really understand the joy of accomplishment, of challenge, and of excellence." They were excited to have their own "home."

The finished campus had a separate kindergarten building, a multipurpose room and two special education rooms. There were also 20 self-contained classrooms arranged in three groups with each group containing two grade levels. The faculty workroom and library were located in the administration building.

A computer laboratory was an exciting feature of the new school, as it was the first of its kind in the school district. It was called WICAT, named after the company that provided the program, and was used as a diagnostic tool to assess students' levels in math and reading. It operated like a fancy workbook: Once assessed, students were placed into an individualized instruction program and then used spreadsheets at their ability level.

Participation in sports was encouraged. There were courts for basketball, tennis and volleyball, as well as a baseball diamonds and a football/soccer field. After a slow beginning during the first year, Mountain View coaches and student athletes became very competitive. By year three, the Golden Bears began capturing first place rankings in area and district events including volleyball, cross-country, baseball and football. Mountain View would witness the beginning career of David Carr, then a sixth grade student, who went on to star as quarterback of the Fresno State Bulldogs and is now a professional football player with the National Football League.

The official ribbon cutting and cornerstone laying ceremony with members of the statewide Masonic Lodge were held the morning of November 30, 1990. A time capsule, containing school memorabilia, was placed in a cavity behind the school's dedication plaque, and the buildings "dedicated to the young people who are our future." Mountain View's first cheerleaders participated in the ceremony by performing and shoveling dirt for pictures.

Principals

After Derby, only three others have held the role of principal at Mountain View: Kristie Wiens, Ricci Ulrich and the school's current principal, Monica Everson.

Recognized Excellence

Mountain View Elementary has received:

>> National Blue Ribbon School Award (1994, 2001)

>> State Distinguished School Award (1993, 1997, 2006)

>> California Blue Ribbon Nominee (1994)

>> California Business for Education Excellence Foundation's Star Schools Award (2009)

>> CSU Fresno's Bonner Center Character for Education's Virtues and Character Education Award (2000)

PINEDALE ELEMENTARY SCHOOL

By Earlene Holguin

The history of Pinedale Elementary School must start with the history of the community of Pinedale itself. Before its start, the entire area of land on which Pinedale was built was agricultural land, but world and local events would play a big part in shaping this tiny community's history.

In existence from 1921 until 1933, the Sugar Pine Lumber Company developed the Pinedale community to house its many employees. Nestled today in a tiny pocket of northwest Fresno, near the bluffs overlooking the San Joaquin River, the community served as one of the most successful lumber producing communities in the nation. Sugar Pine Lumber was a world-wide company, and sugar pine lumber from the Pinedale mill was shipped across the globe.

The townsite of Pinedale, exclusive of the lumber mill complex, was developed around 1922 by the Gorham Land Company of Santa Monica. Arthur Fleming and Robert Gillis, executives with the Sugar Pine Lumber Company, were noted to have been involved with Gorham. The town was developed to provide housing for the mill's workforce and their families.

Population of the town was estimated to start at 2,500, with numbers projected to grow to 5,000. The majority of the residents were expected to be sawmill workers and support staff.

As a result of the booming logging industry and the growing number of Pinedale residents, the Pinedale School District was formed February 8, 1924, to serve students through eighth grade from portions of the Fort Washington, Bullard, Wolters and Lincoln school districts amidst controversy. Both Bullard and Wolters districts approached the Fresno County Board of Supervisors protesting the new boundaries created by the addition of Pinedale which consequently took students away from their districts. The plea to retain their territory was unsuccessful.

Pinedale's first school, built in 1924, was a two-story wooden structure built approximately three blocks from the current school site at Sugarpine and Spruce avenues in Fresno.

On July 26, 1935, Pinedale District elected to join the Clovis Union High School District, and began sending all of its students to Clovis Union High School for grades nine through 12. Until that time, students could choose between Fresno high schools and Clovis Union High.

In 1952, a new Pinedale Elementary School, which remains today though nearly double its original size, was designed by Ernest Kump, Sr., renowned regional architect, and built by Lewis C. Nelson and Sons for $496,856. The campus included 14 classrooms, plus two kindergarten classrooms and a home economics room, as well as an administrative office, multipurpose room and a library. Replaced by the new school, the original 1924 Pinedale schoolhouse was purchased by a local Catholic church and moved to its grounds.

Fluctuating enrollment

Throughout its existence, Pinedale has seen its enrollment numbers significantly fluctuate.

The community of Pinedale was altered when the Sugar Pine Lumber Company filed for bankruptcy in the early 1930s. The population decreased as unemployment increased and property values plummeted. Property values in the area dropped to a low of $7.50 to $15 per lot. School enrollment waned, but rebounded when the properties of the Sugar Pine Lumber Company were sold at auction to the Pensacola Company of Los Angeles which subsequently sold all the land by 1941 to the Valley Compress Company, once again bringing increased employment in the community.

By 1955, the community needed a second school to accommodate enrollment and built Nelson Elementary School, located approximately one mile west of Pinedale Elementary School. Nelson's initial enrollment in 1957 was composed of students in fourth through sixth grades, with Pinedale Elementary serving grades kindergarten through third, and also seventh and eighth.

> **ESTABLISHED:** 1924
> **GRADES:** K-6
> **MASCOT:** Bald Eagle
> **COLORS:** Red, white and blue
> **MOTTO:** "It's All about Pinedale Pride"
> **LOCATION:** 7171 N. Sugarpine, Pinedale
> **ACREAGE:** 15

"This was unique to Pinedale at that time because classes were departmentalized," said Duane Barker, local historian and retired Clovis Unified administrator, who began his teaching career at Pinedale Elementary in 1958. "Pinedale was structured so that classes, which included math, social studies, English, science and P.E., were taught by different teachers, the students were required to transfer from one room to the other." Barker also added that at that time, seventh and eighth grade boys were required to take a class period of woodshop each day, and girls had to take home economics.

In 1959, residents of the Pinedale District voted to join six other districts in unifying as Clovis Unified School District.

In 1969, Clovis Unified opened Clark Intermediate School and all seventh and eighth grade students in the district began attending the new school. Another change occurred when an expansion of Nelson Elementary was completed in 1976. Both Nelson and Pinedale schools were now able to serve a full complement of kindergarten through sixth grade students.

By 1977, due to a declining enrollment, all of the community's students were consolidated into one school, attending Nelson Elementary. At that time, Pinedale Elementary began housing the Clovis Adult Nursing School for several years. Miramonte Elementary students spent September 1978 through January 1979 at Pinedale while their school was being built. Pinedale next housed Lincoln Elementary students starting in September 1979 until their permanent school was completed in 1983, during which time, Pinedale Elementary was temporarily renamed Lincoln Elementary. In 1983, CUSD's alternative education program inhabited the site until 1984. At the same time, space was leased to Fresno Unified special education classes from 1983 to 1984. It was then used as a second and third grade overflow site for students from Cole, Lincoln and Nelson elementary schools, and later, from Fort Washington Elementary School. At that time, Pinedale Elementary was also a walk-in school for the immediate Pinedale area students in first, second and third grades. In the 1989-90 school year, Pinedale served as a temporary home for the 650 students of Mountain View Elementary as their permanent school at Maple and Alluvial avenues was being constructed. Meanwhile, Pinedale was ready to serve its own students again as of 1989-90. Because Mountain View students were housed at the Pinedale facility at that time, Pinedale's students were rerouted to brand-new Valley Oak Elementary at Champlain Drive and Friant Road for 1989-90. By the 1990-91 school year, Pinedale was open again to house its own students.

> ## Recognized Excellence
>
> Pinedale Elementary has received:
> >> State Distinguished School Award (1997)

Principals who have served at the helm of Pinedale Elementary have included John Reep, Homer Kearns, Carl Drow, Dan Langpaap, Norm McTeer, Janice Davis, Dave Derby, Tom Lutton, Joe Faria, Allan Harris, Rick Talley, Nancy Akhavan and the current principal, Allison Hernandez.

Ambassador Sanchez, Pinedale alumnus

Pinedale Elementary School boasts an alumnus recognized on an international level, Phillip V. Sanchez, who served as a U.S. ambassador to Honduras then Colombia. Ambassador Sanchez, born in Pinedale July 28, 1929, attended Pinedale Elementary School, graduated from Clovis High School, and went on to receive both bachelor's and master's degrees from California State University, Fresno. He received the university's Distinguished Alumnus Award in 1977.

Among other political posts he has held, Ambassador Sanchez served as a trustee for Clovis Unified School District from 1961 to 1963.

Today, he remains a resident and strong supporter of the Pinedale community.

Student, community resources

Pinedale Elementary continues to serve as the hub of its small community. One unique service offered by the school is that it is home to one of only three CUSD Children's Health Centers, which is located on Pinedale's grounds and serves the local community. Services offered include immunizations, tuberculosis skin tests, sports screenings, preschool and first grade physicals, and is a safety net for underinsured and insured children. In addition, there is no charge to Medi-Cal patients for sick visits, complete physical examinations and immunizations.

CUSD's three busy health centers on the campuses of Fancher Creek, Pinedale and Tarpey elementary schools are considered models throughout the state. District officials estimate the district would have an average of more than 2,000 more student sick days per year without treatment provided by the centers.

Pinedale Elementary also benefits from the service of the Neighborhood Resource Center, operated by Clovis Unified, which serves both the Pinedale and Nelson elementary schools and the surrounding community. In addition to after-school tutorial assistance, the Center offers assistance in the areas of medical and dental screenings, emergency food and clothing, and assists with emergency housing. After-school literacy programs for adults, tutorial reading with community volunteer assistance, Book Buddies, and sports programs are also monitored by the Neighborhood Resource Center.

A place in history

Where once the community of Pinedale existed surrounded by agricultural fields, over time the City of Fresno has grown and expanded until Pinedale is now completely surrounded by commercial and residential property within the City of Fresno. This growth has led many to question what is to become of this close knit, small community. On February 6, 2007, the city of Fresno, in part, answered that question when it adopted the Pinedale Neighborhood Plan, ensuring the Pinedale community will stay residential until the year 2025. Newly installed sidewalks in the neighborhood community are evidence of the benefits of that residential plan.

"I Am PInedale"

In 2003, former Pinedale Elementary School Principal Allan Harris wrote "I Am PInedale," the Pinedale pledge which added to the ideals of intellectual growth, and school and community pride and support:

I Am PInedale

PInedale Pride
The "I" is always capitalized. Why?
Because, I am Pinedale.
Say it again!
I am Pinedale.
So, wherever you go,
Whatever you do,
Don't forget,
Pinedale is YOU!

RED BANK ELEMENTARY SCHOOL

By James Benelli

The morning sun brightens the proud campus of Red Bank Elementary School early; it is one of the easternmost schools in Clovis Unified School District.

The modern campus, built in 1991 on Locan Avenue between Shaw and Barstow avenues, bears no hint of the school's rich history that spans more than a century. The original district, known as Red Banks, so named for the color of the soil in the area, was organized August 3, 1874.

E. B. McCabe was Red Banks' first teacher; his pay was three dollars per student per month. The location of the first Red Banks schoolhouse is described in *Public Schools of Fresno County Volume One 1860-1998* as:

> The 1891 Thomas H. Thompson Official Historical Atlas Map of Fresno shows the location of the school on the northeast corner of Sierra and Dockery avenues on land owned by Clovis M. Cole. A photograph of Red Banks, published in the *Clovis Tribune* on December 24, 1915, pictures a small wooden building with a simple front porch. A windmill stands close to the school. In 1915, the teacher was Shirley Price.

The Red Banks District was one of the seven elementary schools to come together in 1899 to back the creation of Clovis Union High School District.

The first documented enrollment numbers show that Red Banks' average attendance in 1904 was 10 students. In 1917, the school lapsed due to low enrollment, but reopened again four years later. The aging Red Banks schoolhouse was rebuilt near Del Rey and Herndon avenues in 1921 through funding from a $15,000 bond issue. Two decades later, enrollment had declined so much that the school closed at the end of the 1943-44 school year.

With the end of World War II, consolidation was a common trend among schools in the Clovis area and in 1945, Red Banks District was annexed into Jefferson District to form Jefferson Union District.

The new Red Banks

The name Red Banks and memories of its school community faded over the years until parents and school administrators in Clovis Unified began planning a new school to be built in the southeastern part of Clovis. In studying the history of the area to be served by the new school, the story of Red Banks was revived, becoming the basis for the new school name. Red Banks Elementary, built at the corner of Locan and Temperance avenues in Clovis, opened in 1991.

The new school was needed to relieve overcrowding at Mickey Cox, Jefferson and Dry Creek elementary schools, and first opened to students in the 1990-91 school year at a portable campus just to the east of Clovis High School. Sue Van Doren, Ed.D., was principal.

> **ORIGINALLY ESTABLISHED:** 1874 (Red Banks District)
> **RE-ESTABLISHED:** 1990 in portables; 1991 in its permanent facility
> **GRADES:** K-6
> **MASCOT:** Bobcats
> **COLORS:** Red and black
> **MOTTO:** "Excellence in Education"
> **LOCATION:** 1454 Locan Avenue, Clovis
> **ACREAGE:** 15

During the first year of operation, the school's office staff commented about the school's name, remarking that answering the phone "Red Banks Elementary School" seemed awkward. "As the year went on, parents and teachers agreed," said Van Doren. "Before we moved to the new campus on Locan, we asked the governing board for permission to change the name to 'Red Bank' and they approved the change."

Ground breaking for the new school was held February 7, 1991. Schoenwald-Oba-Morgensen-Pohll-Miller, Inc. designed the new buildings that were built by DMC Construction, all for a cost of $9 million. When it opened, the school had 24 classrooms, a multipurpose room and an administration building.

The new elementary school was completed later that year. Van Doren and the faculty and staff moved out of their temporary classrooms and into their new school over the Thanksgiving weekend 1991. They all worked together, on their own time, and managed to open to students the following Monday. The beautiful new campus was a welcome change from the crowded temporary classrooms they had been using while the new school was being built.

The staff and faculty bond extended beyond just a working partnership, they were a family. Van Doren guided their enthusiasm, expecting the very best from not only her teachers and staff, but from the parent community as well. Her approach to leading her teachers was simple: Get out of their way, and let them teach. The teachers' dedication to the children and their professional skills combined with love, proved to be an unbeatable combination.

Michelle Steagall, Ed.D., assumed the position of principal in 1997 when Van Doren became assistant administrator for the Buchanan Area schools. With Steagall's departure in 2002, Kevin Peterson became the school's principal, a position he still holds today.

PAWS

Unique to Red Bank is the PAWS program, Promoting Awareness Within our School, designed to inspire under-represented students to excel in leadership, academic achievement and community service. The program, started in 2002, builds awareness of various cultures and promotes understanding of differences between groups.

Cultivating nature

Two innovative programs on campus, the Birds of Prey project and the Eco Center, were created to provide students with hands-on ecological and environmental lessons.

The Eco Center was started in the mid-1990s by then-Student Activities Director Kathy Adolph. She and a group of students volunteered their time after hours and at lunchtime to plant flowers. "The students worked in the Eco Center and around the campus," said Adolph. "We had several large gardens that we maintained and would plant flowers around the campus. We also did composting."

Then-sixth grade teachers Charley Ford and Gayle Peck were instrumental in forming the innovative Birds of Prey program in which, through grants and the aid of a wildlife specialist, injured birds of prey are taken in and sixth grade students nurse them back to health. When the birds are strong enough, the students release them back into the wild. Passing the torch through the generations, each year, the sixth-graders teach the lessons they have learned to the younger children, stressing the importance and responsibility of caring for wildlife.

> ### Recognized Excellence
> Red Bank Elementary has received:
> >> National Blue Ribbon School Award (1994)
> >> State Distinguished School Award (1993, 1997, 2002, 2006)
> >> California Blue Ribbon Nominee (1994)
> >> California Business for Education Excellence Foundation's Scholar Schools Award (2009)
> >> CSU Fresno's Bonner Center Character for Education's Virtues and Character Education Award (2000, 2004)

The school has a flight cage large enough that the recuperating birds have room to fly. If the birds are babies when they are taken in, the students care for them in the classroom until they are strong enough to move to the cage. One bird, a barn owl named Larry, was so badly injured when he arrived at the facility that he was never strong enough to return to the wild, and spent his life at the school, helping to promote the program.

Molten glass reminder

A strong sense of community and support has been a constant at Red Bank. Never was this more evident than in the days following the tragic terrorist attacks on the World Trade Center and Pentagon on September 11, 2001.

That day, Principal Steagall stood in front of the school and met parents as they brought their children to school, the same as she did every day. She gave the parents the option of taking their children out of school for that day, and also said that any parents who wanted to stay at the school with their children would be welcomed. Many did stay to watch the events of the day unfold on television.

Later, at Christmastime, the school community gathered together in appreciation to send hundreds of homemade baked cookies to the New York City Fire Department, as well as to the Clovis Fire Department. The students received a thank-you letter from the fire fighters at Engine House E-37 in New York, along with a piece of molten glass recovered from Ground Zero, and the tangled wreckage of what had been one of the towers. Today, the framed letter and molten glass can be found mounted to the wall of the school's main office as a permanent reminder of how 9-11 touched the Red Bank community.

RIVERVIEW ELEMENTARY SCHOOL

By Carol Lawson-Swezey

Riverview Rams charge to success

When Riverview Elementary opened in August 2002, it was a collaborative labor of love, enthusiasm, and hard work for the students, staff, parents and administration. A diverse stream from Copper Hills, Maple Creek and Garfield elementary schools fed into the pool of students.

Riverview, located on the corner of Chestnut and Behymer avenues just east of Willow Avenue, began with 605 students. Today, it has approximately 750. The school was named for its close proximity to the San Joaquin River. The school's architectural design, created by Darden Architects, was unique to the district in 2002, with 26 classrooms housed in one building with an enclosed hallway. Harris Construction built the school.

"Opening a new school is a labor of love," said Riverview Principal Kristie Wiens, who opened the school. "It took a quality, professional team of educators, working with highly enthusiastic students and supportive parents, all bringing with them great ideas from their former schools and creating new ones as well for Riverview Elementary."

One of the first orders of business was to choose the school colors and mascot. Students were involved in developing a list of choices for both, and then voted. Red, blue and gold were selected as the school colors and Rams as the mascot. During the first year, the Riverview educational team created the school's motto, "Rams Are Charging to Success," and students also came up with another motto, "Rams Rock!"

Educational priorities

Before the new campus opened, the parent advisory board, students and school staff met throughout the summer to create the school's mission statement. It states that "Riverview will provide a quality education through exemplary programs, services and activities that empower all students to maximize their full potential in mind, body and spirit." "We labored over every word," Wiens said.

Since opening the school in 2002, the Riverview community of students, parents, support staff, teachers and community members have been inspired through the challenge to create something special at the campus. Looking back on the last seven years, according to Wiens, the following specific conditions have contributed most to the overall success of Riverview: 1) caring, enthusiastic, dedicated, skilled staff; 2) high expectations and standards for all; 3) a well defined standards-based curricular program; and 4) a strong parent/school partnership. These strengths have grown directly from the needs of the community and a common sense of purpose among students, parents, staff and community members. Riverview serves as a focal point in the lives of children, academically, culturally and recreationally. Since its inception, Riverview has distinguished itself as one of the top-performing schools in CUSD and Fresno County. With a California Academic Performance Index (API) of 934 in 2009, Riverview has demonstrated sustained growth of 97 points in seven consecutive years. Students, parents and staff continue to take pride in their high performance, and each year strive to improve upon their already outstanding results.

ESTABLISHED: 2002
GRADES: K-6
MASCOT: Rams
COLORS: Red, blue and gold
MOTTO: "Rams Are Charging to Success"
LOCATION: 2491 E. Behymer, Fresno
ACREAGE: 17

Going the distance

Riverview students celebrated a major accomplishment in June 2009 when the school's first group of kindergartners graduated from sixth grade. That year, the Riverview Rams dedicated their yearbook to the "Riverview Charter Ram Team," which included 22 staff members and 43 students who were there from the school's beginning in 2002. Each individual was recognized as a "thoroughbred" Ram whose outstanding efforts contributed to Riverview's success. Special Charter Ram Team t-shirts were created displaying the name of each individual. A coveted Charter Ram Team photograph was taken which is now proudly displayed in the Riverview school office. It was an exciting milestone for the Riverview community.

United we stand

"Riverview's strength lies in its solidarity," Wiens said. With Riverview's diversity viewed as a strength, student, parent, staff and community involvement in school activities has been a priority. The Student United Nations of Riverview and the leadership students work collaboratively

Recognized Excellence

Riverview Elementary has received:

>> State Distinguished School Award (2006, 2010)
>> California Business for Education Excellence Foundation's Honor Roll School Award (2007, 2009)
>> CSU Fresno's Bonner Center Character for Education's Virtues and Character Education Award (2004, 2008)

with staff, community members and parents involved in Riverview's Intercultural Diversity Advisory Committee as well as the Parent Teacher Club to plan multicultural events on campus. Activities and events have included cultural presentations and performances, the Passport to Diversity Fashion Show, diverse art lessons and projects, and a multicultural food fair representing cuisine from the seven continents. The events are designed to enhance students' educational experiences to promote tolerance, acceptance and unity in diversity.

"We have a consistent focus on always doing what's best for kids," Wiens said. "We realize our efforts empower all students and maximize their potential."

RONALD W. REAGAN ELEMENTARY SCHOOL

By Marjorie M. Allen

"Grand and great"

"We are the showcase of the future. And it is within our power to mold that future — this year and for decades to come. It can be as grand and great as we make it." This quote from a 1974 speech given by then-California Governor and later U.S. President Ronald W. Reagan, was read by Assistant Superintendent Linda Hauser, Ed.D., at the October 5, 2005, ground breaking ceremony for the new Clovis Unified elementary school to be named in honor of Reagan.

The district's thirtieth elementary school, located on the corner of Ashlan and Leonard avenues, opened in August 2006 to complete the Reagan Educational Center already comprised of Reyburn Intermediate School, Clovis East High School and the McFarlane-Coffman Ag Center. Of the comprehensive K-12 educational center Hauser said, "Here our students will have the opportunity to access a first-class education beginning in preschool through high school graduation."

Reagan Elementary, a neighborhood school which today is nestled between farm houses, orchards, row crops and encroaching subdivisions, occupies 15 acres out of the 160-acre educational center.

Plans for the school were approved at the October 13, 2004, governing board meeting.

Harris Construction served as the contractor while Darden Architects designed the Reagan Elementary School site to make use of some of the existing parking and playfields used at the temporary portable campus housed on the site before the school was built. The portables were located along Leonard Avenue, just east of where Reagan currently sits. The portable school was designed to serve as an overflow campus and had been used by neighboring Freedom Elementary during its first semester of operation in 2003 as the students waited for the completion of their new school. When the portables were vacated by the students, the site was used as a professional development campus until it was removed for the construction of Reagan Elementary. The portables' parking lot is all that remains today, providing convenient parking for visitors attending athletic events on the school's athletic fields, which now sits where the portables were located.

> **ESTABLISHED:** 2006
> **GRADES:** K-6
> **MASCOT:** Timberwolves
> **COLORS:** Navy blue, hunter green and silver
> **MOTTO:** "Reagan Elementary – It's in Every One of Us!"
> **LOCATION:** 8300 E. Ashlan, Clovis
> **ACREAGE:** 15

Busting at the seams

Enrollment projections for nearby Freedom Elementary were expected to top 900 students in the 2005-06 school year. To accommodate the influx of students for that year, portable classrooms were added to the campus until Reagan Elementary opened in 2006-07 only 1.8 miles away. The attendance area for the new school was created within the existing boundaries of Freedom Elementary and parts of Temperance-Kutner and Miramonte elementary schools, and was adopted at the May 25, 2005, CUSD Governing Board meeting with little fanfare, having already been extensively discussed in the community. When the school opened, more than 200 former Freedom Elementary students were part of the newly formed student body.

At Reagan's ground breaking ceremony, Madison Kwalwasser, a Freedom student who would attend Reagan its inaugural 2006-07 school year as a fourth-grader, read the following acrostic she had written in celebration of her new school:

R: *Reagan Elementary School will be the best.*
E: *Exceptional students will ace the tests.*
A: *A new beginning for students and teachers.*
G: *Great fun and learning for all boys and girls.*
A: *All who attend Reagan Elementary School*
N: *Naturally will love it and think it is cool!!!*

Principals

Principal Todd Bennett opened the new school doors to its first students on August 21, 2006. Bennett took over the position in March of that year and devoted his time to staffing the school, ordering curriculum material, as well as supplies, and meeting with Reyburn and Clovis East principals and students to choose school colors and a mascot. Bennett left the district after his first year at Reagan, and Tom Judd assumed his role as the new principal on August 9, 2007. Judd was at Reagan until May 1, 2008, when he took a position as principal of CUSD's Alternative Education Community Day School programs.

Robb Christopherson, Ed.D., who serves as Reagan Elementary's principal today, stepped in upon Judd's departure, determined to create leadership continuity, and to build strong new traditions and a culture of excellence at the school.

Unity

To promote unity among the three schools at the Reagan Educational Center, students in the new Reagan Elementary attendance area recommended adopting the mascot and colors shared by Clovis East High School and Reyburn Intermediate School thus making Reagan's mascot the Timberwolves, with the school colors of navy blue, hunter green and silver.

When the campus first opened, it did not have grass, which would mean nowhere for students to play during their recesses. The problem was soon eliminated when Clovis East offered a portion of its athletic field to the Reagan students.

In 2009, Reagan had the highest growth on state standardized testing in the district, raising its Academic Performance Index score from 816 in 2008 to 855 in 2009. (The state sets 800, on a 1,000-point scale, as the minimum desired API target for all schools to meet.) The school celebrated its growth not only overall, but also in all subgroups comprising its diverse population. This success was a significant factor in the school's receiving its first-ever California Distinguished School Award in 2010.

Recognized Excellence

Reagan Elementary has received:

>> State Distinguished School Award (2010)

Upon being informed that the school was selected for the prestigious honor Christopherson said, "Our Timberwolves deserve the best: the most rigorous curriculum, the nicest facilities, and the most caring and committed adults that education has to offer. This award validates our success in those areas. More than the award itself, however, the real reward comes from the success of our students. They earned this distinction!"

SIERRA OUTDOOR SCHOOL

By Kimberly Sherman

Called to serve

In 1965, as part of his pledge to help the impoverished in America, President Lyndon B. Johnson created the Five Mile Job Corps housed in a sectioned-off piece of land owned by the U.S. Department of Agriculture in Stanislaus National Forest in Sonora, California. The Five Mile Job Corps was designed for men ages 16 to 21 who, while in residence, would be trained in vocational skill sets as they prepared to become productive workers upon their departure.

After a scant four years, the program was disbanded due to lack of funding. In 1970, various agencies turned down the lease of the property, until the site superintendent called a friend at the Fresno County Office of Education and described the positive attributes of the woodsy compound.

The original concept for an outdoor environmental education program was formed, the name was changed to the Regional Learning Center, and a long-term lease was established between the Fresno County Office of Education and the Stanislaus National Forest. From 1970 to 1988, the educational program attracted students from both Fresno and Clovis unified school districts.

A time of transition

With funding an issue in the late 1980s, the lease was offered to a host of agencies. Dr. Floyd B. Buchanan, CUSD's then-superintendent, flew the school board up to the facility on a helicopter. After taking a tour, Buchanan decided the outdoor program was a great learning opportunity and needed to be continued. Concerned about the demise of the Regional Learning Center project and its effect on students, CUSD subleased the property in the fall of 1988. The program was restructured and more marketing was implemented to help foster the school's success.

In December 1988, management of the property was turned over to CUSD employees and the husband/wife team of Jack and Carol Bohan.

Basketball camps, service club retreats and community college programs were among the various organizations that flocked to the picturesque site nestled deep within the forest. The outdoor education program alone served nine to ten thousand Central Valley students in any given school year.

From December 1988 to June 2001, the couple nurtured and enriched the outdoor education program, but management of the property under a lease instead of actual ownership was a barrier to much-needed maintenance and significant physical improvements that were critical to the proper upkeep of the site.

In February 1991, plans were set into motion to obtain ownership of the federal property. But an intense letter-writing campaign and trips to Washington, D.C. to fight for the site were abruptly halted when the first Gulf War efforts took priority. With momentum lost, ownership was not to be at that time.

ESTABLISHED: 1965
LOCATION: 15700 Old Oak Ranch Road, Sonora
ACREAGE: 27.1

Another decade passed and by June 2001, as the Bohans prepared to retire from their positions, the center was showing wear around the edges. The school had been in operation over 30 years and seen more than 300,000 occupants mill through the grounds to spend time in the tawny redwoods; yet had little to show by way of significant maintenance and site improvements.

With the Bohans' departure, Buchanan High School's then-science department chair, Mike Olenchalk, jumped at the opportunity to use nature as a backdrop to teaching instead of his limited classroom laboratory. He took over the position of director, and, today, still serves as head of the facility.

Taking ownership

During President Bill Clinton's administration, the federal Educational Land Grant Act (ELGA) had become available. Dubbed HR 150, the grant allowed for the transfer of land to school districts to be used for educational purposes. The ELGA grant program was in transition, however, proving an obstacle for CUSD. The quest for ownership, again, remained stagnant.

In October 2001, CUSD administration and Olenchalk renewed their determination to fight for land ownership in order to restore the grounds and, again, began wrangling for ownership. With help from sponsor U.S. Congressman George Radanovich and senate co-sponsor U.S. Senator Dianne Feinstein, bill HR 3401, designed specifically for transition of ownership to CUSD, was unanimously approved.

On December 17, 2002, President George W. Bush signed into law the conveyance of 27.1 acres to CUSD.

Moving forward

Olenchalk says that the deed transfer to CUSD "enabled an influx of bond measure money and deferred maintenance money which has allowed us to complete five to six million dollars worth of improvements."

Between 2005 and 2009, all seven dorm facilities were completely renovated. The kitchen dining hall was remodeled and space was nearly doubled to allow seating for 300 guests. A 100,000-gallon water tank was also added for fire suppression.

During this time, the facility was renamed to better reflect its focus. In 2006, the official title was changed from Regional Learning Center to Sierra Outdoor School at Five Mile Creek. Monikers have since arisen: SOS or, as local elementary school students endearingly call it, simply "Sonora," so nicknamed for the town in which it is located.

Today, while most outdoor school facilities are run by county offices of education, CUSD and Los Angeles Unified School District are the only two districts in the state that operate outdoor school facilities. A completely self-funded entity, SOS is accredited through the California Outdoor Schools Association (COSA). This accreditation ensures that the program offered is providing a certain level of quality and that curriculum is aligned to state standards in the sciences.

All told, 31 Clovis Unified elementary schools and nearly 120 other schools throughout California visit SOS each year, along with a variety of other organizations interested in a positive, educational three- to five-day experience surrounded by nature.

Nearly 75 percent of visitors served by SOS come from outside CUSD. The outdoor school serves attendees from counties including San Francisco, Alameda, San Mateo, Marin, Sonoma, Amador, Calaveras, Contra Costa, El Dorado, Fresno, Kings, Madera, Mariposa, Merced, Monterey, Napa, Placer, Sacramento, San Benito, San Joaquin, San Luis Obispo, Santa Clara, Santa Cruz, Stanislaus and Tuolumne. The per-student cost includes meals, lodging and instruction, and may include extras such as beaded necklaces, depending on the teacher's choice of classes. Extra ventures, such as a tour of nearby Mercer Cavern, may cost extra.

With up to five schools attending SOS at any given time, a staff of qualified individuals is the key to a smooth-running facility. The school employs 19 full-time staff members including maintenance, custodial and kitchen employees, naturalists, office staff, and administration, all of whom live just off site. In addition, six to seven naturalist interns help run programs. These interns are college graduates who have generally majored in environmental science or recreation administration. A maintenance worker, two program coordinators and interns live on site.

While other outdoor schools offer a fixed four- to five-day schedule, at SOS each experience is unique in that teachers are given a custom menu of classes to choose from in order to provide their students with an optimum experience. Diana Copeland, Gettysburg Elementary's guidance instructional specialist, has been overseeing her school's sixth grade annual trek to SOS for several years and reiterates that "teachers teach the California content science standards throughout the year and the SOS trip reinforces many of the standards taught in fourth through sixth grades." There are 11 day classes to choose from, each running in three-and-a-half-hour chunks. Afternoon and evening classes round out the immersive schedule, which can last from three to five days, depending on what the attending school chooses for its students.

Class titles include "Talk about Trees," "Wilderness Skills," "Forest Life," "Earth and Beyond," "High Ropes," "People of the Sierra," "Pond Life," "Raptor Conservation," "Rocknazium," "Silent Mile Nature Walk" and "Team Challenge." The SOS teachers use a hands-on, discovery-based approach and offer human relation activities that foster leadership development, team building, and interdependence skills.

Because SOS is a self-funded facility, catering to outside organizations over the summer months is crucial. The grounds are an ideal location for camps, conferences, retreats and meetings. Olenchalk says that they are "trying to navigate the current economic crisis and provide stewardship for this part of the forest."

The benefits of this unique school are many, said Olenchalk. "We have served nearly 400,000 kids," he said. "For school districts to promote SOS and embrace it as a rite of passage for their sixth-graders is incredible."

SIERRA VISTA ELEMENTARY SCHOOL

By Linda Robertson

Sierra Vista Elementary School was built in the early 1950s on land donated by the Underwood family. It was constructed for $240,081 by Lewis Nelson and Sons, based on the architectural designs of Horn and Mortland. The neighborhood school has been located at 510 Barstow Avenue, between Minnewawa and Pollasky avenues, since its inception.

When it opened, Sierra Vista, along with Weldon Elementary, was part of the Clovis Elementary School District. The school was built, in part, to accommodate the growing downtown Clovis community, as well as to replace the aging Clovis Grammar School, which was condemned and dismantled in 1952.

Students attended their first classes at Sierra Vista on September 3, 1953. Pine trees and junipers lined the walkways leading to the 12-room building, with specific offices for the principal, nurse and secretary. There was also a small kitchen that served as a lunchroom for staff and faculty. Cedar trees and crepe myrtles provided additional beauty and aroma to the welcoming grounds.

Originally, Sierra Vista classes consisted of students in kindergarten through eighth grade. However, the number of grades taught throughout Sierra Vista's history has varied based on the needs of the neighborhood. When Clovis Unified School District was established in 1960, Sierra Vista's enrollment was 360 children in kindergarten through sixth grades, with 12 teachers. In 1965, Sierra Vista again began serving kindergarten through eighth grade students, with an enrollment of more than 900 students accommodated by portable classrooms. Because the school was overcrowded, some of Sierra Vista's students in grades seven and eight were bused to nearby Cole Elementary School in the 1968-69 school year. The concern of elevated enroll-ment was alleviated in 1969-70 with the opening of Clark Intermediate School, which taught all CUSD seventh- and eighth-graders. At that time, Sierra Vista reduced its classes to kinder-garten through sixth grades.

Renovation of the playground was completed in 1963, adding fencing, a sprinkler system and baseball backdrops. Ten classrooms, one additional kindergarten, a library, and a teachers' lunchroom were added that same year and the small multipurpose room was renovated to be-come full-size.

In 1997-98, Sierra Vista reached its maximum facility capacity of 587 students. The school underwent major repair and modernization on the first and second grade wings. The library media center doubled in size, and a teachers' workroom was added. In addition, classrooms were wired for five Internet stations.

A new administration building was constructed at Sierra Vista between 2003 and 2006 at the same time the kindergarten rooms were expanded.

Today, after the multiple renovations and additions, Sierra Vista has 20 classrooms, three offices in its administration build-ing, two kindergarten rooms, a music room, a band room, a speech room and a multipurpose room. The campus also housed one of three CUSD Children's Health Centers which was later moved to a much-needed larger facility at Tarpey Elementary in January 2007.

ESTABLISHED: 1953
GRADES: K-6
MASCOT: Vikings
COLORS: Columbia blue and gold
LOCATION: 510 Barstow Avenue, Clovis
ACREAGE: 15

Principals

Bruce Merz was the first principal of Sierra Vista when it opened in 1953. Stu Brown was principal from 1958 to 1960. Daniel Langpaap fulfilled principal duties from 1960-1982, with Tom Lutton in 1966 serving as the only vice-principal Sierra Vista had ever had. Next, Richard Smith, current deputy superintendent for Sanger Unified School District, served as principal. Mike Young was the school's next principal followed by Rick Gold who served in the position for six years, from July 1994 to June 2000. Norm Anderson was principal at Sierra Vista from 2000 to 2001. Jackie Burgan performed the duties of principal from 2001 until she became CUSD's director of child development in June 2007. Cathy Dodd began her term as principal in the fall of the 2007-08 school year, and remains at the helm today.

Go Vikings!

The Viking, a Scandinavian warrior traditionally known for his strength and driving force, was chosen as Sierra Vista's mascot, with the striking colors of Columbia blue and gold giving them motivation and inspiration. Former Principal Langpaap said that when he chose the Viking mascot in 1965, he did so because he liked the alliteration of the "v's" in "Viking" and "Sierra Vista." For 45 years and counting, "Go Vikings!" has been heard throughout the nearby neigh-borhoods of the enthusiastic school.

Originating programs

Two district elementary school events — the elementary school spelling contest and the spring festival of oral interpretation — were originated at Sierra Vista Elementary School and held there for 15 years from 1968 to 1982. The oral interpretation program is still in place at many Clovis Unified schools today.

Sierra Vista has also been innovative in its implementation of Project LEAD, a three-year staff development program that focuses on school reform, consistent instruction, research-based teaching strategies and implanting a self-extending system of improvement. In 2001, Project LEAD earned the school a prestigious Golden Bell Award given by the California School Boards Association.

Recognized Excellence

Sierra Vista Elementary has received:
>> California School Boards Association's Golden Bell Award (2001)
>> Title I Academic Achievement Award (2006, 2007, 2010)
>> California Business for Education Excellence Foundation's Scholar Schools Award (2007)

Celebrating diversity

Sierra Vista proudly embraces the rich cultural diversity in its school and community. The cultural heritage of many diverse ethnicities is celebrated in classrooms throughout the year. These lessons are embedded within the curriculum materials utilized at Sierra Vista. Diversity is recognized and respected as one of the school's greatest strengths. Community outreach is taught to students through the Multicultural Club and the Student Human Relations Council. One way the student groups give to the community is through canned food drives to assist the Salvation Army food pantry.

TARPEY ELEMENTARY SCHOOL

By Carol Lawson-Swezey

Although very little of the original school facility remains today, Tarpey Elementary's slogan could be, "The more things change, the more they stay the same."

For the staff, students and community whose lives have revolved around the neighborhood school, the buildings may have evolved but the school's heart and soul remain the same.

Throughout its history, Tarpey has been family-centered as reflected by the generations of families who have attended the school, the former students now working at the school and a staff who considers one another much more than coworkers; they, too, are family.

A second school for Jefferson Union

In the mid-1950s, with the opening of the area's new North American Aircraft plant just south of downtown Clovis, Jefferson Union Elementary District found itself facing a population boom. To accommodate the growing number of new students crowding Jefferson Elementary, the district built a second elementary school in 1958.

The new school, which opened for the 1958-59 school year, was dedicated on October 23, 1958. It was named after Malcolm F. Tarpey, an Irish immigrant who initially failed in silver mining, but later established a successful ranch in the Clovis area circa 1880, a portion of which later became the site of the new school. Tarpey later became president of the Fresno Irrigation District. The school shares its name with an earlier train depot and Tarpey Village, the school's surrounding neighborhood.

Tarpey Elementary started out with two classroom wings to serve students in kindergarten through fourth grade, with another two wings, the library and administrative building added the following year. At the time, the school had 10 classrooms; today it has 36.

District hub

When Tarpey opened, the Jefferson Union School District office, where Dr. Floyd B. "Doc" Buchanan had been serving as the district's superintendent since 1957, was moved from Jefferson to the new library at Tarpey.

In the 1959-60 school year, Jefferson Union School's last year of separate operation, the district's average daily attendance was 830 students. On December 22, 1959, a unification initiative was passed with six elementary school districts (including Jefferson Union) and Clovis Union High School District consolidating to form Clovis Unified School District. Buchanan would become the new district's superintendent, a role he would hold for 31 years before his retirement in 1991.

Buchanan's office remained at Tarpey, which now served as the district office for the entire Clovis Unified School District. "When Jefferson and Clovis districts unified in 1960, we had to have a place for the district staff and Tarpey was the only location which wasn't used," he said.

The staff of seven employees set up offices in the Tarpey library. After three years, the district office relocated to a remodeled barracks building from Fresno's Hammer Field, which was placed north of the two story building at Clovis High School at Fifth and Osmun streets in downtown Clovis.

Tarpey could never be enlarged to accommodate a more substantial district office because of housing and commercial development springing up around the school in central Clovis.

"We had to do some ingenious things with Tarpey to fit all the equipment in," Buchanan said. "The school was very attractive, with brick facing, and the kids used to go out and pound their erasers against the brick walls to clean them. The chalk dust would get stuck in the crevices."

The district that Buchanan found when he arrived in 1957 bears little resemblance to the district of today. When he first came to Fresno County, students weren't encouraged to read before the first grade and the area had a 40 percent high school dropout rate.

Tarpey was eager to leap to adopt new educational philosophies. Its first-graders made CUSD history as the first group of students as a grade level to make the district's criteria of 90 percent on grade level for reading and math. "That happened around 1970, and that then set a precedent that became an expectation," said Buchanan.

Population explosion

Tarpey's student population has swelled and ebbed over the years, with multiple solutions tried to relieve overcrowding.

In the 1992-93 school year, Tarpey, along with Cole, Gettysburg, Miramonte and Weldon elementary schools, was placed on a year-round, multi-track schedule. It was a difficult and try-

---

ESTABLISHED: 1958

GRADES: K-6

MASCOT: Spartan

COLORS: Red, white and black

MOTTO: "Be the Best That You Can Be"

LOCATION: 2700 Minnewawa, Clovis

ACREAGE: 15

---

ing time for parents, students and school personnel. The decision to try this change was due to growth; overcrowding; obtaining construction funds from the state that required 30 percent of a district's kindergarten through sixth grade students to be enrolled in year-round education; and a need for a bond measure to pass in order to build a new school.

The year-round experiment lasted two years, ending in 1994. Under pressure from dissatisfied parents and the community, the school board voted to return to the traditional schedule. At that time, a school comprised solely of portables opened on the southeast grounds of Clovis High as a site that would temporarily accommodate overcrowding.

During Principal Kevin Peterson's tenure from 1994 to 2001, the state-initiated classroom reduction requirement of 20 students to one teacher resulted in a lack of classroom space to effectively meet the 20:1 ratio. Students in first through third grades were taught in groups of 40 students to two teachers in the same classroom. Portables were brought in until new facilities could be built.

To further accommodate enrollment that was bursting at the seams, the school's entire third grade was bused to a nearby overflow school comprised solely of portables, located on the southeast grounds of Clovis High. Another year, teachers taught double sessions, overlapping between morning and afternoon shifts.

"I remember having to hire seven or eight new teachers," Peterson said. "We pillaged and plundered from the county and other districts to find highly qualified teachers."

With Clovis Unified's consistent enrollment increases over the past 50 years, new CUSD schools have opened and attendance areas have changed. Tarpey's central location has meant numerous boundary changes for its students, with some rerouting to nearby elementary schools and also the secondary schools into which Tarpey feeds. At varying times, Tarpey sixth-graders have advanced to attend Clark Intermediate followed by Clovis High; Kastner Intermediate followed by Clovis West High; Alta Sierra Intermediate followed by Buchanan High (its current track); and Reyburn Intermediate followed by Clovis East High.

A Tarpey-area neighborhood, bounded by Clovis, Shields, Minnewawa and Ashlan avenues, located in the City of Clovis was once a part of the Fresno Unified School District. Residents living in this portion of the City of Clovis, along with an area bounded by Shaw, Peach, East Ashlan and North avenues, had made a decision in the mid-1950s to join Fresno Unified School District. Because of this decision, the neighborhood was not part of the 1959 unification vote to form Clovis Unified. However, as Clovis Unified established its strong academic and co-curricular reputation, residents in this area began to wonder why they weren't a part of the school district that bore the name of their city.

In 1990, residents in the Clovis, Shields, Minnewawa and Ashlan avenue area petitioned to be included in Clovis Unified. Both districts opposed the move: Fresno, because it feared it would set a precedent for neighborhoods to withdraw from the district; Clovis, because it would cause overcrowding at Tarpey. The area's residents were persistent and though it took two years, the area was annexed to Clovis Unified in September 1992.

This move left only the area between Shaw and Winery, and East Ashlan and Peach in the City of Clovis, but not in Clovis Unified. Over the years, residents in this neighborhood continued to wonder why their Clovis address didn't guarantee that their children would attend Clovis Unified schools, and again in 2007, a petition was submitted to the Fresno County Committee on School District Reorganization to move the neighborhood into CUSD. The petition was again opposed by Fresno Unified based on concerns over the negative financial and enrollment impact such a move would have on the district. After initially remaining neutral on the matter, Clovis Unified's Governing Board in 2010 approved a resolution supporting the neighborhood's effort. Facing an uphill battle, residents of the neighborhood saw their petition denied at the local level, and then denied again when they appealed the decision to the state. Today, residents in the neighborhood are considering another attempt to join Clovis Unified.

A lifetime of memories

Like many of the veteran Tarpey teachers, Ann Higgins started her career at Tarpey in 1969 and stayed until her 2004 retirement. The school's library was named after her at that time.

"I loved the community around Tarpey," said Higgins. "I felt like it was a community where I was needed." Higgins still substitutes at the school on occasion. Her sentiments reflect the thread of loyalty and camaraderie which connects those who come and then return through the doors of the 50-year-old institution.

Like Higgins, Debbie Stockle's first teaching job was at Tarpey. She has spent 30 of her 32 years as a teacher at the school. As a novice teacher in 1979, she joined several busloads of other new teachers on a tour of the district.

"Each new teacher interviewed with Doc Buchanan who gave them the pen they signed the contract with," Stockle said. "I remember his parting words were 'Now get out there and sic 'em.'"

Stockle recalls many Christmases when Santa would arrive by a helicopter operated by a local family to distribute candy canes to the excited students.

"The demographics of the area have changed and there are more rentals but the heart is still the same," said Stockle, who retired in 2010.

Heart beats the same

Georgi Leonardo is one of the new kids on the Tarpey block. She has been the librarian for "only" seven years.

"What is unique about our school is how even when its appearance changes, the heart beats the same," Leonardo said. "Same dedication to children and the love of teaching from the staff, same support from the family and community for their children and teachers. I've heard it said by alumni that Tarpey is tough. Tough because there is no silver spoon and if you want to achieve, you must learn."

Leonardo is proud that Tarpey, along with Nelson Elementary, was one of the first schools to use the online version of accelerated reader. Now, all CUSD elementary schools are using the same program. Tarpey also showcased its mentor teachers through the Behind the Glass program, in which new teachers were able to observe veteran teachers through a one-way glass partition.

Recently, the Parent Teacher Club, along with fundraising money, purchased $2,000 worth of books for the library, imprinted with bookmarks honoring the memories of staff members Pam Daw and Mary Gabelica. All who knew the two women speak lovingly of their dedication to the Tarpey community.

Family ties

With over five decades of serving the Tarpey community, the lives of many in the district have intertwined with the school.

Clovis Unified school board member Elizabeth J. "Betsy" Sandoval has served on the district board for 26 out of the last 29 years. She has lived in the Tarpey area for longer than that, and still lives in the home she bought in 1965, where she raised her three children. She was a room mother and parent club president and recalls many afternoons visiting with neighbors outside the school while waiting for her kids.

"Tarpey was smaller and quieter, but it's really not that much different now. I still see parents walking their kids to school and the staff works very hard to ensure the kids get what they need. It's important to have a staff who understands the demographics of their school," Sandoval said. All three of Sandoval's children attended Tarpey and now work for the district.

Stockle also noted the multi-generational nature of the school. "I've been fortunate enough to have taught several generations of families here at Tarpey," she said. "It's always nice when kids return to say I was their favorite teacher and they hope they can be like me."

Tarpey's current Guidance Instructional Specialist Sharron Vermillion also has returned home. She spent her entire elementary school education, from 1968 to 1974, at Tarpey and one of her favorite teachers was Ann Higgins. She remembers Higgins letting the class cozy up to the windows to watch a torrential rain and fourth grade teacher Karen Ramsey reading to the kids in a dim, hot room as they lay their heads, covered with wet paper towels, on the desks with only a swamp cooler for relief.

One of Tarpey's current students lives in the same room in the same house that Vermillion grew up in as a child.

"I remember myself in so many of the situations I see the kids in," Vermillion said. "I love telling kids how the school used to be and reliving their excitement in doing the same things I used to do. I feel so blessed to be back where I started. There's been a lot of history built. Lots of things taught and learned. I've had parents say that it's a choice for staff to be here and they can see that daily."

Golden anniversary

Tarpey commemorated 50 years as a school in the 2008-09 school year. Many of the school's alumni and staff returned to the familiar grounds for the celebration.

"The anniversary celebration was the same day as our school carnival and it was pouring rain but that didn't stop anyone," Stockle said. "All the alumni kept coming out to talk to me and we all got soaking wet."

That was then, this is now

Darrin Holtermann, Tarpey's principal since 2009, joins a long line of leaders who have had to hit the deck running. Other principals have included: Donald Clause (1958-1962), Stu Hof (1962-1965), Clyde Willis (1965-1969), Sidney Belt (1969-1971), Ralph Lockwood (1971-1980), Pete Reyes (1980-1986), Janice Davis (1986-1988), Norman McTeer (1988-1990), Richard Smith (1990-1994), Kevin Peterson (1994-2001), Bryan Wells (2001-2006) and Robyn Castillo (2006-2008).

The school just recently broke the 800 mark on the state's Academic Performance Index, showing a 60 point growth in the past four years. More than 100 students attend the ACES (After-school Co-curricular Education and Safety) program, which offers literacy, academic enrichment and tutoring by teaching fellows from California State University, Fresno.

Serving the community

Always focused on its neighborhood, Tarpey offers family wellness classes, migrant education, Spanish and Hmong literacy (a quarter of the school's students come from homes in which English is not the primary language), a state-of-the-art technology lab and after-school intervention labs. The Clovis police department also sponsors activities during and after school.

"The school is a huge community resource," Holtermann said. "There are people here after school, playing on the playground, and on the weekends, it becomes like a public park, with families having picnics and parties."

Unique to Tarpey is that it is home to one of only three CUSD Children's Health Centers, which is located on the school's grounds and serves the local community. Services offered include immunizations, tuberculosis skin tests, sports screenings, preschool and first grade physicals, and affordable care for sick children without insurance. In addition, there is no charge to Medi-Cal patients for sick visits, complete physical examinations and immunizations.

CUSD's three busy health centers on the campuses of Fancher Creek, Pinedale and Tarpey elementary schools are considered models throughout the state. District officials estimate the district would have an average of more than 2,000 more student sick days per year without treatment provided by the centers.

The tie that binds

The underlying sentiment connecting all who have Tarpey in their blood is the family bond. Everyone agrees that working at Tarpey is more, much more, than just a job.

"The staff among us who stayed there went overboard to be part of the community," said Higgins. "We put in lots of extra hours. It was nothing to have the entire staff still there at 6 P.M. The thing that kept me at Tarpey was that we weren't all separate entities of staff, students and parents, it was a very close cohesive group."

"There's such a sense of family and community," Leonardo added. "No matter what happens, we all pull together. We all have the same common goal: educating the students."

TEMPERANCE-KUTNER ELEMENTARY SCHOOL

By Naoma Hayes and Susan Sawyer Wise

Rural Temperance-Kutner Elementary School is a little bit city and a lot country. Today, T-K boasts the only remaining horse-parking zone in Clovis Unified.

"We are a country school," said current Principal Randy Hein. "We see the mountains and fields from our school. Horses graze in the fields next to us. A big bull guards the south side of the school and looks through our fence at the children. Chickens come on site each morning; red tail foxes and several cats live near or on the campus. A Hmong family grows produce on the north side of our school. We can walk across the street for a basket of strawberries at lunchtime," she explained.

The quiet country school is one of the last in the district to retain the rural nature of its early days, when Temperance Colony merged with Kutner Colony to create a school to meet the needs of both communities.

Temperance Colony School District

Temperance Colony, located in the square bounded by today's Fowler, McKinley, Temperance and Belmont avenues, bore the moral stamp of its developer and one of early Fresno County's most prominent citizens, Moses J. Church (1819-1900), from the name to the character of its inhabitants.

The colony was born in late 1877 when Church, who founded the Fresno Canal and Irrigation Company, sold 20-acre parcels equipped with accessible irrigation. "Temperance" was selected as the name based on Church's insistence that colonists agree to follow other moral and character stipulations as dictated by Church, an Adventist opposed to the consumption of alcohol. Colonists had to agree not to make or sell alcohol and abstain from having alcoholic beverages in their homes. They were allowed to only plant grapes that would be used for the table or for raisins, but never for wine.

The Temperance Colony School District was organized June 12, 1878. The Thompson Official Historical Atlas Map of Fresno 1891 placed the colony's first school at today's Olive and Armstrong avenues, where present-day Temperance-Kutner Elementary School now sits.

Temperance Colony School's average attendance in 1904 was 46 students and 47 the following year. By 1948, the district's last year of separate operation before joining with Kutner Colony School District, enrollment had almost doubled to 85 students.

The Clovis Union High School District was established June 27, 1899. Temperance and the six other participating elementary school districts in the Clovis area — Jefferson, Clovis, Garfield, Red Banks, Mississippi and Wolters — were united to the new high school, but they retained their status as separate districts serving younger students.

A new brick building school with a Mission Revival façade was built in 1912 consisting of two rooms, a belfry and a tile roof. The school replaced the original 1878 facility and was built in the same location. In 1948, the building was condemned upon the discovery of cracks in the walls and was eventually demolished. A temporary 20- by 40-foot school was erected to house students while plans for a permanent facility were underway.

Part of the solution to their student housing problem was solved when Temperance Colony and Kutner Colony formed a union July 1, 1949. A new school located across the street from the original Temperance school was dedicated in April 1950.

Kutner Colony School District

In the late 1880s, families of Danish, German and Swedish descent settled the area around what is today Highland and McKinley avenues in Kutner Colony.

Adolph Kutner (1836-1902) was a local land owner, grain merchant and partner in Kutner-Goldstein and Co.'s general merchandise stores located in Fresno and several other San Joaquin Valley communities. It was one of the largest mercantile businesses in California. He also served as president of the Farmers' National Bank of Fresno and of the Kutner Colony Company.

He left his home of Russian Poland at age 16 for the United States. Upon his arrival in the U.S., he followed various careers and ultimately ended up in Fresno in 1874 where he partnered with Sam Goldstein, a previous acquaintance of Kutner's. He amassed considerable wealth, but donated liberally, helped build Kutner Colony School and establish many churches, and gave to individuals in need.

TEMPERANCE COLONY
ESTABLISHED: 1878
KUTNER COLONY
ESTABLISHED: 1892
TEMPERANCE-KUTNER
ESTABLISHED: 1949
GRADES: K-6
MASCOT: Trojans
COLORS: Royal blue and burgundy
MOTTO: "We Believe We Can and We Will"
LOCATION: 1448 N. Armstrong Avenue, Fresno
ACREAGE: 15

In those days, immigrants like Kutner were banned by law from returning to Russia. He longed to visit his homeland, and the U.S. government stepped in on his behalf so that the Russian law was suspended to allow him to return to his native Russia. But Kutner, a noble man, would not take advantage of any exceptions afforded to him alone, and he died in August 1902 having never returned to his birthplace.

The children of the families of Kutner Colony first attended school in 1891 in a small, one-room wood cabin, but after a fire in the cabin, a new school facility was needed. As relayed in John Allan Dow's *History of Public School Organization and Administration in Fresno County, California*, Kutner Colony student Hans N. Hansen recalled in a *Fresno Bee* article the fate of the wood cabin school: "There were 40 students in the one room until the potbellied stove exploded. Thomas E. Maxwell was the teacher who, along with the pupils, formed a lunch bucket brigade to put out the blaze." Hansen graduated from Kutner School in 1899. He later became a rancher near Kings Canyon Road and served as a trustee of Kutner Colony District from 1910 to 1913.

On February 29, 1892, Kutner Colony School District was established with residents funding a new schoolhouse through a $2,200 bond. The school was situated on land donated by Kutner and was constructed by Fresno contractor John Jasper and residents of the colony. The facility, which boasted double oak doors and a bell imported from an eastern factory, was widely praised. The school opened in September 1892 to the 40 displaced students and their teacher, Mr. Maxwell.

By 1912, enrollment had increased due to Kutner Colony's prosperity, propelling the community to build a new contemporary-style stucco facility. Most notable were the two pronounced arches leading to two separate front doors. Inside were two rooms and a basement. The new school was placed on the same site as the 1892 school which was salvaged and relocated to the far side of the schoolyard where it was used for 40 years as a part-time classroom and community center, even serving as the local Red Cross headquarters, and a location for patriotic meetings and Liberty Bond drives during World War I.

Kutner Colony School District had originally aligned with Sanger High School in an agreement that Kutner graduates would attend Sanger beginning their ninth grade year. However, on February 28, 1928, Kutner shifted to the Clovis Union High School District.

In 1948, county school administrators ordered that the Kutner Colony schoolhouse be abandoned due to damage. During the 1948-49 school year, Kutner's last year of separate operation, nearly 70 students were enrolled with Roberta Winslow serving as the school's last principal.

With both Kutner Colony and Temperance Colony facing student housing problems, it was decided that a unification might be in order. In August 1948, Kutner Colony residents voted 64 to three to unite with Temperance Colony, which became effective as of July 1, 1949.

By 1961, the 1912 Kutner Colony School was reported to have begun crumbling; today neither the 1892 nor the 1912 schoolhouses are in existence.

Temperance-Kutner Union District

With both Temperance Colony and Kutner Colony schools wrought with structural damage, the two districts formed Temperance-Kutner Union District effective July 1, 1949. The two schoolhouses continued to be used until a new school at 1448 North Armstrong Avenue in

Fresno, near the Armstrong and Olive avenues site where the Temperance School was located, was built. The new school was dedicated April 20, 1950. The first principal was Phillip Tomb and enrollment averaged 210 students.

Located on seven acres, the school included 12 classrooms, offices, nurse's station and teachers' lounge. Darden Architects, Inc. designed the school that was built by Lewis C. Nelson for $130,000.

The school bell that was used when the school was first built still hangs in the roof of T-K's old main office building.

With growing enrollment, additional classrooms were constructed in 1953, 1956, 1962 and 1967, the same year a library was added.

Temperance-Kutner Elementary

Temperance-Kutner Union District joined six other individual school districts in the Clovis Union High School District to consolidate to form Clovis Unified School District effective July 1, 1960. At that time the school's name became Temperance-Kutner Elementary School, or "T-K," as it is familiarly known.

Principals who have served at T-K include Lloyd Harline, Terry Allen, Pete Reyes, Cheryl Rogers, Ginger Thomas and, currently, Randy Hein.

Harline, who served as the school's principal from 1962 to 1980, recalled the strength of the families and the staff. "I think my favorite memory was the wonderful people I worked with from the parents to the faculty," he said. "When I started at T-K, the district had recently unified and there were hurt feelings but everyone was very supportive and we came out stronger in the end. It was exciting to be a part of a putting the district together then building it up. Students were expected to achieve and goals were high. It was a very exciting time."

The inclusion of competitive athletic teams for the fourth- through sixth-graders in the late 1960s was also a highlight for Harline. "We hadn't had sports at the elementary level before," he said. "Students had to learn how to win and learn how to lose. The first thing we did was we had to get coaches so we drew from the staff. When we would hire new teachers we would also ask if they could coach. Coaching required extra work, extra hours, but that was the kind of dedication we had. We pulled together to make sure our co-curricular programs worked. It was a neat thing watching sports, academics, the fine arts and other activities take shape. They gave students self-esteem and discipline."

Everyone got involved; Harline even played piano for the students in the choir.

Four-way stop

What could have been a tragedy at T-K turned into a unique civics lesson for T-K students after a 1984 traffic accident. One Saturday evening, a car, driving too fast through the intersection of Olive and Armstrong avenues, plowed into T-K's Room 1.

"Parents were upset, asking what if this had happened during the day," said Allen who was serving as principal at the time. "We ended up making a civics lesson for students out of the incident. We went to local government and pleaded for a four-way stop to prevent any future accidents. We had our stop signs within a week."

Changing demographics, meeting needs

When Ginger Thomas arrived as T-K's principal in 1994, the affluent school's boundaries had just changed. "T-K's demographics changed significantly at that time," said Thomas. "There was a high Hmong population. Bilingual programs were needed and an English as a second language curriculum was introduced. The dynamics were changing and there was tension." Debate was ongoing as to whether separate bilingual classrooms should be created with all English learners together or whether balanced integrated classrooms should exist.

Thomas' priority was unifying T-K families, holding numerous multi-cultural events to promote camaraderie and education.

"We all pulled together and worked together," Thomas said. "It's good to have diversity."

The Temperance-Kutner community was soon unified through its recognition as a National Drug Free School for the 1994-95 school year. "The award really looks at programs and how the school is addressing needs of the community, and the different activities schools do to engage kids. We highlighted our connection with local law enforcement; the sheriff was doing outreach with us. We were working with the community in many ways. Winning this award was a big boost for our community at a time when we really needed it," Thomas said.

With the changing needs of students, T-K has continued to provide programs that best serve its population.

T-K was the first school in the district to offer the English Learner Newcomers Academy for newly immigrated students from Thailand. The program ran for four years. It has also implemented Exceptional English Learner programs.

The Reading Recovery Program includes four trained specialists serving more than 120 students needing reading assistance since the program began. To further help with reading, the school's READ 180 Reading Intervention Lab is adapted from an intensive, nationwide reading intervention program that helps educators confront the problem of adolescent illiteracy and special needs reading on multiple fronts using technology, print and professional development. The program directly addresses individual needs through differentiated instruction, adaptive and instructional software, high-interest literature, and direct instruction in reading, writing, and vocabulary skills.

In early 2007, Clovis Unified was awarded funding to operate after-school programs at seven elementary schools, including Temperance-Kutner. The After-school Co-curricular Education and Safety (ACES) program began in February of that year. The program provides students in grades kindergarten through six with literacy, academic enrichment and safe constructive opportunities from the time they are released from school until 6 P.M. every day.

Participation in the program is on a scholarship basis and is free of charge to participating families. It is considered to be a privilege and attendance is mandatory. Students are able to complete homework as well as experience karate, art, dance, percussion and computers. Participating students must attend three hours per day, five days per week. Enrollment is limited to 120 students.

In 2002, T-K was awarded a Distance Learning Grant for $150,000 to create a technology lab complete with computers, TV monitors, widescreen screens for video projections and other distance learning opportunities.

A sense of community

Many families in the community have seen three or more generations attend T-K, a number of whom have farmed and lived on the land for years.

"They take great pride that their children can come to T-K," said Hein. "Our students are the best. They are kind and respectful. They appreciate having an opportunity to learn and study at a school where so many staff members care about them. T-K takes care of T-K…food baskets, Christmas presents, money, clothing, shoes, books and furniture are available and shared with families in need."

The school's motto, "We believe we can…and we will," reflects the sense of community at T-K. "We have a school pledge to work hard and take care of each other. We say the pledge to open each new school day," said Hein. "When people visit our campus they notice students stand to answer questions in complete sentences. Students greet and shake their teacher's hand before going into class. Everyone says 'hi' to everyone else. On state standardized testing days, our students dress for success. Seeing a student in a suit or party dress on testing days is not uncommon. Those who do not have suits may get a haircut or something else special; they all know it is a special day and dressing for success is something they all can do."

T-K is unique for being the only CUSD school to which all students are bused. Neighborhoods and individual homes sit at a distance from the school which is surrounded by narrow country roads unsafe for pedestrians and bicyclists. Also unique is that T-K currently maintains the highest diversity in student population in the district.

Recognized Excellence

T-K Elementary has received:

>> National Drug-Free Schools Program Award (1995)
>> State Distinguished School Award (2008)
>> Title I Academic Achievement Award (2007)
>> Scholastic's READ 180 All-Star Award Student Winner (2007)
>> Scholastic's READ 180 National Outstanding Educator of the Year (2008)

Secret Garden School

The school offers a variety of activities such as sports, drama, choir, chess club and gardening in which children have planted flowers, bulbs, and even an orchard. "Some of the oldest and grandest trees in CUSD are still thriving at T-K under the care and concern of our Garden Club," said Hein. "T-K is often referred to as the Secret Garden School. Students and staff take great pride in planting flowers and caring for our site. Since I have been at T-K we have added 64 new trees and countless rose bushes, flowers, shrubbery and brick planter areas."

VALLEY OAK ELEMENTARY SCHOOL

By Carole Grosch

Where there were tall oak trees

Beautiful, strong oak trees once grew in the area where Valley Oak Elementary makes its home. The school site sits on the bluff overlooking the San Joaquin River bottom where Valley Oak trees still flourish along the river banks. The majestic trees were an inspiration to the naming committee which submitted to CUSD's Governing Board their recommendation of honoring the trees' symbolic strength, stability, character and endurance through the bold name "Valley Oak." The board voted and agreed to the suggested name.

Due to increasing residential development in northeast Fresno near the popular, upscale Champlain Drive and Friant Road area in the late 1980s, a new school was needed for the growing number of students moving into the new neighborhoods. Octagon of Visalia designed the school and it was constructed at a cost of $6.9 million by Schaal Lechner Corporation. Facilities include 22 classrooms, an administrative office, a multipurpose room, a snack bar and a library media center.

Today, attached to the library, is a computer lab using Thin Client technology, which is a low maintenance, low cost solution to providing student computer labs using a centralized server. Here, students have access to lessons and activities developed by the teachers and a library technician.

In September 1989, with Dick Sparks as Valley Oak's first principal, the school was ready to receive students formerly from Fort Washington Elementary School. Not only was it a memorable year because it was the school's first, it was also the only year students from Pinedale Elementary School were bused to Valley Oak. The Pinedale Elementary facility was being used that year by Mountain View students who were waiting for their permanent school to be built. Valley Oak had the highest enrollment of all district elementary schools that year.

"That was one of the high points of my career," said Sparks. "We were the biggest school in the district after welcoming the Pinedale community; we had about 900 students that first year. I thought the Pinedale students would be thrilled to be at a new school but Pinedale is their school. But it turned out to be wonderful; everyone embraced each other."

One of the first orders of business in establishing Valley Oak's identity was to choose the school colors and mascot. Students helped develop a list of choices for both, and then voted. Columbia blue and gold were selected as the school colors and "Wildcats" as the mascot. When the school opened, the motto was "Wildcats Are Awesome!"

Teamwork

Everyone involved with Valley Oak works together to create a high quality-learning environment where the needs of all students are addressed. Family support plays a key role in high student achievement, as does the dedication of the school's teachers.

ESTABLISHED: 1989
GRADES: K-6
MASCOT: Wildcats
COLORS: Columbia blue and gold
MOTTO: "Wildcats Are Awesome"
LOCATION: 465 E. Champlain, Fresno
ACREAGE: 15

The community surrounding Valley Oak is very much a part of the school's team and is extremely supportive of the school, staff and students. Though Valley Oak's enrollment has consistently been on the smaller side of CUSD schools, students and staff have found great fundraising success — for items such as school supplies, sports equipment, trophies and new technology — through the support of its community.

"The school considers itself a community of learners," said former Principal Sharon Uyeno. "We work as a team with the staff, students and community to optimize student learning potential and do it with high standards. Our school is known historically for its high performance." Other past principals, among them Ken Wulf, Dave Derby, Rosalie Baker and Eimear O'Farrell, and the current principal, Jennifer Watson, have maintained this standard, as have faculty and staff including Karen Doris, Daphne Johnson, Cindy Mortensen and Nancy Swain who have been on staff since opening day.

"As principals, staff and faculty have come and gone one thing has remained constant, that attitude of looking at obstacles, challenges and even opportunities with that 'can do' attitude," said Mortensen. "I think the people that work or have worked or volunteered at Valley Oak have always had the sense that they matter. And really, we all have and do matter! We have mattered to the children, to the parents, to the teachers and staff, to the community, and to each other. Valley Oak Elementary has mattered to many."

One of the focuses of the campus is to help others. During the months of November and December, the Parent Teacher Club (PTC) assists the Student Council in holding drives for food, books, toys and clothes. Throughout the year, members of the PTC work together to provide school supplies, fill technology needs, help coach clubs and athletic teams, answer phones, and anything else that might be needed.

Staff and students also keep each other uplifted. "Laughter is a part of our history and present. Our school is filled by it," said Mortensen. "I think I have laughed every day of my 21 years at Valley Oak and sometimes it was through the tears of a stressful day. Laughter has been an essential ingredient to the recipe of Valley Oak's success. It costs nothing and keeps us all coming back for more."

Cultivating the arts

Valley Oak does not lack for classes in the visual or performing arts. There are opportunities to participate in orchestra, band, choir and an art docent program set up by community volunteers.

In February 1997, Valley Oak was selected as one of 36 schools in the nation, and one of six in the state, that received a combined total of $15 million as part of the Arts Partner Schools effort funded by grants from the Annenberg Foundation, the Getty Education Institute and other private and public sources. Valley Oak's strong emphasis on art prompted teacher Nancy Swain to apply for the grant and was, she said, one of the major reasons the school was chosen to be part of the nationwide, five-year program aimed at improving education through the visual arts.

Valley Oak received $150,000 over the five-year period, with Clovis Unified also contributing $5,000 a year in direct funding and in-kind contributions.

The money was spent on teacher training and curriculum development and supplies. The teachers worked as grade level teams to integrate art education across the curriculum. One year, the teachers focused on making artist boards to accompany the core artists that had been assigned to each grade level. Another year, grade level units were created that centered on the theme "An Enduring Idea." Art textbooks were also purchased for all grades to serve as a teacher resource for the future after the grant had expired. The last year of the grant, a sculpture was commissioned by local artist Margaret Hudson so that the school could have its own piece of public art. The sculpture, which honors the arts in education, stands nearly 30 inches high and depicts three children: one holding a paintbrush, one holding a book and one holding a horn.

Recognized Excellence

Valley Oak Elementary has received:

>> National Blue Ribbon Award (1994, 2001)
>> State Distinguished Award (1993, 2000, 2004, 2008)
>> California Blue Ribbon Nominee (1994)
>> California Business for Education Excellence Foundation's Scholar Schools Award (2005, 2008, 2009)

Valley Oak was later chosen as a partner in conjunction with the Fresno Metropolitan Museum for the Visual Thinking Strategies Program. The intent of the program was to gain input to help create a children's discovery museum in the Fresno area.

CLOVIS UNIFIED SCHOOLS
BY YEAR ESTABLISHED

1866	Dry Creek Elementary	1989	Gettysburg Elementary (opened in portables in 1987)
1869	Fancher School		
1874	Red Banks School	1989	Valley Oak Elementary
1875	Fort Washington Elementary	1990	Fancher Creek Elementary re-established (opened in portables in 1989)
1878	Temperance Colony School		
1883	Garfield Elementary		
1884	Jefferson Elementary	1990	Mountain View Elementary
1887	Letcher	1991	Alta Sierra Intermediate
1892	Temperance Colony School	1991	Liberty Elementary
1895	Clovis Grammar	1991	Red Bank Elementary re-established (opened in portables in 1990)
1899	Clovis High		
1909	Lincoln Elementary		
1911	Friant Elementary	1993	Buchanan High
1947	Dry Creek Elementary re-established	1994	Garfield Elementary re-established
		1995	Maple Creek Elementary
1949	Temperance-Kutner Elementary	1996	Cedarwood Elementary
1949	Weldon Elementary	1996	Copper Hills Elementary
1952	Pinedale Elementary	1999	Reyburn Intermediate
1953	Sierra Vista Elementary	2000	Clovis Elementary (opened in portables in 1999)
1956	Nelson Elementary		
1958	Cole Elementary	2000	Center for Advanced Research and Technology
1959	Tarpey Elementary		
1968	Clovis Adult School	2000	Century Elementary
1969	Clark Intermediate	2000	Clovis East High
1975	Gateway/Alternative Education	2002	Riverview Elementary
1976	Clovis West High	2003	Freedom Elementary
1979	Miramonte Elementary	2004	Fugman Elementary
1980	Kastner Intermediate	2005	Woods Elementary
1980	Mickey Cox Elementary	2006	Reagan Elementary
1983	Lincoln Elementary re-established (opened at Pinedale Elementary in 1979)	2007	Bud Rank Elementary
		2007	Clovis North High
		2007	Granite Ridge Intermediate
1988	Sierra Outdoor School at 5 Mile Creek		

CLOVIS UNIFIED GOVERNING BOARD TRUSTEES SINCE UNIFICATION IN 1960

1960-1961	James B. McCrummen
1960-1961	William B. White
1960-1963	Einar P. Cook
1960-1963	William F. McFarlane
1960-1965	James E. Oliver
1960-1965	F. L. "Kelly" Parks
1960-1974	Everett G. "Bud" Rank, Jr.
1961-1963	Ambassador Phillip V. Sanchez
1961-1973	Alfred P. Biglione
1963-1964	J. D. Eugene "Gene" McGaughy
1963-1975	Ralph J. Lynn
1963-1985	Claude B. Shellenberger
1964-1971	Douglas R. Dresser
1965-1977	Calvin F. Wise, D.D.S.
1965-1987	John E. Coffman
1971-1979	Sara Jane "Sally" Kayser
1973-1981	Mike C. Vuicich
1975-1987	John W. Davis
1975-1989	Gerald G. Walker
1977-1989	Pat V. Ricchiuti, Jr.
1979-1987	Paul C. Anderson
1981-1993, 1996-present	Elizabeth J. "Betsy" Sandoval
1985-1993	Jan M. Biggs
1987-1991	Allen O. Clyde, D.P.M.
1987-1991	Ralph E. Lockwood, Jr.
1987-1991	Richard V. Powers
1989-1990	David J. Daniels
1989-1993	Naomi P. Strom
1990-1991	Christine A. "Kris" Maul
1991-1992	William C. "Clint" Barnes
1991-1996	R. Kent Kunz
1991-2008	Susan M. Walker, D.H.Sc.
1991-present	Ginny L. Hovsepian
1992-2008	Richard P. Lake, C.P.A.
1993-1996	Robert H. Rowley
1993-present	Sandra A. Bengel
1993-present	Jim Van Volkinburg, D.D.S.
1996-present	Brian D. Heryford
2008-present	Christopher S. Casado
2008-present	F. Scott Troescher

PHOTO GALLERY

Clovis Elementary School Afternoon Kindergarten Students, April 17, 1952.
Photo Courtesy of Margaret Beltran

Clovis Grammar School, built in 1918 at Second Street and Pollasky Avenue in downtown Clovis. The building was demolished in 1952. Photo taken circa 1925. *Photo Courtesy of the California History and Genealogy Room, Fresno County Public Library*

Clovis Union High School's first campus. Located on the corner of Fifth and Osmun streets in Clovis, the schoolhouse was financed by a school bond in 1902. The new wooden building opened to students in 1903. Photo taken October 1908. *Clovis Unified School District Archives*

Clovis Unified celebrates 25 years of unification at a gala event at Selland Arena in 1985.
Clovis Unified School District Archives

PHOTO GALLERY

Fort Washington Elementary School, built in 1906 at Friant Road and Copper Avenue. Photo taken circa 1925. *Photo courtesy of the California History and Genealogy Room, Fresno County Public Library*

Fort Washington Elementary School students. Everett G. "Bud" Rank, Jr., who would serve as trustee on the Fort Washington-Lincoln Union District Board and later on the Clovis Unified Governing Board, is pictured in the front row, second from the right. His older sister is in the second row, above Rank's right shoulder. Photo taken in the 1930s. *Photo Courtesy of Everett G. "Bud" Rank, Jr.*

Fort Washington Elementary School, built in 1906 at Friant Road and Copper Avenue. Photo taken in the 1930s. *Photo Courtesy of Everett G. "Bud" Rank, Jr.*

Dry Creek Elementary School, constructed in the 1920s in the town of Academy. Photo taken circa 1925. *Photo Courtesy of the California History and Genealogy Room, Fresno County Public Library*

Kutner Colony Elementary School, built in 1912 near Highland and McKinley avenues. It was the second of two school structures to occupy the site and is no longer in existence. The Kutner Colony District was created in 1892, and was consolidated with the Temperance Colony District to form the Temperance-Kutner Union District, effective July 1, 1949. Photo taken circa 1925. *Photo Courtesy of the California History and Genealogy Room, Fresno County Public Library*

Jefferson Elementary School, built in 1907, was the second schoolhouse constructed at this Shaw and Fowler avenues site. The structure was removed in 1949 when a new campus was built in its place. Photo taken circa 1925. *Photo Courtesy of the California History and Genealogy Room, Fresno County Public Library*

PHOTO GALLERY

Nees Colony Elementary School, built in 1912 at Nees and Armstrong avenues. When Dry Creek District and Nees Colony joined to form Dry Creek Union District in 1947, this schoolhouse was used to educate all the district's students. Photo taken circa 1925. *Photo Courtesy of the California History and Genealogy Room, Fresno County Public Library*

Pollasky Elementary School, built circa 1910 on Friant Road. The structure was later moved to the Fort Washington Elementary School campus at Friant Road and Copper Avenue, where it was destroyed by fire sometime after 1950. Even though both Pollasky organizations (the district had organized twice) were located in the Sierra Union High School District, most of the students attended Clovis High School. Photo taken circa 1925. *Photo Courtesy of the California History and Genealogy Room, Fresno County Public Library*

Students at Red Banks District School, April 13, 1897. *Photo Courtesy of Gene Griffith*

Scandinavian Elementary School, built in 1908 near the intersection of Shields and Sierra Vista avenues. With Scandinavian School District's annexation to Fresno City Unified School District effective July 1, 1960, Scandinavian's 17-square mile district was removed from the new Clovis Unified School District. Photo taken circa 1925. *Photo Courtesy of the California History and Genealogy Room, Fresno County Public Library*

Red Banks Elementary School, located at Herndon and Del Rey avenues. Built in 1921, this was the second campus built by the Red Banks District in roughly the same location. The school was abandoned in 1944, due to a declining enrollment, and its later disposition is unknown. Photo taken circa 1925. *Photo Courtesy of the California History and Genealogy Room, Fresno County Public Library*

BIBLIOGRAPHY

ARTICLES IN PERIODICALS

California School Board Journal:
March 1972

Clovis Free Press, Clovis-Academy Edition:
February 17, 2004

Clovis Independent, Clovis, California:
August 31, 1966
June 1979
February 4, 1981
October 17, 1984
September 19, 1988
November 9, 1988
December 7, 1988
May 31, 1989.
August 9, 1989
October 31, 1990
November 2, 1990
November 23, 1994
October 11, 1995
June 21-27, 2002
February 6-12, 2004
July 16, 2004
August 20, 2004
September 22, 2006

Clovis Tribune, Clovis, California:
April 13, 1917

CUSD Today, Clovis, California:
September 20, 2001
October 5, 2001
October 20, 2001
November 5, 2001
November 20, 2001
December 5, 2001
December 20, 2001
January 20, 2002
February 5, 2002
February 20, 2002
March 5, 2002
March 20, 2002
April 5, 2002
April 20, 2002
May 5, 2002
May 20, 2002
June 5, 2002
June 20, 2002
September 20, 2002
October 5, 2002
October 20, 2002

November 5, 2002
November 20, 2002
December 5, 2002
January 20, 2003
February 5, 2003
February 20, 2003
March 5, 2003
March 20, 2003
April 5, 2003
April 20, 2003
May 5, 2003
May 20, 2003
June 20, 2003
October 20, 2003
October 5, 2004
October 15, 2004
November 15, 2004
March 15, 2005
May 25, 2005
August 20, 2005
October 5, 2005
October 20, 2005
February 5, 2006
February 20, 2006
April 15, 2006
May 20, 2006
June 20, 2006
September 15, 2006
August 20, 2006
October 5, 2006
November 5, 2006
August 5, 2007
August 25, 2007
October 25, 2007
January 15, 2008
August 2008
May 5, 2008
June 2008
November 2008
January 15, 2009
August 20, 2009
September 2009
October 2009
December 2009
January 2010
February 2010
April 2010
May 2010

DramaBiz Magazine, Gillette, Wyoming:
January 2009

Fresno Bee, Fresno, **California:**
November 15, 1939
April 19, 1985
April 23, 1990
July 12, 1990
July 30, 1990
July 31, 1991
September 2, 1993
June 22, 1995
February 9, 1996
February 29, 1996
October 9, 1998
September 17, 1999
January 13, 2000
March 14, 2006
October 15, 2006
November 12, 2007
December 21, 2007

Mountain Press, **Auberry, California:**
December 24, 1986

North News **(Clovis North High Student Newspaper), Fresno, California:**
March 2010

PRNewswire, **Dallas:**
October 19, 2001

San Francisco Chronicle, **San Francisco:**
August 27, 1902

PERSONAL INTERVIEWS
(Telephone, in-person, email)
Allen, Terry. October 12, 2009, April 10, 2010, May 2010.
Amparano, Linda. October 13, 2008.
Anderson, Norm. February 17, 2010.
Andrews, Julie. April 15, 2010.
Archer, Christine. November 17, 2009.
Barker, Duane. May 28, 2008, April 16, 2010, May 2010.
Barkman, Judy. January 4, 2010.
Bass, Bobbie. April 28, 2010.
Bernhardt, Christy. December 2009.
Bishop, Dave. September 22, 2009, March 6, 2010.
Bitter, Annette. November 4, 2010, April 11, 2010.
Blizzard, Devin. December 2009, May 5, 2010.
Borges, Sylvia. July 10, 2008, April 28, 2010, April 29, 2010.
Bos, Peg. October 2, 2007, October 25, 2007, June 18, 2009, April 3, 2010, April 8, 2010.

Bradley, Terry, Ed. D. May 2010.
Brosi, Doris. December 2009.
Buchanan, Floyd, Ed.D. December 6, 2007, July 23, 2008, September 3, 2008, September 15, 2008, February 27, 2009, March 22, 2010, April 5, 2010, May 2010.
Casado, Valerie. December 2009.
Cawthorne, Karen Swartz. January 27, 2010.
Christopherson, Robb. November 2, 2009.
Chute, Alice. August 1, 2007, June 12, 2009.
Coffman, John E. May 28, 2010.
Condley, Diane. February 26, 2010.
Cook, Aaron. June 18, 2009, August 16, 2009, August 25, 2009, August 26, 2009, September 14, 2009, October 29, 2009.
Copeland, Diana. April 16, 2010.
Couchman, Dawn. December 2009.
Cox, Shelby. August 8, 2009, August 20, 2009, September 7, 2009.
Darrow, Rob. May 26, 2010.
Derby, Dave. November 16, 2009, March 9, 2010.
Dias, Ken. May 3, 2010.
Dille, Scott. December 2009.
Dodd, Cathy. April 13, 2010.
Dorrell, Wendi. May 18, 2010.
Dunnicliff, Stacy. January 26, 2010.
Enos, Mary. April 13, 2010.
Erickson, Suzi. December 2009.
Feasel, Shirley. February 19, 2010.
Fey, Michelle. May 2010.
Fisher, Susan. May 18, 2009.
Fritsch, Melissa. February 11, 2010.
Garner, Debbie. February 12, 2010.
Gatzman, Bob. May 12, 2010.
Gray, Anne. June 15, 2009.
Hansen, Chris. April 15, 2010.
Hansen, Robert. November 20, 2009, December 10, 2007.
Hein, Randy. May 25, 2010.
Hernandez, Janet. April 29, 2010.
Hernandez-Serpa, Lupe. October 10, 2007.
Herrera-Facio, Isabel. November 20, 2009.
Higgins, Ann. May 2010.
Hintergardt, Colin. October 16, 2007, October 29, 2007, November 2, 2007, December 3, 2007.
Hirayma, Satoshi "Fibber." October 5, 2009.
Holtermann, Darrin. May 2010.
Houngviengkham, Sing. December 5, 2007.
Hovsepian, Ginny L. May 4, 2010.
Johnson, Phyllis. January 18, 2010.

Judd, Kim. April 19, 2010.

Judd, Tom, September 22, 2009, March 8, 2010.

Kemp, Jodi. February 22, 2010.

Kilburn, Carol. March 17, 2010.

Kismet, Gina. July 21, 2009.

Lane, Candace (Russell). April 10, 2010.

Langpaap, Daniel. February 9, 2008, May 2010.

Lawrence, Shannon. September 2009.

Leonardo, Georgi. May 2010.

Lewis, Carol. September 30, 2008, April 21, 2010, May 24, 2010.

Lindsey, Ann. June 23, 2009.

Lindsey, Dennis and Floyd Buchanan, Ed.D. May 29, 2009.

Linenbach, Carole. May 2010.

Lozano, Ray, January 29, 2010.

Lutton, Tom. April 2010, May 2010.

Lynn, Ralph J. December 16, 2008.

Marshall, Mary Grace. November 30, 2009.

Martin, David. April 9, 2010.

McElhaney, Charlene. February 22, 2010.

McShea, Julie. February 12, 2010.

Mele, Jessica. December 2009, April 29, 2010.

Nax, Natalie. April 17, 2010.

Nitschke, Cliff. April 27, 2010.

Olenchalk, Mike. April 23, 2010.

Oraze, Roger. May 13, 2010.

Otta, Christen. June 1, 2009.

Parker, Erin. January 27, 2009.

Parks, Barbara. September 17, 2009, March 8, 2010.

Parra, Debbie, Ed.D. September 2009, December 2009.

Pena, Susan. May 2010.

Pessano, Dan, February 9, 2010.

Petersen, George. October 5, 2009.

Petersen, Tony. December 2009.

Peterson, Kevin. June 17, 2009, May 2010.

Prandini, Carlo, Ph.D. May 18, 2010.

Putnam, Carol. September 16, 2009.

Rank, Everett G. "Bud." July 30, 2008, July 31, 2008, August 3, 2009, April 15, 2010, May 4, 2010.

Rank, Judy. September 4, 2009.

Rhodes, Ellen. October 9, 2009.

Rodriguez, David. May 23, 2008.

Sample, Tom. December 11, 2007.

Sanchez, Ambassador Philip V. January 19, 2009.

Sanchez, Robert. October 5, 2009.

Sandoval, Elizabeth J. "Betsy." May 2010.

Schmalzel, Ed. April 19, 2010.

Schultz, Tom. August 26, 2009, August 30, 2009, September 16, 2009.

Sells, Pam. December 10, 2007.

Shroyer, Donald, Ed. D. November 17, 2009.

Sieckowski, Marcia. February 23, 2010, March 1, 2010, March 8, 2010.

Simmons, Karen. May 19. 2009.

Smith, Tracy. October 30, 2009.

Sparks, Dick. May 18, 2009, May 17, 2010.

Staebler, Chad. December 2009.

Steagall, Michelle, Ed. D., October 30, 2009.

Steele, Scott, February 1, 2010.

Stockle, Debbie. May 2010.

Stockle, Linda. January 28, 2010.

Swain, Nancy. January 21, 2010, March 10, 2010.

Tiftick, Geoffrey. December 5, 2007, October 23, 2007.

Ulrich, Ricci. January 28, 2010.

Uyeno, Sharon. January 28, 2010.

Van Doren, Sue, Ed. D. October 15, 2009, May 2010.

Vermillion, Sharron. May 2010.

Wagner, Troy. November 16, 2009, December 15, 2009.

Walker, Gerald G.. May 4, 2010.

Watson, Jennifer. December 18, 2009.

Watson, Rick. April 26, 2010.

Weil, Steve. October 6, 2009.

Wells, Melissa. February 9, 2010.

Wetzel, Donna. April 15, 2010.

Wiens, Kristie. December 2009.

Wright, Tom. April 3, 2010.

Young, Janet, Ed.D. May 12, 2010.

UNPUBLISHED MATERIALS

Devorak, George P. *Recollections of a Big White School by a Student 1913 to 1921*, Unpublished.

Hill, Elaine. *History Memories – Jefferson Elementary School 1884-1984*, "The Jefferson Story." Editors Jean Andreis Berry and Georgette Andreis. Unpublished, 1984, p. 21-24.

Ikeda, Dale. "Remembering Pinedale and Ambassador Phillip V. Sanchez." Unpublished, 2009.

Lemmon, Alma Dawson. *History Memories – Jefferson Elementary School 1884-1984*, "Jefferson Remembered." Editors Jean Andreis Berry and Georgette Andreis. Unpublished, 1984, p.13-15.

Reyburn, Glenn William. "Biography of Joseph Davidson Reyburn." July 1952.

Reyburn, G. M. *History Memories – Jefferson Elementary School 1884-1984*, "Jefferson School Was Established in 1884." Editors Jean Andreis Berry and Georgette Andreis. Unpublished, 1984, p. 4-10.

Smith, Albert D. *History Memories – Jefferson Elementary School 1884-1984*, "An Old Bell Speaks." Editors Jean Andreis Berry and Georgette Andreis. Unpublished, 1984, p. 2-3.

BOOKS

Atkin, William T. and Malcolm Johnson. *The History of Clovis: 50 Years of Progress.* Clovis, CA: M. Johnson, 1962.

Clough, Charles W., et al. *Fresno County in the 20th Century, Vol. II.* Fresno, CA: Panorama West Books, 1986.

Dow, John Allan. *History of Public School Organization and Administration in Fresno County.* Dissertation presented to University of Southern California, 1967.

Durham, David L. *Durham's Place Names of Central California.* Clovis, CA: Quill Driver Books/Word Dancer Press Inc., 2001.

Eaton, Edwin M. *Vintage Fresno, Pictorial Recollections of a Western City.* Fresno, CA: Huntington Press, November 1965.

Fresno County Centennial Committee., et al. *Fresno County Centennial Almanac – A Century of Progress.* Fresno. Fresno County Centennial Committee, 1956.

Johnston, Hank. *Rails to the Minarets: The Story of the Sugar Pine Lumber Company.* Corona Del Mar, CA: Trans-Anglo Books, 1980.

Lester, Carole. *Friant.* Fresno, CA: Fresno Historical Society, May 13, 2008.

Lewis Publishing Company. *A Memorial and Biographical History of the Counties of Fresno, Tulare and Kern, California.* Chicago: Lewis Publishing Co., 1892, p. 346.

Preston, Brenda Burnett. *Andrew Davidson Firebaugh and Susan Burgess Firebaugh: California Pioneers.* Del Mar, CA: Rio Del Mar Press, 1995.

Rehart, Catherine M. *The Heartlands Heritage: An Illustrated History of Fresno County.* Heritage Media Corp: September 25, 2000.

Rehart, Catherine Morison, William Secrest Jr., J. Randall McFarland, and Elizabeth Laval. *Celebrating the Journey: 150 Years of Fresno County and Beyond.* Fresno, CA: Fresno County Office of Education, 2007.

Robertson, Donald B. *Encyclopedia of Western Railroad History, Volume IV: California.* Edited by Wayne Cornell. Caldwell, ID: Caxton Press, April 1, 1998.

Secrest, William B. *California Feuds: Vengeance, Vendetta and Violence on the Old West Coast.* Fresno, CA: Word Dancer Press, October 1, 2004.

Shallat, Tom. *Water and the Rise of Public Ownership on the Fresno Plain, 1850 to 1978.* Fresno, CA: Public Works Department, City of Fresno, 1978.

Smith, Wallace. *Garden of the Sun: A History of San Joaquin Valley, 1772-1939.* Los Angeles: Lymanhouse, 1939.

Strother, Deborah Burnett. *Clovis California Schools: A Measure in Excellence.* Bloomington, IN: Phi Beta Kappa, 1991.

Temple, Bobbye Sisk, editor. *Public Schools of Fresno County 1860-1998 Vol. 1.* Fresno, California: Historical Homes Committee. Fresno, CA: Fresno Branch American Association of University Women and Fresno County Superintendent of Schools, 2000.

Thickens, Virginia. "Pioneer Colonies of Fresno County." M.A. Thesis, University of California, 1942. 51.

Vandor, Paul E. *History of Fresno County, Vol. I.* Los Angeles: Historic Record Company, 1919.

Waltz, Georgia, and Eva Burns Lyons. *A Summer in the Sierras.* Fresno, CA: Sierra Printing and Lithograph Company, 1962.

CUSD-PRODUCED MATERIALS

Barker, Duane. *Clovis High School – 100 years of Existence.* 1998.

Buchanan, Floyd B. and Clouse, Donald L. *Historical Listing of Trustees of the Area Now Comprising the Clovis Unified School District.* January 1964.

Buchanan, Floyd, Ed.D. *Historical Overview of Clovis Unified School District.* Edited by Nancy McNeil. Written, late 1980s.

Chedister, Arthur W. *Those Were The Days*, "Grain Farming and Clovis Beginning." Compiled by Clovis Adult Education, Clovis Unified School District. Unpublished 1976.

Clark, Merle. *Those Were The Days*, "The Methodist Church." Compiled by Clovis Adult Education, Clovis Unified School District. Unpublished, 1976, p. 50-52.

Clovis High School yearbook – 1920-21, 1944-45, 1952-53, 1959-60, 1968-69, 1969-70.

Clovis Unified School District Governing Board Resolution No. 2925. "In the Matter of Naming the Elementary School at Leonard & Powers Avenues." May 10, 2006.

Clovis Unified School District. *Legacy in Education.* Annual Report 1990-91.

Clovis West Athletics Department. "The History of Clovis West Athletics." Received April 21, 2010.

Coles, Harold L. Letter to James E. Oliver. October 24, 1960.

Crystal Award Nomination Form 2009. Nomination of Dave Bower.

Hintergardt, Colin. Cedarwood Elementary's 2001-02 California Distinguished School Application. Section II: School Synopsis.

Hintergardt, Colin. Cedarwood Elementary's 2005-06 California Distinguished School Application. Section III: School Programs and Processes.

Kastner Talon. "Special 25th Anniversary Edition." September 22, 2005.

Martin. Walter G. 1960. Letter to Mr. E. G. Rank, Jr. October 24, 1960.

Mickey Cox Elementary School – School Accountability Report Card 2007-08.

Mickey Cox Elementary School yearbook – 1981-82, 1988-89, 1997-98, 1998-99, 1999-00. 2002-03, 2007-08.

Miramonte Elementary School – School Accountability Report Card 2007-08.

Naming of School at Maple/Teague Site. March 11, 1992.

Reyburn Intermediate School – School Accountability Report Card 2007-08.

Sanchez, Ambassador Phillip V. Letter to Mr. Everett G. Rank. November 3, 1960.

Thun, Jessie Myers. *Those Were The Days*, "Mrs. Thun Reminisces." Compiled by Clovis Adult Education, Clovis Unified School District, Unpublished, 1976. 94

White, William B. 1960. Letter to Walter G. Martin. October 21, 1960.

Wulf, Ken. Mickey Cox Elementary School. California Department of Education – California School Recognition Program. 2004 Distinguished Elementary School Application.

Zylka, Claire Baird, Ken Greenberg, and Jessie Myers Thun. *Images of an Age: Clovis*. Fresno, CA: Pacific Printing Press. 1984.

ELECTRONIC SOURCES

Bonner Center for Character Education official website. education.csufresno.edu/bonnercenter. Accessed February 13, 2010.

Bureau of Reclamation History Program Denver, Colorado: "Research on Historical Reclamation Projects: The Friant Division" by Robert Autobee. usbr.gov/dataweb/html/friant.html. Accessed May 15, 2008.

California Business for Education Excellence official website. www.cbeefoundation.org. Accessed October 14, 2009.

Century Elementary School official website. www.clovisusd.k12.ca.us/century/. Accessed December 14, 2009.

Clark Intermediate School official website. www.clovisusd.k12.ca.us/clark/. Accessed December 17, 2009.

Clovis Adult School official website. www.clovisadultschool.com. Accessed November 13, 2009.

Clovis Elementary: "The Way We Were"; "The Rebirth of Clovis Elementary." clovislem.cusd.com/history.htm. Accessed November 13, 2009, April 14, 2010.

Clovis High School official website. www.chs.cusd.com. Accessed April 2010.

Clovis North High: "Built on a Strong Foundation" and "CNEC Mission." cnec.cusd.com/mission.htm. Accessed January 2010.

Clovis North High: Academic Decathlon Team. cnec.cusd.com/Academic%20Decathlon.htm. Accessed March 2010.

Clovis Unified Programs Description. CUSD.com/programs. Accessed March 2010.

Cole Elementary official website. cole.cusd.com/. Accessed November 1, 2009.

Copper Hills Elementary: "History." copperhills.cusd.com/history.htm. Accessed November 13, 2009.

CUSD Project SMART Detail. www.volunteermatch.org/search/org89243.jsp. Accessed February 26, 2010.

Darden Architects, Inc. www.dardenarchitects.com. Accessed March 2010. Dry Creek Elementary: "Panther Express" newsletter. clovisusd.k12. ca.us/dcpanthers_express.htm. Accessed December 4, 2007.

Dry Creek Elementary: "Parent/Student Handbook 2007-08." clovisusd.k12. ca.us/dcHandbook%20Web?DC. ParentHandbk.07.08. Accessed December 4, 2008.

Early Literacy Intervention. literacy-for-all.com. Accessed April 13, 2010.

Ernest J. Kump, Sr. www.historicfresno.org/bio/ kumpsr.htm. Accessed April 14, 2010.

"Fred L. Swartz" by John Edward Powell. historicfresno.org/bio/swartz.htm. Accessed March 2010.

Freedom Elementary official website: freedom.cusd.com. Accessed December 2009.

Fugman Elementary official website
qp.clovisusd.k12.ca.us/QuickPlace/
fugmanelem/Main.nsf/h_Toc/a512cda7d89
5857b882571e40062d13a/?OpenDocument.
Accessed January 2010.

Garfield Elementary official website.
garfield.cusd.com/. Accessed December 2009.

Gettysburg Elementary official website.
gettysburg.cusd.com/. Accessed
December 2009.

Historic California Posts: Camp Pinedale.
www.schoolfolks.com/school/38899.
Accessed September 2008.

James S. Fugman Elementary-School: Great
Schools Rating and Summary. greatschools.
org/california/fresno/13972-James-S.-Fugman-
Elementary-School Great Schools. Accessed
January 15, 2010.

Jefferson Elementary School: School
Accountability Report Card.
cusd.com/schools/06_Clovis%20USD_
Jefferson%20ES.pdf. Accessed November 13,
2006, November 9, 2007.

Kirkman, Frank. Mountain Meadows
Massacre site: "John Fancher Cattle
Brand." 1857massacre.com/MMM/
johnfanchercattlebrand.htm.
Accessed April 2010.

Kirkman, Frank. Mountain Meadows Massacre
site: History. 1857massacre.com.
Accessed April 2010.

Maple Creek Elementary: "About Us."
maplecreek.cusd.com/facts.htm. Accessed
September 2009.

Maple Creek Elementary: "Recognition."
maplecreek.cusd.com/recognition.htm.
Accessed September 2009.

McDonald II, Douglas Shaver. "Fresno Flume
and Irrigation Co. – Individuals Who Shaped
the Sierra"; "Cannonball: A Biography of C.B.
Shaver." www.sierrahistorical.org/archives/
cbshaver.htm. Accessed November 2007.

Mountain Meadows Massacre.
mountainmeadowsmassacre.com. Accessed
April 2010.

Mountain View Elementary official website.
mv.cusd.com. Accessed November 15, 2009.

Nelson Elementary Roadrunners: "Mission Vision
Goals." nelson.cusd.com/mission.htm. Accessed
January 2009.

Olson, Bud. Local History Project 1998-2001:
"Elementary School Series 13:126." www.efchs.
org/_126es.html. Accessed December 11, 2007.

"Project S.M.A.R.T.: A Clovis Unified School
District Mentoring Program."
qp.clovisusd.k12.ca.us/project_smart.
Accessed February 22, 2010.

Riverview Elementary official website.
riverview.cusd.com. Accessed December 2009.

Sierra Outdoor School and Conference Center
official website. sos.cusd.com/default.htm.
Accessed April 19-23, 2010.

Tarpey Elementary: "About us." www.clovisusd.
k12.ca.us/tarpey/abouttarpey.htm. Accessed
May 2010.

trulia.com/schools/CA-Fresno/Clovis_North_
High_School/. Accessed February 2010.

United States Air Force Thunderbirds: "History."
www.airforce.com/thunderbirds. Accessed May
2010.

United States Bureau of Reclamation: "Joint Study
of Big Dry Creek Reservoir Modification."
www.usbr.gov/mp/sccao/storage/docs/phase1_
rpt_fnl/tech_app/01_big_dry_creek.pdf.
Accessed October 2009.

Valley Oak Elementary official website:
qp.clovisusd.k12.ca.us/LotusQuickr/vo_
homepage/Main.nsf/h_Toc/1dd50003ca0378ad
8825706e005c3841/?OpenDocument. Accessed
December 21, 2009.

Weldon Elementary: "Ensign Library Media
Center." www.clovisusd.k12.ca.us/weldon/.
Accessed January 14, 2010.

Woods Elementary: "Principal's Message."
woods.cusd.com/principal.htm. Accessed
February 13, 2010.

MISCELLANEOUS

Focus on Learning WASC Accreditation Report
2006-07, Chapter I: Student/Community
Profile and Supporting Data and Findings.

Focus on Learning WASC Accreditation Report
2006-07, Chapter II: Student/Community
Profile: Overall Summary from Analysis of
Profile Date.

Focus on Learning. WASC Self–Study Report
1997-98.

Smith, Ephraim K. and John Edward Powell.
*An Assessment of the Historical Significance of
Clovis Union High School 1920.* Prepared for the
County of Fresno. April 1981.

INDEX